Between 1934 and 1941 Stalin unleashed what came to be known as the 'Great Terror' against millions of Soviet citizens. The same period also saw the 'Great Retreat', the repudiation of many of the aspirations of the Russian Revolution. The response of ordinary Russians to the extraordinary events of this time has been obscure. Sarah Davies's study uses NKVD and party reports, letters, and other evidence to show that, despite propaganda and repression, dissonant popular opinion was not extinguished. The people continued to criticise Stalin and the Soviet regime, and complain about particular policies. The book examines many themes, including attitudes towards social and economic policy, the terror, and the leader cult, shedding light on a hugely important part of Russia's social, political, and cultural history.

POPULAR OPINION IN STALIN'S RUSSIA

POPULAR OPINION IN STALIN'S RUSSIA

Terror, propaganda and dissent, 1934–1941

SARAH DAVIES

University of Durham

CAMBRIDGE
UNIVERSITY PRESS

PUBLISHED BY THE PRESS SYNDICATE OF THE UNIVERSITY OF CAMBRIDGE
The Pitt Building, Trumpington Street, Cambridge CB2 1RP United Kingdom

CAMBRIDGE UNIVERSITY PRESS
The Edinburgh Building, Cambridge CB2 2RU, United Kingdom
40 West 20th Street, New York, NY 10011-4211, USA
10 Stamford Road, Oakleigh, Melbourne 3166, Australia

First published 1997

Printed in the United Kingdom at the University Press, Cambridge

Typeset in Baskerville 11/12¼ pt

A catalogue record for this book is available from the British Library

Library of Congress Cataloguing in Publication data
Davies, Sarah Rosemary.
Popular opinion in Stalin's Russia : terror, propaganda,
and dissent, 1934–1941 / Sarah Davies.
p.   cm.
Includes bibliographical references (p.   ) and index.
ISBN 0 521 56214 7 (hb). – ISBN 0 521 56676 2 (pb)
1. Public opinion – Soviet Union.
2. Soviet Union – Politics and government – 1936–1953 – Public opinion.
3. Soviet Union – Social policy – Public opinion.
4. Soviet Union – Economic policy – Public opinion.
1. Title.
HN530.Z9P835   1997
303.3'8'0947 – dc 21   96–49928   CIP

ISBN 0 521 56214 7 hardback
ISBN 0 521 56676 2 paperback

Transferred to
Digital Reprinting 1999

Printed in the
United States of America

For all those who spoke out

Contents

x   *Contents*

Tables

Acknowledgements

This book is the product of archival research in Russia carried out during the halcyon years of 1992–3, when large numbers of highly classified documents were made available to researchers for the first time. For allowing me access to these, I am grateful to the archivists at all the institutions where I worked, but especially to Taissa Pavlovna Bondarevskaia and the late Irina Il'marovna Sazonova at TsGAIPD SPb.

The doctoral thesis from which this study evolved was supervised by Mary McAuley and David Priestland, who both gave enormous amounts of their time and energy to advising, criticising, and encouraging me. It is largely thanks to their dedication and enthusiasm that the book has materialised.

Many other people were generous with their advice at different stages of the work. My thesis examiners, Chris Ward and Catherine Andreyev, made stimulating suggestions on how to improve the work, as did Catherine Merridale, who read and commented on the whole manuscript. Sheila Fitzpatrick, whose own research on the social and cultural history of the 1930s has been an inspiration, offered extensive and invaluable criticisms.

I would like to thank all those who have commented on work in progress or helped in other ways, in particular John Barber, Cathryn Brennan, Mary Buckley, Bob Davies, Paul Dukes, David Hoffmann, Anthony Kemp-Welch, Hiroaki Kuromiya, Natalia Lebina, Gábor Rittersporn, Lewis Siegelbaum, Boris Starkov, Robert Thurston, and the participants of the University of Chicago's Workshop on 'Letters' in 1996. I am also grateful to my teachers at St Andrews and SSEES for encouraging my interest in all things Russian.

My colleagues at Durham have been more than patient. Alex Green put up with this work and with me for far too long – I thank him, and all my friends and family for their support. I would also like to thank Cambridge University Press and Michael Holdsworth, John Haslam, and Karen Anderson Howes. Last, but not least, I wish to acknowledge the financial assistance of the Leverhulme Trust, the British Academy, the British Council, the Pirie–Reid Fund, and the Thomas Reid Institute at the University of Aberdeen. None of these institutions or individuals bears any responsibility for the mistakes and shortcomings of the work, which are mine alone.

Chronology

1934

26 Jan.–10 Feb.	Seventeenth Party Congress
18 Sep.	USSR joins League of Nations
25–8 Nov.	TsK plenum decrees end of bread rations effective from 1 January 1935
1 Dec.	Assassination of Kirov
December	Local soviet elections

1935

15–16 Jan.	Trial of Zinoviev, Kamenev, and others
Jan.–Mar.	Mass expulsions from Leningrad
17 Feb.	New model *kolkhoz* charter adopted
30–31 Aug.	Stakhanov's record
22 Sep.	Military ranks restored
25 Sep.	End of rations on meat, fats, fish, etc.
14–17 Nov.	First All-Union Conference of Stakhanovites Stalin's speech 'Life has become better, life has become merrier'
29 Dec.	Decree ending restrictions on access to higher education on the basis of social origin

1936

12 June	Draft of new Constitution published
27 June	Decree 'In defence of the mother and child'
18–24 Aug.	Trial of Zinoviev, Kamenev, and others
September	Ezhov succeeds Iagoda as head of NKVD
Autumn	Harvest failure in many regions
5 Dec.	Adoption of new Constitution

1937
6 Jan.   Abortive population census
23–30 Jan.   Trial of Radek, Piatakov, and others
18 Feb.   Death of Ordzhonikidze
25 Feb.–5 Mar.   TsK plenum excludes Bukharin and Rykov
                        from party, and calls for vigilance
31 May   Suicide of General Gamarnik
12 June   Tukachevskii and other generals executed
12 Dec.   Elections to Supreme Soviet

1938
2–13 Mar.   Trial of Bukharin, Rykov, Iagoda, and others
8 Dec.   Beria succeeds Ezhov as head of NKVD
28 Dec.   Decree on labour discipline

1939
January   Population census
10–21 Mar.   Eighteenth Party Congress announces end of
                        purges
27 May   Decree on measures to prevent squander of
                        public *kolkhoz* land
23 Aug.   Molotov–Ribbentrop pact signed
17 Sep.   USSR annexes eastern Poland
29 Nov.   Winter War with Finland begins
20 Dec.   Stalin prizes instituted

1940
12 Mar.   Peace treaty with Finland
26 June   Labour decree
2 Oct.   Decree on fees for higher classes and *vuzy*, and
                        decree on labour reserves

1941
22 June   Hitler invades USSR

Abbreviations and archive references

GARF	Gosudarstvennyi arkhiv Rossiiskoi Federatsii
GANO	Gosudarstvennyi arkhiv Novosibirskoi oblasti
LP	*Leningradskaia pravda*
P	*Pravda*
RR	*Russian Review*
RTsKhIDNI	Rossiiskii tsentr khraneniia i izucheniia dokumentov noveishei istorii
SP	Sheila Fitzpatrick, *Stalin's Peasants. Resistance and Survival in the Russian Village After Collectivisation*, Oxford, 1994
SR	*Slavic Review*
ST	J. A. Getty and R. Manning (eds.), *Stalinist Terror. New Perspectives*, Cambridge, 1993
TsGA SPb	Tsentral'nyi gosudarstvennyi arkhiv v Sankt Peterburge
TsGAIPD SPb	Tsentral'nyi gosudarstvennyi arkhiv istoriko-politicheskikh dokumentov Sankt Peterburga
TsKhDMO	Tsentr khraneniia dokumentov molodezhnykh organizatsii

The archival reference system has been adopted for the sake of conciseness. Throughout, all references are from TsGAIPD SPb unless otherwise specified. The references are to *fond* (collection), *opis'* (inventory), *edinitsa khraneniia* or *delo* (file), *list* (folio). Thus 24/2v/2600/ 3 refers to *fond* 24, *opis'* 2v, *edinitsa khraneniia* 2600, *list* 3. In the case of letters and documents reporting on popular opinion, I have indicated the provenance and date of a file according to the following system: p = a party source (information and agitprop departments); k = a Komsomol source; n = an NKVD source; l = a citizen's letter (except in the case of intercepted letters reproduced by the NKVD which are classified as 'n'). Thus 'p/34' refers to a party file dating from 1934.

Glossary and notes on the text

agitprop	agitation and propaganda
artel'	cooperative
batiushka	'little father' (often applied to tsar)
bezbozhnik	member of the 'League of Godless' (pl. *bezbozhniki*)
chastushka	popular, often four-lined verse (pl. *chastushki*)
edinolichnik	individual peasant farmer (pl. *edinolichniki*)
ezhovshchina	campaign of mass terror in 1937–8 named after NKVD head, Ezhov
gorkom	*gorodskoi komitet*: city committee (of party)
intelligent	member of the intelligentsia (pl. *intelligenty*)
ispolkom	*ispolnitel'nyi komitet*: executive committee
ITR	*inzhenerno-tekhnicheskii rabotnik*: engineering/technical worker
khutor	consolidated farm (pl. *khutora*)
khutorianin	khutor dweller (pl. *khutoriane*)
kolkhoz	*kollektivnoe khoziaistvo*: collective farm (pl. *kolkhozy*)
kolkhoznik	member of the *kolkhoz* (f. *kolkhoznitsa*, pl. *kolkhozniki*)
Komsomol	Kommunisticheskii soiuz molodezhi: Communist League of Youth
k.	kopek(s)
krai	administrative region
kraikom	*kraevoi komitet*: regional committee (of party)
kustar'	cottage industry
lishenets	disenfranchised person (pl. *lishentsy*)
muzhik	Russian peasant (colloquially, man)
narodnik	member of nineteenth-century populist movement

NEP	Novaia ekonomicheskaia politika: New Economic Policy
nizy	lower classes, those at the bottom
NKIu	Narodnyi komissariat iustitsii: People's Commissariat of Justice
NKVD	Narodnyi komissariat vnutrennikh del: People's Commissariat of Internal Affairs
obkom	*oblastnoi komitet*: regional committee (of party)
oblast'	administrative region
oblispolkom	*oblastnoi ispolnitel'nyi komitet*: regional executive committee (of soviet)
OGPU (GPU)	Ob"edinennoe gosudarstvennoe politicheskoe upravleniie: Unified State Political Administration (Secret Police)
okrug	administrative region
PPO	*pervichnaia partiinaia organizatsiia*: primary party organisation
raikom	*raionnyi komitet*: district committee (of party)
r.	ruble(s)
RSFSR	Rossiiskaia sovetskaia federativnaia sotsialisticheskaia respublika: Russian Soviet Federative Socialist Republic
sel'sovet	*sel'skii sovet*: village soviet
sluzhashchii	employee, white-collar worker (pl. *sluzhashchie*)
soratnik	comrade-in-arms (pl. *soratniki*)
Sovnarkom (SNK)	Sovet narodnykh komissarov: Council of People's Commissars
SR	Socialist Revolutionary
SSSR	Soiuz sovetskikh sotsialisticheskikh respublik: USSR
Torgsin	Shop trading for hard currency and precious metals (pl. Torgsiny)
TsIK	Tsentral'nyi ispolnitel'nyi komitet: Central Executive Committee
TsK	Tsentral'nyi komitet: Central Committee (of party)
TsKK	Tsentral'naia kontrol'naia komissia: Central Control Commission (of party)
verkhi	upper classes, those at the top (s. *verkha*)
VKP(b)	Vsesoiuznaia kommunisticheskaia partiia

	(bol'shevikov): All-Union Communist Party (Bolsheviks)
vozhd'	chief/leader (equivalent of *Führer*; pl. *vozhdi*)
VTsIK	Vserossiiskii tsentral'nyi ispolnitel'nyi komitet: All-Russian Central Executive Committee
vydvizhenets	upwardly mobile cadre (pl. *vydvizhentsy*)

The transliteration system followed is that of the Library of Congress. Certain Russian words with accepted English equivalents will be given in the English form, for example, Bolshevik, rather than *bol'shevik*, and soviet, rather than *sovet*.

Unless otherwise noted, all locations are in Leningrad and Leningrad region.

Introduction

How do we recover the thoughts and values, hopes and beliefs of 'ordinary people'? So often their voices have been silenced by the rich and powerful. In Stalin's Russia, this process of silencing was particularly insidious. Not only were people literally silenced – shot, or incarcerated in concentration camps for expressing unorthodox views – but also the entire Soviet media eliminated virtually all reference to heretical opinion. Dissonant voices were written out of history by the Stalinist scriptwriters – but not forever. In letters and top secret documents, hidden in the archives, these voices were preserved. The aim of this book is simple: to 'release' them, and allow them to speak for themselves as far as possible. However, inevitably the selection and organisation of the material will have left its mark. What follows is just one of many possible interpretations that could, and should, be undertaken.

This book focuses on popular opinion during a formative and momentous period of Soviet history. The years 1934–41 witnessed both the 'Great Retreat' and the 'Great Terror'.[1] The term 'Great Retreat', coined by the sociologist Timasheff, symbolises the repudiation of many of the values and aspirations of the Russian Revolution of October 1917. In the words of Stalin's arch-enemy, Trotsky, the Revolution had been 'betrayed', and had given way to a 'Soviet Thermidor'.[2] The Russian Revolution, carried out under the banner of socialism and the liberation of the working class, was followed by a bloody civil war, portrayed as a class struggle of the poor and exploited against the rich capitalists. During the war, the Bolshevik Party established a 'dictatorship of the proletariat' and introduced 'war communism', a series of measures including the nationalisation of industry, a grain monopoly, the abolition of free trade, and rationing. The Bolsheviks won the civil war, but, in the face of mounting social disaffection, were forced to abandon war communism in 1921 and introduce the New Economic Policy (NEP). Free trade was reintroduced, and only heavy industry, banking, and foreign trade remained under state control.

The economy, shattered by war and revolution, began slowly to recover. However, NEP society was riddled with contradictions. A 'bourgeois' stratum flourished, epitomised by the petty capitalist 'nepmen' who flaunted their wealth in nightclubs and restaurants. With the growth of the party and state apparatus, it seemed to many, including Trotsky and the opposition which crystallised around him, as if the country was being run by a new 'bureaucracy'. Relations between the party and the proletarians it claimed to represent were strained, and unemployment continued to blight workers' lives. The peasants, meanwhile, were being encouraged by Bukharin to 'get rich'. Their reluctance to supply the towns with grain precipitated an economic crisis which heralded the end of NEP.

NEP was both economically unviable and ideologically unacceptable to the leadership. In 1928, Stalin, who had secured power following the death of Lenin after outmanoeuvring his rivals Trotsky, Kamenev, and Zinoviev, launched a new 'revolution from above' in many ways as far-reaching as that of 1917. It entailed unprecedentedly rapid industrialisation carried out according to 'five-year plans', the first of which operated from 1928 until the end of 1932. New factories and even cities sprang up, the industrial workforce doubled, and the bureaucracy expanded. The collectivisation of agriculture was initiated in 1929, with peasants forced to join *kolkhozy* en masse. Millions of peasants were shot or resettled in Siberia for resisting the policy. The massive opposition to collectivisation by so-called kulaks led to a partial retreat, and complete collectivisation was not accomplished until the eve of the 'Great Patriotic War' (1941–5). The period 1929–32 also experienced Cultural Revolution – utopianism, social and cultural experimentation on a grand scale, and a class war against those of non-proletarian origins. The result of all these measures was not utopia, however, but social and economic turmoil and the famine of 1932–3 which claimed the lives of millions.

In 1933–4, a new course was adopted. Stability, rather than revolution, was the watchword. More realistic targets were set for the second five-year plan, and concessions were made to the peasants. The emphasis on class war was moderated in favour of propaganda and policies promoting the unity of the 'whole people'. Proletarian dictatorship was replaced by a Constitution which guaranteed everyone over eighteen the right to vote in secret elections for a Supreme Soviet, including those previously disenfranchised because of their social origins. Hierarchical rather than egalitarian values were actively encouraged through the promotion of Stakhanovite workers and other heroes. Specialists were now rewarded rather than persecuted. A new elite emerged, and a new ethos of consumerism. Religion was tolerated (within limits), stable family values were encouraged, and education, law, and the arts reverted to tradition. The Cultural Revolution was definitely over, and with it the privileges of workers, who were now expected to tolerate working practices in some ways reminiscent of those under capitalism. At the same time, in the international arena, the USSR sought alliances with capitalist states, and in 1939 went so far as to sign a non-aggression pact with fascist Germany.

Yet this partial retreat to conservatism and tradition was accompanied by a new 'revolution', in the form of the Great Terror, which had the effect of bringing down many of the elite and creating a climate of acute instability. Its origins lay in the still unexplained murder of Leningrad party boss, Kirov, on 1 December 1934. The murder was officially attributed to Stalin's old opponents, Kamenev and Zinoviev, and was used by Stalin to launch a crackdown in early 1935 on thousands of former 'oppositionists' and 'class enemies', particularly in Leningrad. In mid-1936, terror struck again. Kamenev and Zinoviev were sentenced to execution in the first of many show trials in which prominent party figures were accused of spying and wrecking. For a number of reasons the terror escalated into what has become known as the *ezhovshchina*, after Ezhov, the head of the NKVD, who organised the terror against millions of innocent citizens in 1937–8.[3]

This dramatic tale is well known. What has been unclear until now and what this study seeks to address is the way in which 'ordinary people' responded to the Great Retreat and Great Terror. The focus is deliberately upon the views of subordinate groups in general, rather than one particular social category, because the opinions expressed cannot be clearly attributed to precisely defined groups. In any case, the a priori categorisation of social groups reveals more about the assumptions of scholars than it does about the identities and ideas of those alleged to constitute them. The determinist notions that skilled workers automatically possess a revolutionary class consciousness, that peasants are naturally backward and petty-bourgeois, and that white-collar workers have different interests to blue-collar workers are all too redolent of Bolshevik ideology. In reality, peasants, workers, *sluzhashchie*, and low-level party members often spoke a similar language, albeit with different degrees of competence. Clearly their concerns were not always identical, and this work reflects such differences with separate sections devoted to the particular interests of peasants, workers, or women. Even confining the study to subordinate groups is somewhat artificial and presupposes a rigid dichotomy between those with power and those without. In this period of social flux and purging, those at the top could easily end up at the bottom, and vice versa, and *some* views expressed by members of the elite may not have differed much from those of the 'lower classes'.

An analysis of popular opinion in this period must take into account the role of propaganda and coercion in Soviet society. This was a period of unprecedentedly intense and uniform propaganda, and of censorship taken to absurd degrees. The propaganda pervaded every sphere of public communication, including the media, the arts, and education. Its main messages, intoned with monotonous regularity, proclaimed that life in the Soviet Union was unequivocally rosy in contrast to the pitiful existence of workers living under capitalism, that in the USSR the whole people allegedly enjoyed satisfying jobs and high living standards, endorsed the policies of the party and Stalin to whom they were devoted, and believed in socialism with a Stalinist face. The standard formula accompanying the newspaper publicity for a policy or event proclaimed that 'all the workers of Leningrad/Moscow/the USSR (or wherever) greeted the decision/policy/verdict with pleasure/approval/satisfaction'. The heavily censored media were forbidden to publish material about real feelings at the grassroots. In 1927 the censor classified information on the 'political mood [*politicheskie nastroeniia*]' alongside news about strikes, demonstrations, disorder, and similar manifestations of discontent as information which could not be printed lest it damaged the 'political-economic interests of the USSR'.[4] Unacceptable views were referred to only occasionally and obliquely in public as 'the survivals of capitalism in the consciousness of the people', 'the psychology of the petty proprietor', 'petty-bourgeois feelings', and 'outbursts [*vylazki*] of the class enemy'.

As well as propaganda and censorship, the regime also relied on repression to block alternative ideas. People were charged with the crime of 'anti-Soviet agitation' (the notorious article 58.10) for expressing opinions which seemed to the authorities to be aimed at 'the overthrow, subversion, or weakening of' Soviet power.[5] This was an elastic definition and the numbers of those sentenced under article 58.10 fluctuated considerably. In lenient periods, the numbers were relatively small, but during collectivisation and the terror of 1936–8 many thousands of people were sentenced.[6] During the terror, convictions were even possible for statements such as 'The loan is voluntary. I don't want to subscribe 150 r., only 100', or 'in Greece there are many types of fruit, and in the USSR few'.[7] At the peak of the terror, thought crime became institutionalised when a statement such as 'I wish Stalin was dead' was deemed to be equivalent to actually committing a terrorist act, and was supposed to be prosecuted accordingly.[8]

So what was the effect of these measures? Were ordinary people reduced through a combination of repression and propaganda into either regurgitating the official discourse, or keeping their silence? Or was there any significant dissonant popular opinion in Stalin's Russia?

Although historians have broached this question, they have been stymied until recently by a lack of sources.[9] Most investigations have focused on the views of the intelligentsia, since the sources are richer for this group. The debate has centred on the sometimes unproductive wrangle between adherents of the 'totalitarian' model of Soviet society and so-called revisionists, a debate which has dominated the field to such an extent that other perspectives have been rather marginalised.

There is no need to rehearse in detail the arguments of both sides, except in so far as they touch on the question of popular opinion.[10] Proponents of the 'totalitarian' model *tend* to ignore society,[11] which they regard as being atomised and under the absolute control of the Soviet state. They stress the latter's use of propaganda and coercion, and imply that the 'masses' were either brain-washed into conformity or were silent but implacable opponents of the regime. By contrast, revisionists portray society as an active and autonomous force, not merely an adjunct of the state. In their concern to overturn the 'totalitarian' orthodoxy about the terrorised, disaffected, and zombie-like masses, some revisionists attempt to demonstrate the existence of a social basis of support for Stalin amongst, for example, upwardly mobile cadres (*vydvizhentsy*), Komsomol members, and Stakhanovites, all of whom, it is suggested, actively endorsed the regime.[12] Although this interpretation provides a refreshing alternative to the totalitarian perspective, it is sometimes taken to extremes. For example, one historian argues that most ordinary people did not feel terrorised in this period except at the worst moments of 1937, that they exercised the freedom of speech (within limits), and enjoyed the right to criticise and complain. He concludes that many workers were probably loyal to the regime.[13]

While it seems appropriate to jettison the stereotype of the 'terrorised masses', claims about workers' loyalty appear less well founded. Just because workers did not feel terrorised, and continued to criticise managers and so on, it does not follow that they were always satisfied with the Soviet regime or its policies. Indeed, the large amount of criticising and complaining going on might imply quite the contrary. Recent research on both workers and peasants indicates that they did indeed feel oppressed and adopted many tactics of passive resistance.[14]

Evidently it is time to reevaluate the whole question of popular opinion, to get away from the totalitarian insistence on the atomised, voiceless masses, without moving to the other extreme of painting a socialist realist picture of satisfied and contented workers and peasants singing in unison 'life has become better, life has become merrier'. Clearly along the continuum from active consent to active resistance/dissent were a range of heterogeneous positions. There were few absolute 'conformists' and 'dissenters'. In practice, people's views were far more ambivalent and contradictory: opposition to one policy or facet of the regime was quite compatible with support of others, a tendency which has been noted by historians of other authoritarian societies. Detlev Peukert shows that in Nazi Germany 'diverse forms of criticism and "grumbling" were quite capable of existing side by side with partial recognition of the regime or at least with passive acceptance of authority', while Luisa Passerini's oral history also highlights the ambivalence of popular attitudes in Fascist Italy.[15]

In his recent important work on the new Soviet city of Magnitogorsk in the 1930s, Stephen Kotkin rejects the totalitarian/revisionist, opposition/support dichotomy, and is aware of the tactical use of language by ordinary citizens. However, he is inclined to take propaganda at its face value, overemphasising the popular tendency to 'speak Bolshevik' (i.e. to use the official language).[16] He denies that a Great Retreat occurred and makes the provocative claim that 'To the vast majority of those who lived it, and even to most of its enemies, Stalinism, far from being a partial retreat let alone a throwback to the Russian past, remained forward-looking and progressive throughout.'[17] He also asserts that:

Even the truest of true believers appears to have had regular bouts with private doubt. But few could imagine alternatives. Nor was anyone encouraged to do so. Sealed borders and censorship did their part.[18]

In the only significant study of Soviet propaganda, Peter Kenez argues in a similar vein that the regime

succeeded in preventing the formation and articulation of alternative points of view. The Soviet people ultimately came not so much to believe the Bolsheviks' world view as to take it for granted. Nobody remained to point out the contradictions and even inanity in the regime's slogans.[19]

These conclusions are undermined by the new sources, which reveal that, on the contrary, ordinary people were adept at defeating the censor, seeking out alternative sources of information and ideas in the form of rumours, personal letters, leaflets (*listovki*), and inscriptions (*nadpisi*).[20] They also continued to draw on a variety of rival discourses, including those of nationalism, anti-semitism, and populism, which proved tenacious despite concerted attempts to eradicate them.

Moreover, the official language was used and understood in a far from passive way. As Voloshinov points out, language is inherently flexible and can become an arena in which social conflicts are played out over the meaning of signs: 'every living ideological sign is double-headed like Janus. Every living abuse may become praise, every living truth inevitably will sound like the greatest lie to many others.'[21] This 'janus-headed' character of signs prevented the Stalinist regime from imposing one monolithic interpretation of reality.

This seems to be the point Bakhtin was trying to convey in the late 1930s in his work on Rabelais, which represents, in the view of Clark and Holquist, 'Bakhtin's most comprehensive critique to date of Stalinist culture'.[22] Whether or not Bakhtin deliberately set out to describe his own culture in an aesopian way, some features of this work ostensibly about medieval France do illuminate similar processes underway in Soviet Russia. He describes a society in which the hegemonic class maintains its dominance partly through its ideological diktat. Official culture is characterised by its attempt to present only one 'natural' interpretation of reality. It projects seriousness, retrospectivity, immutability, eternity. It is also associated with fear and violence. However, the monopoly of the official culture of the medieval world is undermined by a second culture of laughter, typified by the carnival. During carnival, official symbols are invested with new meaning, for 'the second life, second world of popular culture is constructed to a certain extent as a parody on the usual ... life, like a "world inside out"'. Its role lies in the desacralisation of all that represented by the hegemonic culture. It breaks all the taboos, mocks the sacred, reverses the hierarchy. It represents equality, utopia, and freedom from fear.[23] So too, in Stalinist Russia, the official discourse, characterised by gravity, a sense of its own permanence and so on, was subjected to carnivalisation in the form of jokes and songs which 'deconstructed' the hierarchies and assumptions implicit in the official discourse, reversing the traditional topography, bringing high down to low and vice versa, emphasising the physical side of life, and using profanities.

This is just one example of the various ways in which the official discourse became a tool in the hands of subordinate groups who reappropriated it for their own purposes. Likewise, officially hallowed words, such as 'revolution' and 'the people [*narod*]' were reclaimed for the expression of dissent. So, while the regime employed *narod* to denote the 'whole people', and thereby to imply unity, dissenters used it in a divisive way to signify the powerless *nizy* (lower classes).

Citizens also couched illegitimate or subversive requests and complaints in terms of the official discourse, protecting themselves by invoking their Constitutional rights, Stalin's words, the working class, and other officially cherished notions. Rigby refers to this practice in his analysis of a 'shadow culture' in the USSR. He argues that 'political hypocrisy' was a 'time-bomb' with a self-fulfilling potential. The collapse of the Soviet regime was facilitated by the existence of an official rhetoric about democracy, rights, and so forth which could be used by those seeking real democracy.[24]

It is not my aim to give the erroneous impression that the official language was always used with purely subversive or cynical intent. There were undoubtedly true believers and fanatics, as chapter 10 will show. It is also likely that some of the less committed sometimes 'welcomed the policies', 'condemned the enemies', or said whatever they were alleged to be saying in newspaper articles reporting so-called 'popular reactions' to various measures. However, 'popular opinion' in this sense is not the main subject of this book. Rather, the objective is to illuminate the hitherto neglected body of dissonant opinion which distorted, subverted, rejected, or provided an alternative to the official discourse.

It is difficult to generalise about the content of this popular opinion, to make categorical assertions about a hypothetical 'Russian popular political culture'. Often the values expressed seem to contradict each other, refusing to fit conveniently into boxes labelled socialist, anarchist, conservative, liberal, or whatever. However, certain themes do feature prominently. Hostility towards officialdom and antipathy towards 'the state' were often expressed. Conversely, there was also a widespread contrary opinion that the state should provide for and look after the people. A paternalist style of leadership was valued highly. Materialism and egalitarianism pervaded many popular statements. 'Socialism' seems to have been favoured and 'class' feelings were very pronounced. Social conservatism was widespread. Politics and the law were treated in various ways: although many were indifferent to them, others took them more seriously. Above all, popular opinion was heterogeneous. People's attitudes depended as much upon the nature of particular policies or issues as upon any coherent worldview. For this reason, and because the sources lend themselves to this treatment, this book is structured thematically. Part I focuses on economic and social questions. Part II considers politics, including international relations, and various aspects of the terror. Part III concentrates on the leader cult. Before we proceed any further, at this stage it is worth examining the sources for the study and considering how these may have affected the representation of popular opinion.

SOURCES

The evidence for this study includes citizens' letters, memoirs, diaries, and newspaper reports. Reports prepared by party agitators on the feedback they obtained from their audiences have also been used. However, the main sources are summaries produced by the NKVD and party (and Komsomol) information departments on popular responses to particular events or policies (*svodki/spetssoobshcheniia o nastroenii*). As this is a large body of untapped and valuable material, it deserves particular attention.

The party, through the various incarnations of its Information Department, and the secret police, through its Secret-Political Department, had been involved in the surveillance of popular opinion since the revolution (and, in the party's case, even before that).[25] The party Information Department was responsible for coordinating the exchange of information between centre and periphery on a variety of subjects, including information on the popular mood.[26] According to a directive of 1934, each PPO was supposed to have a party informant (*informator*), who was required to be politically literate and authoritative, and to have experience of political work with the masses. His job was to analyse both positive and negative aspects of grassroots party organisations in a clear, self-critical, profound, and objective fashion. He was also to be aware of the general mood of workers and to pay particular attention to characteristic events of the day (accidents and stoppages, interruptions to services, various types of feelings). The job entailed maintaining close links with the party secretary, being present at meetings, and liaising with grassroots activists and editors of local newspapers in order to maximise the possibility of obtaining what was described as 'objective' information.[27] This was the theory. In practice, information work was not always accorded a high priority, even in the powerful Leningrad party organisation, although there were some improvements after the Kirov murder, when additional informants were appointed. Even so, in 1939 it transpired that certain PPOs lacked any informants. If the party information system sometimes functioned moderately efficiently in the factories of Leningrad, it was far less effective in the countryside and amongst the intelligentsia.[28] By contrast, the NKVD was able to monitor a far broader range of social groups through its network of paid and unpaid secret agents (*seksoty*).[29]

Party and NKVD informants noted down conversations, rumours, jokes, and other evidence of the popular mood which were compiled into *svodki* (summaries). In the case of the party, the data was sent to the *raikom*, which summarised it for the *obkom*. The Information Department of the *obkom* then compiled a summary on the basis of all the *raikom* reports. Both party and NKVD summaries were classified 'top secret' and addressed to about two to six recipients. For example, Leningrad NKVD reports were usually sent to the first three *obkom* secretaries, the head of the SPO (Secret-Political Department) in Moscow, and occasionally to the president of the *oblispolkom*.

All party and NKVD reports invariably began with the standard formula that 'the majority of the people' had reacted to a policy or event in a 'healthy' way. This was always followed by examples of typical 'correct' opinions, which tended merely to reiterate the official line published in the newspapers. Negative remarks followed the positive comments in a section beginning 'However, alongside this there are certain cases of backward/negative/unhealthy/anti-Soviet/counter-revolutionary statements' (usually about three of these adjectives were employed). Information about the identity of those alleged to be making the remarks was usually provided, such as their name, occupation, and place of work, for example, 'worker Sizova, second galoshes shop, Krasnyi Treugol'nik'. Party and Komsomol affiliation were also mentioned. Other details sometimes highlighted included age, length of work, and any information indicative of the speaker's general political orientation, such as 'recently arrived from the country', 'formerly engaged in trade', 'excluded from the party', 'has relations with enemy of the people', or 'evangelist'. This type of information tended to be more prevalent in NKVD reports, partly because the latter was already involved in the surveillance of 'socially dangerous elements', and partly because of its own preconceptions about the causes of undesirable attitudes. Sometimes, particularly in 1937, a hostile opinion was followed by phrases such as 'has been arrested', 'will be arrested', or 'investigation is being carried out'.

It is hard to know whether party, and particularly NKVD informants, influenced by the general atmosphere of conspiracy which characterised the Great Terror and under pressure from above to exercise vigilance and expose 'enemies', invented or distorted the negative comments in their reports. The temptation to invent remarks, or to report an unverified denunciation must have been great. Informants signed undertakings to provide accurate material, and could be punished for not doing so: in 1932, 180 OGPU informants were given five-year sentences for supplying 'unobjective information'. Informants could also be excluded from the party for failure to adhere to the criteria of objectivity.[30] However, these undertakings may have meant little in 1937.

It is plausible that some genuine expressions of discontent may have been given a more 'counter-revolutionary' gloss by some informants, perhaps by the addition of fictitious praise of Trotsky, threats to kill Stalin, or other such formulae. However, it is also clear that many of the opinions cited in the reports do correspond with those contained in other sources, such as memoirs, diaries, the emigre journal *Sotsialisticheskii vestnik*,[31] censors' reports, and even occasionally the official media.[32] Some of these will be cited in subsequent chapters; however, just one example is a survey of items expunged during the preliminary censorship of the factory press of Leningrad's Tsentral'nyi district in April 1934. The censor removed several items concerning the 'political mood', which editors had included to illustrate undesirable attitudes (publishing such comments was deemed to be equivalent to the outright propagation of anti-Soviet views). One newspaper had intended to print the following *chastushki*: 'Ne poidu ia na sobran'e / Ne poidu na preniia / Skazhem priamo est' zhelan'e / Netu nastroeniia' ('I won't go to the meeting / I won't go to the discussion / I'll tell you straight out there is the desire / but not the mood'); 'Govoriu zhe Vam po russki / Mne ne nravitsia nagruzki / Mne nagruzki po plechu / da rabotat' ne khochu' ('I will tell you in Russian / I don't like duties / I have duties up to here / No, I don't want to work'). Another contained an article on the state loan campaign which reported the words of a person unwilling to contribute: 'The state does not help me, but drags out my last kopeks. Go away, I'm not going to subscribe.'[33] This type of language echoes very closely that of the party and NKVD opinion reports.

The authenticity of the reported opinion can also be verified by comparing it with that from various areas and periods. A comparison of reports in several archives[34] reveals that regardless of where the information was assembled, by whom, and for whom – the centre or the regions, European or Siberian Russia, by party or NKVD workers, for the Kremlin or for the Komsomol – there were certain consistent traits of popular opinion, certain discourses which existed independently of the whims and fantasies of those responsible for the reports. Nor did the discourses of the terror period differ significantly from those of other years. Some opinion reports for the civil war, 1920s, and collectivisation period have already been published, while historians have begun to analyse reports in the context of work on the 1920s and 1930s.[35] These reveal that a body of critical opinion existed throughout the early Soviet period, and that views held by ordinary Russians during the terror did not diverge significantly from those expressed at other times. Similarly, even when the terror had abated, during the 'thaw' of 1939–40, there was still continuity between the views uttered then and those of previous years. In the immediate pre-war period, when serious attempts were made by Stalin and Beria to restore legality and to repair the damaged prestige of the procuracy, courts, and NKVD, there was a corresponding drive to tighten up the accuracy of the opinion reports. Negative comments recorded in an opinion report were checked, and if they were found to be incorrect, this was noted in a subsequent report.[36] The range and substance of opinion in reports prepared in more 'liberal' periods, when falsification was minimised and the fear of punishment less acute, did not differ markedly from that of the years of the Great Terror.

Distortion occurred rather in the manner in which material was selected and analysed. The selection of material was clearly influenced by considerations of what informants and the compilers of reports imagined their superiors wanted to hear at any particular moment. If the regime was particularly concerned with, for example, exposing 'Trotskyists' or 'saboteurs' of the Stakhanovite movement, informants may have made a special effort to record comments expressing pro-Trotsky or anti-Stakhanovite feelings. Reports were compiled because the regime wished to monitor reactions to particular events and policies; thus the subject matter of the reports was already circumscribed. In reports on reactions to the Stakhanovite movement, for example, the majority of recorded comments concerned this issue. Comments and discussion about other non-related questions were generally mentioned only *en passant*. This can convey the false impression that in the week in which a report was compiled, people were talking only about the Stakhanovite movement, or the state loan, or whatever; also, that in the intervals between important events and policies warranting reports, no popular discussion took place. Reporting was very uneven. Weeks could pass without a report, and then a major crisis, such as the murder of Kirov or the outbreak of war with Finland, would precipitate a mass of daily and even hourly reports. Because of this irregularity, it is difficult to plot the dynamics of the popular mood.

Since the choice of subjects warranting reports was dictated by regime priorities, which did not necessarily coincide with the people's own interests (or with those of a future historian for that matter), there are many lacunae. There is an abundance of comment on purely political issues, as it was these which primarily concerned the regime. However, this abundance does not necessarily reflect the actual weight of political subject matter in the discourse of ordinary people. More private concerns, such as those connected with the family and leisure, are hardly represented at all. Likewise, because reports were compiled in relation to specific events and policies, popular opinion about more ill-defined phenomena such as the mass terror of 1937–8 is less well represented. There are of course no 'Summaries of popular reactions to terror'. However, inferences about reactions to this and other phenomena not specifically covered in reports can sometimes be gleaned from reports on different questions.

Analysis of the causes of incorrect opinions was usually superficial in both types of report. The NKVD favoured the 'enemy' theory, identifying those holding hostile views with alleged 'enemies of the people'. Both party and NKVD emphasised the work of 'anti-Soviet/ counter-revolutionary agitators' in spreading rumours and discontent amongst ordinary people. For example, a party report on reactions to the sale of unrationed bread in January 1935 noted that 'counter-revolutionary elements try to use the new system of bread sales and price rises for ordinary slanderous attacks'.[37] However, in some party reports, the party tried to shoulder responsibility for negative views, especially in the case of worker discontent, blaming poor agitprop and 'explanatory work' for workers' failure 'correctly' to understand a particular policy. They sometimes even highlighted the material conditions of workers as a cause of discontent, suggesting that the failure to be paid on time, low levels of pay, inadequate provision of services, and so on were influencing popular opinion.

Party reports differed from those of the NKVD in that they included a large proportion of positive comments. Presumably party officials were keen to demonstrate that their particular organisation was functioning well, and that the propaganda was being absorbed. Unlike the party, the NKVD was concerned primarily with monitoring 'enemies' and the suppression of dissent, and its reports therefore devoted the majority of space to critical comments. However, in both cases the insistence was always that negative comments were in a minority. No statistics were provided so it is almost impossible to establish how widely these opinions were in fact articulated.

Were they in fact in a minority? One solution is to look for other evidence of the scale of discontent. Thus, some letters to party leaders contain overtly 'anti-Soviet' comments similar to those recorded in the reports. These form a tiny proportion of all letters; for example, 15 of 5,638 letters sent to Leningrad party secretary Zhdanov in January 1940 were classified as anti-Soviet.[38] However, this fact alone is not necessarily indicative of the extent to which such views were expressed. In this period it was clearly a far more dangerous and deliberate act to put critical views in writing to a party leader than to make an impromptu remark to fellow workers in the relative safety of the toilets. While explicitly 'anti-Soviet' letters are rare, there are millions of letters and petitions complaining about living conditions, corruption, and so on. While these adopted a loyal tone, and directed their criticism towards local bureaucrats only, they provide evidence of general social discontent which corresponds with the tone of some of the negative opinion.

This is substantiated by the evidence of behaviour, although it is difficult to make a direct correlation between attitudes and behaviour. However, it is clear that there were many infractions of the labour decree of June 1940, that people committed suicide on learning that they were to be prosecuted, and that party members and the judiciary tried to obstruct the decree. This suggests that there may have been a correspondingly high incidence of negative opinion in relation to the decree. Consumption patterns can also be compared with reported popular opinion. If there were complaints about the price of bread or food in canteens after the end of rations, and these were accompanied by a quite substantial decline in the amount of bread and canteen meals consumed, it is plausible that such complaints were quite prevalent. Likewise, the difficulty the party experienced in its collection of state loans suggests that the anti-loan comments reflected widespread opinion.

Statistics on the prosecution of cases of anti-Soviet agitation present a somewhat distorted impression of the numbers expressing dissonant views. A report on arrests and sentences in cases initiated or investigated by police agencies reveals the figures for arrests for anti-Soviet agitation shown in table 1. Quite apart from the intrinsic difficulties of dealing with the regime's statistics on repression,[39] there is a problem in that the regime's definition of what constituted anti-Soviet agitation was constantly changing. Many of the examples in this study, such as complaints about price rises, would not

Table 1 *Anti-Soviet agitation cases*

1934[a]	1935[a]	1936[a]	1937[a]	1938[a]	1939[b]	1940[b]	1941[b]
16,788	43,686	32,110	234,301	57,366	24,720	18,371	35,116

Source and notes: GARF 9401/1/4157/201–3, 205. I am very grateful to Gábor Rittersporn for a copy of these figures. They may not include the cases being processed by the ordinary court system.
[a] Arrests.
[b] Convictions.

necessarily have fallen into the category of anti-Soviet agitation, except perhaps at the height of the terror in 1937–8. Statistics relating to anti-Soviet agitation cases therefore refer only to certain types of negative opinion. In addition, the rise and fall in the numbers of cases prosecuted is not necessarily indicative of anything more than changes in the severity of repression. What can we make of the statement by the USSR Procurator Akulov following Kirov's death in early 1935 that 'an increase in the activity of anti-Soviet elements has been noted in the form of counter-revolutionary agitation, approving not only of the terrorist act against Kirov, but also of the execution of such acts against other leaders of the Party and Soviet government'?[40] This year saw a threefold rise in cases of anti-Soviet agitation. But how far did an increase in the number of cases prosecuted reflect a real increase in negative comment about the *vozhdi* and how far did it reflect the stepping-up of repression?[41] Such statistics are therefore of limited value in attempting to answer this question.

So, given the obstacles to reaching any reliable quantitative conclusions about the extent of dissenting opinion, I will try to focus instead on *typical and recurring themes*, and to indicate whenever an opinion was particularly common or particularly unusual. However, here too caution must be exercised: were the large number of reports of negative comments in relation to the labour decree of 1940 indicative of widespread complaint, or simply of a more thorough and concerted reporting campaign?

It may be that future research will yield more precise data. However, until then, we must be content with a rather impressionistic picture,[42] and perhaps also derive insights from comparative and theoretical literature. For example, Ian Kershaw suggests in relation to similar reports on the popular mood produced by party and state authorities in Nazi Germany that the draconian repression of critical opinion and the accompanying fear of denunciation produced a web of deceit and mendacity in which spoken words concealed real feelings; where people frequently neither said what they meant nor meant what they said; where out of fear they even more frequently said nothing at all. We can safely claim, therefore, that *the reported comment hostile to the regime was but the tip of the iceberg* [emphasis added].[43]

Likewise in Stalin's Russia, many who stayed silent or used the official language on certain occasions may have privately shared the heretical views expressed openly by others.

LENINGRAD

Much of the material on which this study is based comes from Leningrad and Leningrad *oblast'*.[44] It could be argued that Leningrad's particular history made it a more fertile breeding ground for alternative opinion than other regions. More detailed regionally based studies are needed to test this hypothesis. However, work that has been done on other regions, including that by Jeffrey Rossman and Sheila Fitzpatrick, suggests that popular opinion in other regions did not differ very much from that of Leningrad.[45] Nevertheless, the specific character of Leningrad should be borne in mind.

Leningrad *oblast'*, formed in 1927, covered a vast area of 360,400 km². In the period 1934–7, its population (excluding the city of Leningrad) numbered almost 4 million, a figure which declined to about 3.2 million by 1939.[46] Just under half of these lived in the towns of the *oblast'*, some of which were very ancient and had their own large-scale industrial enterprises, often developed from *kustar'* origins. *Kustar'* industry (including porcelain, matches, and paper) continued to play a significant role in the economy, partly because of the proximity of a huge market in Leningrad itself and partly because of the unfavourable agricultural conditions. The *oblast'*, with its poor climate and land covered by forest and marsh, was not an environment conducive to agriculture, especially grain production, and the economy was based largely on fish, timber, and flax. The collectivisation process was slow to take off here, as in other consumer regions, and was complicated by the large number of *khutora* which were difficult to resettle.[47] By 1 March 1930, the *oblast'* had achieved only 23.1 per cent collectivisation, the lowest rate in the country. After Stalin's volte-face on the tempo of collectivisation, this declined to 5.7 per cent.[48] Thereafter the rate rose steadily, reaching

65.2 per cent by July 1934. The real breakthrough came with the issue of the *kolkhoz* model charter in 1935 (see chapter 2) and, by October 1936, 91 per cent collectivisation had been attained.[49] Although clearly affected to a certain extent by its proximity to Leningrad, Leningrad *oblast'* cannot be considered particularly atypical, certainly in comparison with other consumer regions in Russia.

Although founded 'only' in 1703 by Peter the Great, St Petersburg–Leningrad ranks as one of Russia's oldest large cities. In the Soviet period, its population experienced a rapid decline, followed by an equally rapid rise. In 1917 it numbered 2,300,000, but by 1920, the devastation of the civil war reduced it to a mere 740,000. During NEP, it rose steadily and, with the onset of industrialisation, it accelerated to 2,720,000 by 1934, a figure which rose to 3,190,000 by 1939. In the 1930s, it was the seventh largest city in the world, after New York, London, Berlin, Moscow, Chicago, and Paris. The city was first and foremost a major industrial centre. In 1934, 12.6 per cent of the USSR's large-scale industry was located in Leningrad. Large-scale industry in the city employed over half a million workers in 1934–5, a figure which rose steadily throughout this period. Most of these worked in the metal and electro-technical industries (239,722 in 1934). Other major branches included the chemical, textile, sewing, timber, and food industries. The majority of enterprises had been established before the revolution, with a few even dating back to the eighteenth century. Leningrad was also an important cultural centre, home to more than sixty higher educational establishments in 1934, as well as large numbers of theatres, museums, and so on. Its literacy rates were higher than elsewhere in the USSR – 94.6 per cent in 1939.[50]

This, then, was no ordinary city. The representation of western-oriented St Petersburg–Leningrad as a locus of opposition to the more traditional 'Slavophile' Moscow has become something of a stereotype. Nevertheless, it has some basis. The 1905 and 1917 revolutions began in the city. After the capital was moved to Moscow in 1918, the city continued to bear all the hallmarks of a former capital, but was not burdened with the administration that so defined Moscow's identity. It experienced a spate of radical political activity during the civil war and, in 1921, the revolt of sailors at the city's naval base, Kronstadt, and unrest within the city itself precipitated the turn to NEP. During NEP, under the leadership of Grigorii Zinoviev, Leningrad became a stronghold of the opposition movement within the party. With its great Petersburg heritage, the Leningrad party was stronger than most other provincial organisations and relatively independent, and managed to hold out against Stalin until 1926, longer than any other organisation. Kirov was sent in to quell the dissent, and appears to have succeeded. However, there may have been more than a grain of truth in Stalin's allegations after the murder of Kirov that the city remained a nest of former oppositionists and anti-Soviet types. Certainly many former members of the opposition retained leading posts under Kirov, while old aristocrats and members of the intelligentsia lived on in relative tranquillity.

Leningrad may indeed have been a more natural home for heretical ideas than some other parts of Russia. However, it would be wrong to overemphasise the singularity of opinion emanating from the city and its environs. Comparable material from other regions, including Moscow, Novosibirsk, Ivanovo, and Smolensk, does not suggest that Leningrad opinion was unique, except perhaps in its extent and articulateness. Ordinary people throughout Russia (and the USSR) experienced common problems in this period, and probably reacted to them in not too dissimilar ways.

I

Economy and society

CHAPTER I

Workers, the economy, and labour policy

At the end of the 1920s, Stalin launched the Great Leap Forward, an economic revolution of unprecedented speed and magnitude. Although crash industrialisation brought workers certain benefits, such as virtually full employment, it also created enormous hardship. Despite a modest improvement in their living standards during the second five-year plan, the immediate priority for most workers in the 1930s was sheer survival. Unsurprisingly, economic questions featured more prominently than any other issue in popular opinion. This chapter will examine workers' views on subjects such as the end of rationing, state loans, price rises, and shortages. It will also consider their reactions to the main innovations in labour policy: Stakhanovism and the labour decrees of 1938–40.[1]

Workers were acutely aware of fluctuations in their standard of living, frequently comparing prices with wages. It was patently obvious to them whether their own economic situation was improving or deteriorating, and they were not deceived by official rhetoric about rising standards. The rhetoric simply highlighted the disparity between the fictitious 'good life' and their actual situation. Their personal experience of the Soviet economy, with its queues and deficits, led to criticism of the regime's refusal to address such issues publicly. Many of their comments reveal a belief that the state ought to be providing for workers as it claimed it was doing.[2] Workers showed no hesitation in invoking the regime's own ideological claims: for example, they readily deployed the party's own rhetoric on workers' emancipation. When objections were voiced to Stakhanovism or to the labour decrees of 1938–40, it was often on the grounds that these measures were 'exploitative', and reminiscent of 'capitalism'.

Workers' perceptions of their own economic position can only be understood against the background of their changing standard of

Table 2 *Wage differentiation amongst Leningrad industrial workers in 1936*

Percentage of workers within each wage band across all industries

to 140 r.	140.1– 180 r.	180.1– 220 r.	220.1– 260 r.	260.1– 300 r.	300.1– 340 r.	340.1– 420 r.	420.1– 500 r.	500.1– 600 r.
5.5	10.9	14.2	13.7	11.4	9.3	13.3	8.2	5.9

600.1– 700 r.	700.1– 800 r.	800.1– 900 r.	900.1– 1,000 r.	1,000.1– 1,100 r.	1,100.1– 1,200 r.	1,200.1– 1,500 r.	1,500 r. +
3.2	1.8	1.0	0.6	0.4	0.2	0.3	0.1

Source and note: 24/2v/2471/95, 98, 101. The average wages of *sluzhashchie* were less than that of workers, at 279 r. Those of the ITR stood at 583 r.

living in this period.[3] Between 1928 and 1934 the standard of living had declined rapidly. From 1934, this decline halted, although standards never regained their levels at the end of NEP. The relative prosperity of the second five-year plan was followed by the exceptionally lean years of 1938–41. Naum Jasny estimates that, in 1932–3, workers' real wages were only 49 per cent of their 1928 level. By 1937, they had risen to about 60 per cent, falling again to 56 per cent in 1940.[4] While real wages for the average worker were lower than in 1928, this was offset to some extent by an increase in the number of women workers and a concomitant fall in the ratio of dependants to wage earners from 2.26:1 in 1927 to 1.59:1 in 1935.[5] Active promotion of wage differentiation continued in this period, although differentials were perhaps not quite as great as has been imagined. A survey of 396,788 Leningrad workers for October 1936 reveals that monthly wages ranged from less than 140 r. to over 1,500 r., with the average standing at 321 r. (see table 2). The highest average wages were in the metalworking industries (364 r.) and the lowest in the food industry (231 r.). Considering that this survey was carried out after the introduction of Stakhanovism, greater differentials might have been expected, but in fact almost 50 per cent of workers were earning in the range of 220 to 420 r., and only a tiny minority were receiving in excess of 1,000 r.

Most of the average worker's wages were spent on food in this period. Surveys of household budgets of workers in Leningrad show that, while in 1927–8 the proportion spent on food was 43.8 per cent, this rose to 55.9 per cent in 1934 and 58 per cent in 1935. The figure stood at about 55 per cent until 1938, after which statistics are not available. In general, the proportion spent on non-comestible items was lower in this period than at any time between 1928 and 1933. For example, 9.3 per cent of the household budget was spent on clothes in 1935, compared with 13 per cent in 1933, and 17 per cent in 1928.[6] The housing crisis, exacerbated by the influx into the cities during the first five-year plan, continued to be a problem. In 1934–5, the average Leningrad resident occupied only 5.8m² of space (compared with 8.5m² in 1927).[7] There are no published statistics for the later period; however, in the towns of the *oblast'* the average housing space fell from 5.1m² per individual in 1934 to 4.1m² in 1937. Some towns were particularly badly provided for, such as Murmansk, where the figure was only 2.1m²in 1937.[8] It is likely that, in all these cases, workers would probably have occupied even less then the average space. Certainly many continued to live in barracks in this period. The Stakhanovite workers with their own flats were very much the exception.

Other factors, such as virtually full employment, the 'social wage', and cultural benefits, may have compensated to some extent for the decline in living standards since NEP (although workers also lost benefits in this period, such as the right to free medicine). However, in any case, the actual 'objective' economic situation outlined above cannot be *directly* correlated with workers' perceptions of their living standards, which were influenced by other variables, including the disparities between the propaganda vision of prosperity and their own situation, and between their own situation and that of other social groups.

1934–1935: SEVENTEENTH PARTY CONGRESS, BREAD, AND THE END OF RATIONS

After the bleak famine years of 1932–3, the propaganda machine built up to the Seventeenth Party Congress in January 1934 with positive articles and assertions that socialism had been won. *Leningradskaia pravda* included an article 'For a happy, cultured, joyful life!' which began 'How life has changed! Gone are the times when the worker only thought about his daily bread.'[9] The congress sanctioned a new line in economic policy. The first five-year plan had concentrated on building up heavy industry at the expense of the consumer. The dominant ethos had been one of sacrifice and the denial of individual needs even to the point of asceticism. Egalitarianism had prevailed in the initial period of the plan, and sometimes continued despite official injunctions to the contrary. By contrast, the second five-year plan aimed to raise wages, increase production of consumer goods, and stimulate retail trade. Peasants were encouraged to keep more livestock. In his report to the congress, Stalin declared that unemployment had been liquidated, promoted economic relations based on money, and attacked egalitarianism, stressing that a Marxist understanding of equality did not entail levelling in the area of personal needs and everyday life, but rather the destruction of classes. He defined socialism as 'not poverty and deprivation, but the elimination of poverty and deprivation'.[10]

The results of the congress, and Stalin's speech in particular, were propagated quite widely amongst workers during the first half of 1934. Discussion at factory meetings included openly critical comments contrasting the fine words of the congress with the actual food shortages: 'The speeches are good but there's no bread.' Clearly, food remained the highest priority for most workers, and all the talk about cultural achievements, satisfying workers' needs, productivity rises, and so on had little significance for them in the face of this overwhelming need. Criticisms were made even by those willing to accept the achievements. As one worker admitted, 'The working class has grown – that's right, but why do we eat badly – there are not enough food and goods, when will we live to see the end of it, it's time to start getting worried about it.'[11] The questions workers raised concerning the speech reveal some of their concerns. Paradoxically, given the complaints about material deprivation, Stalin's emphasis on future material abundance worried some workers. Although Stalin had been careful to differentiate between Bukharin's call to the peasants in 1925 to enrich themselves (*Obogashchaites'*) and his own 'Make every *kolkhoz* wealthy', people nevertheless wondered what the difference was. There was a fear that if 'the worker raises cattle, and leads a wealthy life, won't it be a return to private property?'[12] Stalin's criticism of downward levelling was evidently directed at this type of egalitarianism and suspicion of wealth. As well as these feelings, and the notion that the regime should be doing more to feed the workers, anti-state, somewhat individualistic language could also be heard. One worker mocked Stalin's calls for people to develop animal husbandry, complaining that he had a cow, and had to give 300 litres of milk to the state for a fixed price, while the state gave him nothing. His comment was typical of the individualistic colouring of some popular opinion. While he spoke out openly, many others exchanged their critical views in private. At the Lenin works, for example, there was widespread criticism of the various taxes, including income tax, insurance, and lotteries. Workers did not feel that they were getting any personal benefit from them. Huge factories were being built, but their own situation was not improving.[13]

Many of the typical concerns of the worker in this period are illuminated in a letter to the party secretary of Tomsk from the middle of 1934. The letter posed twenty-eight questions, the majority of which concerned the material needs of the worker – why was bread so expensive, why could workers not live in the city centre, why were their houses not repaired, why was there no fish for sale? The letter also included a comparison of wages and prices in 1914 and 1934, indicating to what extent the real standard of living had declined. The letter commenced with the question 'Was there ever a time when people thought about bread as much as they do now?'[14] This again was typical, because the most common topic of discussion in 1934 was bread. Despite the assurances of the propaganda that the worker 'no longer thinks only about his daily bread', bread continued to assume a huge symbolic and material importance in everyday life. It had always formed the staple part of the Russian diet, and was (and is) treated reverently (even today, bread is sacred for Russians, who consider it almost immoral to discard old crusts). The reliance on bread meant that the periodic famines had devastating consequences. A succession of famines in 1891, 1921–2, and 1932–3 ensured that anxiety about bread featured prominently in popular discourse of this period.[15] Also, since bread was rationed from 1929 until 1 January 1935, it had acquired an additional significance, as it could be used for the purposes of barter.

The ration system favoured workers above other social groups and industrial workers above other workers. It provided the worker with a feeling of security and, although bread was apportioned in a 'hierarchical' way, distribution was relatively egalitarian, as disparities between norms were not great. However, the system was heavily flawed. Supplies were inadequate, the quality of bread was low, and the prices in commercial shops beyond the means of the majority.[16] Throughout 1934, the government attempted to narrow the gap between the price of commercial and rationed bread in preparation for the complete abolition of rations. In June 1934, the price of rationed bread doubled from 25 k. to 50 k. for a kilogram of rye bread, and although the wages of the low-paid were raised in partial compensation, this failed to alleviate tension.[17] The news of the rise was followed by a spate of rumours reflecting workers' fears and hopes. It was suggested variously that from 15 June prices would fall, that in Moscow there had been no price rise, and that Stalin had heard about workers' consternation and had annulled the decree. The situation in the second half of the year was strained. In August, *Sputnik agitatora* referred overtly to the recent 'sorties [*vylazki*]' of the class enemy in factories, which was the usual cryptic formula for describing any manifestation of hostile or anti-Soviet feeling. In November, workers used the occasion of the forthcoming local soviet elections to push through mandates requesting that bread prices be reduced to their level prior to the price rises in June.[18]

Widespread speculation that the rationing of bread was about to be ended was finally confirmed by the TsK plenum of 25–8 November, which decreed that rations would cease from 1 January 1935, and that bread would be priced at a figure midway between current commercial and state prices. Wages were to be raised for the very poor. The announcement of the plenum's decision coincided with the murder of Kirov, and it is notable that discussion about the murder was sometimes less intense amongst ordinary people than the debate about the end of rations. While some welcomed the decision, and the prospect of greater choice and fewer queues, there was also confusion about the end of a system to which many had become accustomed, a few fears that peasants would buy up the bread, and concern about how the policy would be implemented in practice.

The most hostile responses emanated from the poorest workers, especially those with large families and in which the husband was not earning much. For example, a party member earning 200 r. with a family of seven said 'It's terrible. I don't have enough bread even now. The kids don't eat enough black bread. One has died. Now even more will die. The prices are too high.'[19] Amongst this group, the general feeling was that the compensation would prove inadequate, and that white bread in particular would be beyond the means of the ordinary worker: 'Only the rich will eat white bread, like in the past.'[20] A joke current at the time conveyed workers' apprehension about a decline in living standards: Stalin decided to end the ration system, but, not sure about how to do it, lay down to sleep. The dead Lenin came to him in a dream and said to him, 'Do this: transfer those who were in the first category to the second, the second to the third, the third to the fourth, and send the fourth to me.'[21]

On 1 January 1935 'the toilers of Leningrad joyfully welcomed the free sale of bread'.[22] This, at any rate, was the official version, which as usual reflected only part of the story. The reality was that the cost of bread doubled on average to one ruble per kilogram, that is, a four-fold rise on the price of rationed bread prior to June 1934.[23] As had been predicted, the compensation failed to cover the increased expense, since although the average monthly wage for a working-class family rose by 22 r., bread expenses went up by 31 r.[24] These average statistics conceal the plight of those such as a railway worker, Dobriakov, who had a wife and six children to support on wages of 150 r. per month. The additional compensation of 15 r. to which he was entitled covered only about 10 per cent of his extra bread costs.[25] Food assumed an even greater proportion of the family budget. In the first quarter of 1935, the average spent on food by a Leningrad working-class family rose by 6.3 per cent, to 60.6 per cent of the total expenditure.[26] As workers had anticipated, white bread became less accessible, and in 1935 the consumption of the cheaper rye bread peaked.[27]

Those hit hardest by the end of rations were large families, and those, such as industrial workers, who had received preferential rations under the old system.[28] At the November plenum, Stalin himself had portrayed this system as a no longer tolerable form of positive discrimination in favour of the working class, describing the low price of rationed bread as 'a gift from the state to the working class' and 'a social class ration for the working class'.[29] It is clear that large numbers of workers themselves also believed the new policy was directed against them, and commented that it flew in the face of Stalin's Seventeenth Party Congress pronouncements about improvements in the standard of living of the working class.[30]

The sense of betrayal was compounded by the abolition on 25 September 1935 of rations for meat, fish, sugar, fats, and potatoes, a policy mitigated somewhat for the very poor by a simultaneous reduction in bread prices (from 100 k. to 85 k. per kilogram of rye bread, for example). Low-paid workers complained that this reduction was insufficient, that the policy was unjust and designed to benefit the rich.[31] This was to a large extent true. Since only the rich had patronised the commercial shops in the past, the end of rationing of expensive products worked mainly to their advantage. Jasny concludes that 'the burden of the great rise in the prices of rationed food in the first place fell on the low-wage worker'.[32] Party informants noted a correlation between wage levels and reactions to the policy. At the Svetlana factory it was alleged that most complaints were being expressed in shops where workers earned less than 150 r.[33]

The new policy also affected prices in canteens, which rose by as much as half, putting meals beyond the means of some workers and prompting parodies such as the following 'menu', which appeared at the entrance to the canteen of the Kirov works on 1 October: 'Dinner for the workers: first course – kerosene soup; second course – fresh moss with smetana; third course – swede pudding.'[34] During 1935, the numbers eating at canteens declined drastically, causing the leadership anxiety, not least because the Seventeenth Party Congress had aimed to increase the numbers of people 'enjoying' public catering by two and a half times.[35]

While the abolition of rations was in fact a sign of economic strength, and although the economic climate certainly improved in 1935, with a much better assortment of goods available in the shops, the improvement was felt only by the better off, and so exacerbated social cleavages (see chapter 8). For most ordinary people, 1935 was, as Alec Nove notes, a year in which 'living standards were very grim indeed'.[36] Interestingly, one worker, looking back from the perspective of 1940, pointed to 1935 as the year when life started to deteriorate for workers.[37] The very conspicuous consumption which characterised the mid-1930s, the return to newspaper advertising, the propaganda of the 'good life' all raised and frustrated the expectations of the poor. A letter sent to Zhdanov in June 1935 expresses this clearly. The writer, a worker, described his average day:

I get up in the morning, go to work, cut off a chunk of bread, sprinkle salt on the table, and a glass of cold water, eat it up and get on with work until 12 a.m. We go to the canteen to eat and have some tasteless, disgusting soup or *shchi* [cabbage soup], you eat it and feel sick, it's really disgusting. The price of the first course is quite considerable: 45 k. You have just a first course and leave, the second course is very expensive: 1 r. 55 k. for pork. We can't afford that on such small wages ... So you come home at the end of work, and again have a chunk of bread, salt, and glass of water. You drink a little, and lie down to sleep on that. I can't afford to buy food in the commercial shops, everything is expensive, and so you walk and wander around like a deathly shade, and get very thin and weak.

The writer admitted that now the shops were full of goods, but complained that he and other workers could not buy them, and he appealed to Zhdanov for prices to be halved.[38]

Throughout the dismal year 1935 workers wrote to Zhdanov citing figures to demonstrate the failure of their wages to keep pace with price changes and the end of rations. The refrain running through these letters was that, although now the shops were full, nothing was affordable. While under rations the worker had occupied a privileged position, now he felt second-class. A locksmith who had worked at the Bol'shevik factory for eighteen years told Zhdanov how, eighteen years after the revolution, he was once again hearing those old words, 'I am a worker again, I am in need.' The government had ended rationing and introduced free trade, but the worker could not afford the newly available products. He himself earned 180 r. a month, 30 r. of which disappeared on various taxes and accommodation. The rest was barely sufficient to buy bread for himself and his dependent wife and child.[39] Other workers wrote comparing the cost of living with that in 1913 – showing that while wages had gone up by four times, the price of bread had risen by twenty-seven times – or recalling the 'good life' under Trotsky.[40]

The propaganda began to reflect this popular concern with 'everyday' issues, although in a less subversive manner. In April 1935 *Trud* asked 'When will "everyday" [*bytovye*] questions be raised at workers' meetings?', and urged that issues such as the canteen and labour turnover be discussed openly.[41] Newspapers began to print numerous 'workers' letters' criticising leaking roofs in hostels, dirty canteens, the late payment of wages, and the lack of shops in certain districts. Local bureaucrats were considered culpable for all these problems. These letters expressed some of the real popular dissatisfaction of this period, although they never touched on politically sensitive subjects such as low wages or hunger.

STAKHANOVISM

On the night of 30 August 1935, the Donbass miner Aleksei Stakhanov overfulfilled his quota by 1,400 per cent, inaugurating what would become known as the Stakhanovite movement. Although 'shock work' had been employed since 1929, Stakhanovism differed from the earlier movements partly in its more overt use of material stimuli, ranging from very high wages to flats, holidays, bicycles, and theatre trips, and also in its stress on the 'heroic' image of individual record-breakers. This approach corresponded well with the new consumerism and more individualist philosophy of the second five-year plan.

In the autumn of 1935, Stakhanovism spread throughout industry, not without resistance. In particular, some managers were hostile towards it, and the movement acquired an anti-managerial dimension, as workers were encouraged to criticise and expose those 'sabotaging' its implementation. However, anti-managerial feeling was only one type of worker response to the movement. While some clearly endorsed Stakhanovism, welcoming the opportunities it provided for individual advancement, and complaining when they failed to receive the necessary back-up, others were less enthusiastic. The regime itself was inclined to represent any worker opposition to the movement as limited to envious attacks on individual Stakhanovites. Although these did take place, most objection to the movement amongst workers seems actually to have been based on anxiety about its potential and actual effects on their own wages, employment, and so on.

The representation of leading Stakhanovites in the media certainly did give ordinary workers grounds for resentment and envy. Speeches such as the one made by a Stakhanovite, Likhoradov, at the first All-Union Conference of Stakhanovites in November 1935 must have incensed less fortunate workers. He described how in January 1935 he was earning only 184 r. By September this figure had increased to 1,315 r. However, he declared:

I want to earn even more – two thousand, three and a half, because our Soviet power gives us the chance to work well, earn a lot and live a cultured life. Can't I wear a good Boston suit, buy good cigarettes? I can. Some comrades envy me, but what's that to me?[42]

What effect did this overt celebration of wealth, materialism, and self-advancement have upon workers? There clearly was some resentment at Stakhanovites' meteoric careers. One worker asked in 1936, 'Why did Stakhanov develop the Stakhanovite movement and does not work himself, but is a boss [*nachal'nik*]?'[43] It seems to have been older workers who particularly resented the swift progress of their juniors – 53 per cent of Stakhanovites in Leningrad industry in November 1935 were under thirty years old.[44] At a class in December 1935 at Krasnyi Vyborzhets, Kopylev, who had worked at the factory for forty-four years, complained that young workers with one or two years' experience were being paid so well, taken to see Stalin, and so on. However, it is worth noting that older cadre workers also resisted Stakhanovism simply because the increments for long service and qualifications and *progressivka* (sliding payments) ensured that their wages were already sufficiently high.[45]

Some physical and verbal attacks on Stakhanovites certainly did take place, and the TsK decree of 28 November 1935 'On the struggle against crimes intended to disorganise the Stakhanovite movement' and subsequent procuracy directives were designed to deal with this real, if limited, phenomenon.[46] In fact, 'attacks' were often not very serious, involving jokes at the expense of Stakhanovites, such as 'Oh, you Stakhanovite, let's have a smoke. The work won't go away.'[47] Many alleged attacks, including physical assaults, were not necessarily related to the individual's status as a Stakhanovite, as the legal press itself even admitted.[48]

Thurston argues plausibly that most conflict associated with the movement arose not between Stakhanovites and ordinary workers, but between all workers and their bosses.[49] The extension of Stakhanovite status to up to a third of all workers probably mitigated the problem of envy. To be an ordinary Stakhanovite was not really to belong to an elite, particularly as the status was fairly fluid.[50] Only a tiny minority of Stakhnovites were earning wages comparable to those of Likhoradov, and the prizes Stakhanovites received were more likely to be teapots, chairs, mattresses, and boots than luxury flats.[51]

Workers were less critical of individual Stakhanovites and their achievements than of the wider implications of the movement. They were sceptical about its efficacy for, despite the alleged records, the general economic situation did not seem to be improving much. As one worker, a party member from the Samoilov factory, said in November 1935 'They write that at Skorokhod the worker Smetanin makes 2,000 pairs of shoes on his own, but go and try to find boots – there aren't any.'[52] They were particularly concerned about the threat the movement posed to their own pay and working conditions and frequently drew analogies between the new methods and those of capitalist exploitation.[53] In autumn 1935, unemployment, the raising of norms, and the lowering of wage rates because of increased productivity were predicted and some people deliberately worked less hard in order to keep the norms down.[54] Francesco

Benvenuti argues that the regime itself appears to have been aware of potential worker reaction to norm rises in connection with the movement, and so raged against spontaneous norm-raising by enterprises in October 1935.[55] However, the latter continued regardless, and at the Stakhanovite conference at the end of November, Stalin spoke of the need to raise norms, a decision ratified by the December plenum of the TsK. This only fuelled workers' fears, causing uncertainty and rumour. For example, in January 1936 at the Sudomekh factory, a rumour spread that at the Karl Marx plant workers had earned 1,000 r., so norms had been adjusted, and the new norms were impossible to fulfil. As a result, the norms had been lowered twice but still could not be fulfilled: 'Now there will be a revision of norms in all the factories, probably they will set norms that are impossible to fulfil. Then we'll live more easily and joyfully.'[56]

In April 1936 norms and wage rates were revised in many enterprises throughout Leningrad, and workers sometimes ended up earning less than before, despite Stalin's pledge that increased productivity would push up everyone's earnings. As different factories introduced different norms at different times, worker turnover escalated. Reports at the end of April speak of a 'massive refusal to take on and fulfil new norms; the presentation of collective petitions and departures from factories on a mass scale'. Some workers reacted by venting their hostility on Stakhanovites themselves, calling them traitors. However, there were also examples of solidarity between ordinary and Stakhanovite workers – at one factory the latter declared that, if norms were to be raised, they would give up their Stakhanovite status and leave the factory, since the new norms would reduce the earnings of both types of worker.[57] The propaganda was ridiculed, especially Stalin's slogan that life was becoming merrier and the claims of the December plenum that all workers' wages would rise. Yet again, the workers felt betrayed.

The revision of norms in some factories in July 1936 also caused some antipathy; however, by then the tempo of the movement was beginning to slow down after the first frenzied months of activity. Record-breaking for its own sake was attacked, and the anti-managerial tone was moderated. Norms rose more gradually and were even reduced in some cases in 1937–8. Reports rarely mentioned reactions to Stakhanovism after mid-1936.

1936–1937: 'LIFE HAS BECOME BETTER, LIFE HAS BECOME MERRIER' (STALIN)

This was the refrain which characterised the propaganda of the period 1936–7. Although the average wage was pushed up in this period in connection with the Stakhanovite movement, and life may have become marginally easier for some, the improvement was not sufficient to eliminate complaint. Workers based their judgements on common sense, not on slogans, and the latter often merely served to stimulate discontent: 'Much is written about the achievements of Soviet power, while the reality is that before a worker drank tea with white bread while now he gulps down water, and as for the *kolkhozniki* – there's nothing to say.'[58] Behind the window-dressing, it is clear, as Manning shows, that the economy was already beginning to falter by mid-1936, creating popular discontent which appears to have fuelled the momentum of the purges.[59]

In 1936 the lowering of wage rates in the factories in connection with the Stakhanovite movement, several price rises, and a new state loan all conspired to inflame popular opinion. The revision of norms in April 1936 provoked negative comments about the resulting fall in wage rates, and the failure of the latter to keep up with prices: 'with the revision of norms, instead of 9 r. a day, I only get 6 r., but food is very dear'; 'Before the norm revision I ate porridge, but now I don't get enough for porridge.' Life was not getting better, but worse, 'because it [was] becoming more expensive every day'.[60] On 1 July the government announced a decree on the 'State loan of the second five-year plan (fourth issue) and the conversion of previously issued internal loans'. Bonds earlier sold to citizens at an interest rate of 8–12 per cent with a short repayment period were converted to the lower rate of 4 per cent for twenty years.[61] Loans issued in previous years had never been popular, since workers were expected to contribute about a month's wages. However, in 1936 the additional obligation to convert old loans exacerbated the usual reluctance to subscribe, with party and especially Komsomol members displaying backward (*khvostistkie*) feelings, manifestly failing to provide the necessary 'encouragement' in what was supposed to be a voluntary exercise, and even refusing to subscribe themselves. By 4 July only 47.5 per cent of the required amount had been collected (in districts of Leningrad that provided information), a slower pace than for the loan of 1935. Some workers took collective decisions to subscribe

minimal amounts, citing material hardship as justification. The loan
coincided with yet another revision of norms and, by 8 July, workers
were still refusing to contribute, often arguing 'we don't know if we'll
get so much with the new norms'. Thus, only 44.9 per cent of
workers at the Nogin factory had subscribed by this date, contri-
buting a paltry 38.6 per cent of the required sum.[62]

On 25 July prices on certain items such as shoes were raised
without any public announcement. Agitators, who were not party to
any prior information, were bombarded with awkward questions on
the lines of 'how will the price rises improve the workers' welfare?'
The official discourse was frequently invoked, as people recalled how
the party congress had vowed to bring down prices: 'how does this
correspond with the promises of the Seventeenth Party Congress?'
Some questioners felt that the situation was worse for workers at this
time than during the famine years of 1932–3:

According to the plan, by the last year of the second five-year plan the
material situation should improve by two to three times, but we do not live
any better yet: everything is expensive, and clothes get worn out, and you
can't replace them. A worker with a family eats less bread and meat than in
1932 and 1933.[63]

There was a general sense of having been deceived, particularly as
much of the agitation at the time of the state loan a few weeks before
had stressed that the country was getting richer, and that prices
would soon fall.[64] The disillusionment was exacerbated when new
price rises were introduced in December. Once again, it was left to
agitators to deal with the hard questions, and they reported that the
question of the contradiction between this policy and the promises of
the party congress was raised by large sections of the population.[65]

By 1937, plan targets were not being met and the economy was
facing a looming crisis.[66] Famine in the countryside in the winter of
1936–7 caused an influx of peasants into the city in search of bread,
and the retail system failed to function properly. Shortages became
more widespread. Even stalwarts of the regime were worried about
the economic situation at the beginning of 1937. One wrote to
Zhdanov casting doubts on Stalin's words: 'The question of whether
we have reached a wealthy and cultured life has not yet been decided
completely, I think.' He continued that it was necessary to provide
the people not only with expensive products, but also with cheaper
varieties. He himself was unable to buy writing paper and pens, or

ordinary boots since, firstly, they were too expensive and, secondly, there were none in the shops anyway. The queues for bread were worrying, especially because no one, not even the local party organisations, seemed to understand why they were happening. He finished, 'We must take into account that there are many good things too, i.e. achievements, but I am not writing about them, because you already know what they are.'[67]

The state loan of July 1937 was entitled the 'Loan for the strengthening of the defence of the USSR', and the agitation campaign emphasised the duty of every citizen to contribute towards the nation's defence. However, it rapidly became clear that, as in 1936, some workers and communists were disinclined to put this noble ideal above their personal interests.[68] Some justified their refusal in terms of the official discourse on wrecking:

The loan is not compulsory for every worker. I earn 250 r. and spend 300 r. on food. So find some for the loan. I'll only subscribe 100 r. and that's too much. Anyway there's no point to the loan. At the top there are a lot of wreckers who'll wreck the loan.

Others tried to 'trade' with the officials, whom they knew were under pressure to collect the requisite amounts. At Krasnyi Treugol'nik workers said that they would only subscribe if they could have somewhere to live, a holiday, and so on.[69] Newspaper articles openly pointed to factories where many workers had not subscribed weeks after the issue. The articles blamed the factory administration. For example at the First Bread Factory, where more than 200 of the 823 workers had not subscribed by 20 July, the president of the factory committee, Lavrikov, had purportedly said 'I don't have time now to deal with the loan. The factory committee reports and elections are approaching. Let others get on with that.'[70] Such articles did not attempt to delve more deeply into the causes of popular reluctance to subscribe, for this would have meant admitting the financial hardship of many workers, and the dearth of enthusiasm for causes such as the defence of the motherland.

Newspaper reports did not mention the connection between popular dissatisfaction with economic policies and more general hostility towards the regime; however, it is clear that the two were closely related, and that the regime was well aware of this. For example, the May Day demonstration in 1937 encountered a marked lack of enthusiasm. People questioned why they should go to the

demonstration when there was nothing to eat, and meetings at
factories to celebrate the day attracted little support. At the Kirov
factory, only 30 of the 500 workers from the first shift came to the
meeting, and 60 of the 2,000 from the second shift. Only 20 of the
1,000 workers of the Fifth Hydro-Electric Power Station turned up to
their meeting.[71]

This link between poor economic performance and anti-Soviet
feeling was discussed candidly by party officials at meetings. At a
party conference at Krasnyi Treugol'nik on 23 January 1937, the
secretary of Kirovskii district, Kasimov, explained the impact of
shortages of galoshes (the factory's main product) on popular
opinion. When a worker, *intelligent*, or peasant could not find
galoshes, he became dissatisfied: 'Moreover that consumer does
not see Krasnyi Treugol'nik, comrades Vasil'ev, Konstantinova,
Denisov, he says "Soviet power! The power has changed, but there
are no galoshes! That's how good Soviet power is!"[72] This recognition that support for the regime rested to a large extent on its ability
to satisfy the consumer seems to have lain at the root of much of the
party leadership's anxiety during this period. It was clear that the
tide of popular opinion was turning against the regime because of
continued economic failure. This must at least partly explain the
policy which became particularly pronounced in 1937 of directing
popular hostilities away from 'Soviet power' and towards individuals,
such as the above-mentioned Konstantinova, secretary of the party
committee of Krasnyi Treugol'nik, who was purged on 19 June
1937.[73]

1938–1941: PRE-WAR SLUMP

The third five-year plan, which ran from 1938 until the outbreak of
war, envisaged greater investment in the defence industry at the
expense of consumer goods. This, when coupled with the havoc
wrought by the purges, created an extremely unfavourable economic
climate. Whereas there had been a modicum of justification for the
use of the slogan 'life has become better, life has become merrier' in
1936–7, such a refrain was wholly inappropriate for the third five-
year plan period, as even the regime came to recognise. The popular
mood was summed up in a letter of April 1938 from a foreman, who
had been a worker since before 1917. He demanded *glasnost'* and an
end to the charade of 'life has become better':

In fact, there's been twenty years of our power. Fifteen to sixteen of these have been peaceful construction. There were many difficulties, failures. The party warned the people that these were temporary difficulties, that after the fulfilment of the two five-year plans there would be everything in abundance. The people struggled with zeal, overcame difficulties. Socialism has been built in the main. As we embark on the third five-year plan we shout at meetings, congresses, and in newspapers 'Hurray, we have reached a happy, joyful life!' However, incidentally, if one is to be honest, those shouts are mechanical, made from habit, pumped by social organisations. The ordinary person makes such speeches like a street newspaper-seller. In fact, in his heart, when he comes home, this bawler, eulogist, will agree with his family, his wife who reproaches him that today she has been torturing herself in queues and did not get anything – there are no suits, no coats, no meat, no butter.

The writer noted that the words 'Life has become better, life has become merrier' were now cited ironically, usually when people were experiencing some difficulty. He admitted achievements, and the need for defence, but asked that the most basic necessities be made available, at any price. Wondering why there were no strikes and revolutions in fascist Germany, he concluded that presumably this was because German workers had everything they needed. He also confessed that he wanted to join the party, but only when leaders openly spoke up in the press and explained to the people why they were experiencing difficulties and when there would be enough of everything.[74]

In fact, the press did reduce their incessant incantations of the slogan 'life has become better' and even began to write publicly about the problem of discontent, mainly in order to assist agitators who were finding it increasingly difficult to justify the blatant shortages to workers. In September 1938, *Sputnik agitatora* published the 'correct' answers to the tricky questions 'Why are there some- times not enough products and consumer goods in the shops?', and 'Why are there queues?' Agitators were supposed to focus on the failure of heavy industry to fulfil its plans, the bad work of trading organisations, and the problem of speculation.[75] However, despite this guidance, many agitators failed to provide satisfactory answers. One agitator explained the queues in 1939 in the following, far from convincing way, 'Our country is big, with a population of 170 million, while England, for example, has a small population, and thus there are no queues there.'[76]

Queues and shortages were the hallmark of this period. The

queues contained large numbers of disaffected people, and served as fertile breeding grounds for discontent and the spread of rumours. For example, at the end of September 1938, the militia noted queues for clothes, shoes, and cloth in the centre of Leningrad ranging in size from 1,500 to 6,000 people. Those waiting would complain 'You stand in a queue and don't get anything.'[77] In this period workers advocated the reintroduction of rations and closed shops. Women from the Rabotnitsa factory stated at the end of 1938:

There are such huge queues for manufactured goods that we workers cannot buy anything for the [October] holiday. The struggle against speculation is very weak. We must end speculation and at least introduce a ration system on goods or else open closed shops at the factories, so that we factory workers could get something for ourselves.[78]

This was a demand which became more pronounced in 1939–40. However, in order to combat the deficits, the government resorted instead to a policy of continually raising prices. In January 1939, unified prices were introduced for consumer goods, which meant an effective doubling of prices on many products, accompanied by protests from workers.[79] This measure failed to eradicate queues, however. People noticed that the situation had worsened even relative to the mid-1930s: 'Why is there nothing in the USSR, even compared with 1936?'[80] The government loan campaign in August 1939 encountered the usual opposition. Some activists refused to carry out the campaign and there were cases of open agreement between workers to subscribe a lower amount. For example, in the tenth shop of the No. 7 Works, Sysoenkova gathered a group of workers and told them to 'maintain unity', as a result of which each of them subscribed only 50 r. A couplet spread round this factory 'Nalogi, nalogi. Nalogi davai, a osen' pridet shtany prodavai' ('Taxes, taxes. Pay taxes, and when autumn comes, sell your trousers').[81]

With the outbreak of war in September, the food situation deteriorated as people began to hoard. In October, rumours abounded that it would worsen as Soviet produce was sent to Germany, and the newly occupied west Ukraine and west Belorussia.[82] An attempt was made to improve supplies in time for the anniversary of the revolution, but this was largely invalidated by hoarding. The outbreak of the Winter War with Finland at the end of November and the government's prohibition on the sale of flour and bread in the countryside in December meant that, by the end of 1939, huge queues and shortages were endemic in Leningrad and the towns of the *oblast'*.

The Winter War exacerbated already low morale. Many factories in Leningrad were unable to operate because of the lack of power. In January 1940 people hoped and believed that rations would be introduced to cope with the crisis but, as one party member argued, the government clearly would not adopt rations since that would entail actually providing food for the people, food which evidently did not exist. What actually happened was another round of price rises in Leningrad at the end of January, resulting in an increase in 'anti-Soviet conversations', and dissatisfaction amongst even party and Komsomol members. Some party secretaries were at a loss as to how to explain the situation. One argued that the *raikom* itself should explain to workers, many of whom were earning only half their wages because of stoppages at the factories. They should answer the workers' questions as to why there had been enough food in 1914–17, but not during this war. Such negative comparisons with the tsarist regime were common at this time, while others drew analogies between the First World War's precipitation of revolution and the current situation: 'the people are suffocating in queues. It's an outright mockery of the people. I remember how in 1916 the people were mocked likewise and then the revolution occurred.'[83]

The demands for *glasnost'* from the grassroots became more vociferous. An unpublished letter to *Leningradskaia pravda* from January 1940 complained about the deficits, queues, and the stoppages which halved workers' pay:

No, comrades, you must change this situation of payment without fail and you must not ruin the worker completely, he's not guilty, give him work and he will work honourably, and if there's no work because of the [lack of] power, then pay him 100 per cent of the average wage ... We could live for a while even in these conditions if you, in a Bolshevik way, admitted all your failings. For you must explain why there is nothing in the shops, or if something does appear, then it's 50 per cent more expensive. I hope that we'll hear soon on the radio or read in the paper – as often we read in the paper and hear on the radio about foreign powers – how there prices have gone up on some goods.[84]

On 25 January, the party committee of the Bol'shevik factory received an anonymous letter, supposedly from fifty workers. The letter complained about the agitators who were trying to explain the price rises. It said that the party lied 'like the Mensheviks':

If your explanations about transport and other things do not convince anyone, then you should tell the workers straight away that your pork, sausage, rice, and sugar are being sent to Germany. Let the fascists enjoy it and get better, while the entire working class has got used to walking with an empty stomach.[85]

The price rises did little to solve the problem of queues, partly because considerable quantities of money remained in circulation. The regime resorted to repressive measures, using the militia to fine speculators and those standing in queues outside shops before opening time. People found ways of circumventing this, however, by standing in groups at bus stops and at other shops, waiting until the shop opened, and then rushing en masse to it and forming a queue.[86]

Popular ingenuity was also exhibited in spontaneous attempts to introduce unofficial forms of rationing, despite explicit instructions from the centre forbidding this practice. For example 'closed' shops were set up, by attaching people from one particular neighbourhood to a shop and preventing others from shopping there. Closed distribution points were also created within enterprises, and the quantity of goods that a customer could purchase at any one time ('norms') were set at a lower level than that sanctioned by the centre.[87]

Although the economic situation was at its most catastrophic during the winter of 1939–40, conditions remained grim throughout 1940–1. More price rises on basic foods were introduced in April 1940, causing panic and complaints from both low- and well-paid workers. In an unusual departure from its normal formula of blaming anti-Soviet and backward individuals for hostile comments, the NKVD noted that even those loyal to the regime were discontented. By this time, the party had virtually abandoned its explanatory work in many factories and enterprises.[88] In May 1940, new work norms were established. Further price rises came into effect in July 1940. In October, bread prices rose, and the norms of bread and other food which could be sold to any individual were reduced, provoking comments that 'government which lowers norms, raises the prices of food, leads an aggressive policy should be sacked' and the warning that 'if you deprive the worker of everything, no one will work for you, everyone will leave'.[89] The regime was aware that the workers no longer had any stimulus to work. There were no longer consumer goods for which they could strive if so inclined. Valuable labour time was wasted in queues. The only way to ensure productivity was to resort to ever more coercive disciplinary measures – this was the rationale behind the introduction of the labour decree of June 1940.

THE LABOUR DECREES OF 1938 AND 1940

While Stakhanovism had relied heavily on material stimuli to motivate workers, labour policy during the third five-year plan was based primarily on coercion. By this time, the shortfall in labour was becoming acute. Labour discipline had allegedly fallen to catastrophic levels in 1937.[90] The first half of 1937 witnessed one and a half times more cases of absenteeism than the first half of 1936. At some factories, up to 400 workers did not turn up every day, especially in the summer.[91] These problems continued into 1938[92] and, in an attempt to combat them, the government issued the decree of 28 December 1938 which imposed penalties for absenteeism and lack of discipline (including fines, evictions, and dismissals), and reduced maternity rights. Labour books were introduced to try to curb turnover and keep a check on discipline.

According to the NKVD, the announcement of the decree encountered 'numerous negative remarks', especially concerning the compulsory dismissal of absentees and those late for work. The decree was felt to be an infringement of workers' rights, of the gains of the revolution, and of the rights enshrined in the Constitution. Some spoke up openly at meetings. One worker at the Kirov works said 'I am voting against this law. Only in fascist Germany do they throw workers out onto the street. Do you think that all those present will vote? They are also against it, but they are afraid to say so openly.' Much dissatisfaction was also expressed, especially by women, regarding the clause on maternity rights.[93]

After the decree, cases of lateness and absenteeism continued, and workers were dismissed from their jobs accordingly. The dismissals particularly incensed long-standing cadre workers, who resented being treated as unreliable workers. At the Kombinat im Kirova, one worker, Fedorov, was sacked for being thirty minutes late, even though he had worked at the factory for twenty years and had received no reprimands. The female workers in the shop protested to the party secretary: 'we've worked all our life, gone to work [on time], and suddenly we oversleep in our old age, so surely you're not going to sack us all?' An atmosphere of tension prevailed amongst cadre workers;[94] nevertheless, the majority of those sacked, according to a report of July 1939 on turnover at Leningrad enterprises, were 'backward', 'young', or 'from the country'. This report actually criticised the excessive use of administrative measures to deal with the problem, which had resulted in numerous sackings. Thus, in the five months following the decree, 6,765 people had been sacked from the Kirov works, 4,572 of them for absenteeism. At the Molotov works, 1,288 workers had been sacked, or a third of the workforce. People deliberately tried to get sacked as a way of leaving the factory, and then they were taken on at new factories without any problem. The labour book system was clearly ineffective, and the shortage of labour meant that workers continued to control the market.[95]

Although this report suggested that administrative measures were ineffective and should be replaced with educational work, the regime resorted once again to the coercive approach. The decree of 26 June 1940 was issued supposedly at the behest of workers and under the auspices of the trade union council (the party and government deliberately tried to disassociate itself from this manifestly unpopular policy). It criminalised absence from work, including lateness of twenty minutes or more, and introduced an eight-hour working day. Timasheff argues that 'Since war was already raging in the West and threatened to spread to Russia, all these measures were willingly accepted by a population permeated by patriotic sentiment.'[96] An NKVD report of 21 October 1940 also noted that 'the main body of workers greeted the decree with enthusiasm. We have only isolated instances of anti-Soviet phenomena amongst the skilled workers.'[97] These conclusions seem rather rose-tinted, given other evidence.

The number of people suffering as a result of the decree was considerable: from 26 June 1940 until 1 March 1941, 142,738 people in Leningrad were sentenced to corrective labour for periods of up to six months under the decree. These included 3,961 communists and 7,812 Komsomol members.[98] The courts and prisons were overwhelmed. Nor did the decree make much difference to discipline in many factories, since workers continued to be late and play truant. In the Bol'shevik works, statistics for the third quarter of 1940 revealed that discipline had actually deteriorated since the second quarter. Several factories were failing to fulfil their plans. These facts cast doubt on the alleged widespread support for the decree.[99]

Likewise, the epidemic of suicides in the second half of 1940 do not appear to be symptomatic of enthusiasm. On learning that they were to be tried, it was not uncommon for workers to hang themselves, take poison, or throw themselves from windows, often leaving behind notes confessing their distress at being considered criminals for arriving a few minutes late for work usually because of the vagaries of public transport. One, Vasilieva, from the No. 7 Works, took iodine and opium, leaving a letter to her relatives:

I beg you not to cry for me, but be happy. Now he who is born must cry about this life, and he who dies must rejoice. Mummy, I'm sorry, but I cannot live on this earth any longer ... no one in our family has ever been put on trial, even long ago, and now I'll be tried, and I can't stand it.

Another worker was sentenced to forced labour for four months after being drunk at work. Before hanging himself, he left a note: 'Please do not blame anyone for my death. I have lived sixty-seven years. In 1940 I've been accused. Look for me in the attic.'[100]

The period following the decree witnessed a flurry of political protest. This included open political speeches, the spread of rumours and leaflets, and calls for strikes. The theme of revolution and rebellion emerged more strongly amongst workers than at any other time in this period. Leaflets and inscriptions announced 'Soon we'll strike' and 'Down with the government of oppression, poverty, and prisons.'[101] Rumours spread about strikes at other factories: at the Kirov works 500 people with fifteen planes and an armoured train had allegedly been gathered, and in Moscow and Donbass workers had already demonstrated.[102] Workers spoke of having a 'second revolution', of an 'outburst of dissatisfaction', of the 'people rising up', of a '*bunt* [uprising] against the government'.[103] It was felt that the people's patience was exhausted, that only a small shove was needed to push them over the edge, and that 1940 or 1941 would witness the end of Soviet power.[104] The NKVD, clearly perturbed by the upsurge in popular protest, gave the hostile reactions a counter-revolutionary colouring, attributing them to 'Trotskyists', 'anarchists', 'Mensheviks', and 'SRs', and ending their report of 28 September with ominous words reminiscent of 1937–8: 'In the immediate future we will be carrying out arrests of the most active counter-revolutionary elements, and also strengthening measures to reveal the anti-Soviet underground.'[105]

The reality behind the NKVD rhetoric was not political programmes, but rather plain dissatisfaction with the policies of the regime and, above all, a sense of injustice and exploitation. There was little mention of Trotsky or other symbolic figures, apart from Lenin; the constant theme of numerous comments was that all the gains of the revolution had been squandered, that the rights enshrined in the Constitution were being violated, that the country was regressing to capitalism, fascism, or even a 'second serfdom'.[106] Such comments revealed that even those who had hitherto been basically loyal to the regime, who had supported the ideals of the revolution and Constitution, who had believed that the workers were living in socialism – even these were now turning against the regime. It is interesting how often Constitutional rights were invoked in 1940: 'This decree is an infraction of the point in the Stalin Constitution, which points clearly to only a seven-hour day. Yes, that means we are not going forward to communism, but are retreating backwards'; 'the decree enserfs the workers. Where is the freedom of the person given in our Constitution? Where is justice?'[107]

The roots of much of the political activism appear to have lain with party members. Some party members, especially old Bolsheviks, were disturbed by the decree, partly because it seemed to contradict all the dreams of the revolution. Others objected to it because it meant losing skilled workers. Attempts to protect the latter were widespread, despite condemnation from on high. The decree was also resented because it created tension in the workplace. As one activist complained at a meeting at Krasnaia Znamia, 'Since the decree, there is an atmosphere of nervousness, a worker cannot rest properly now, but goes home and looks at his watch worrying about being late for work.' Communists advocated different methods of motivating workers, such as interesting them in their work and giving them more, rather than less, freedom. The alienation of certain party members surfaced particularly at the time of the October revolution anniversary. Some party committees made few preparations for the event, with the result that at many meetings only half those invited appeared. At the Kirov works, no members of the party committee turned up at the celebratory meeting on 4 November.[108] Other workers seem to have been aware of and influenced by the disaffection of party members. A worker from the Izhorskii works said:

Yes, I know even many communists who are just as dissatisfied as me, but the whole problem is that we talk to each other in some corner, but we need a strong organiser, and there isn't one. But we only need one shove, i.e. war, and the front line would break and everyone would go to those communists and turncoats, even women from the countryside would take up rakes, scythes, brooms, and go.[109]

This awareness of dissatisfaction within the party, and the fact that many thousands of communists and Komsomol members were among those sentenced under the decree, may have encouraged workers to hope for some form of organised protest.

By the end of 1940, the existence of worker dissatisfaction was being openly admitted. At a meeting organised by the party committee of the Kirov works, an old worker tried to raise morale:

There's no point hiding the fact that there are moaners amongst the workers. I want to say one thing to these moaners: when we workers, and many of us were Red partisans in our time, were fighting for Soviet power, sometimes we did not have a dry crust of bread, but we did not moan on and on. But now everything belongs to the worker.[110]

Such exhortations do not seem to have been particularly effective. Negative feelings continued, and all kinds of rumours spread, many focusing on the fate of workers who had been imprisoned under the decree. Workers' reactions suggest that in some ways this decree affected them more than the terror of 1937. Rumours highlighted the torture which was supposedly being inflicted upon imprisoned workers. One worker refused to subscribe to the 1941 loan, saying 'I won't give money for the construction of prisons for the working class.' The word 'sport' was deciphered by workers as 'Sovetskoe pravitel'stvo okruzheno rabochikh tiur'mami' ('Soviet government is surrounded by workers' prisons') and 'Sovetskoe pravitel'stvo organizovalo rabochii terror' ('Soviet government organised a worker's terror').

In these circumstances, party organisations appear to have abandoned the struggle against anti-Soviet attitudes. In February 1941, the Leningrad organisation-instructor department noted that anti-Soviet and unhealthy feelings were flourishing unchecked at the city's enterprises. It claimed that 'some anti-Soviet elements have let themselves go to such an extent that they brazenly and in the hearing of others slander the Soviet government, party and leaders'. Among party secretaries there was a growing sense of the futility of explanatory work.[111] It had been just about possible to justify the shortages, loans, end of rations, price rises, and Stakhanovism, but how was it possible to explain away the irony of mass imprisonments of workers by a regime whose claim to legitimacy lay in a doctrine which called for the working class to rise up and throw off its chains? The particular significance attached to ideology by the party left it especially vulnerable to popular criticism when it failed to live up to the claims of this ideology.

CHAPTER 2

Peasants and the kolkhoz

In 1917 Russian peasants had a single overwhelming aspiration – land. The Bolsheviks recognised this and, badly needing peasant support, on the night after the October revolution issued the Decree on Land, which abolished private ownership of land and called for its general redistribution. Despite this initial congruence of interests, relations between the Soviet regime and the peasants soon began to go sour. This was partly because the peasant had always lived in a self-contained world (*mir*), and strongly resented the interference of 'outsiders'. Clashes inevitably ensued as the Soviet regime was self-professedly interventionist, with ambitious plans for eliminating what it considered the 'idiocy of rural life'. However, the main bone of contention was the state's forced requisitioning of grain during the civil war. The serious resistance which this provoked was one of the factors behind the introduction of NEP and free trade in grain.

NEP was in some ways a relatively golden age for peasants. Although they were obliged to pay taxes, which caused some resentment, otherwise they were left much to themselves. Communists 'were rare birds in the countryside of the 1920s' and the peasant attitude to the regime in this period seems to have been one of indifference, rather than hostility.[1] Since peasants were under no compulsion to sell grain, and state grain prices were very low, they tended to produce just for subsistence, or else to hoard grain in the hope of pushing up prices. Agriculture remained at a primitive level, reliant on implements such as the wooden plough and the sickle.

All this meant that the towns were simply not being adequately fed. In an attempt to resolve the dilemma, the regime embarked upon collectivisation and in 1929 Stalin called for complete collectivisation and the liquidation of the 'kulaks' (rich peasants), who were blamed for hoarding grain. Peasants resisted fiercely, sometimes resorting to killing their livestock or burning their houses rather than join the collective farm. The regime was forced to back down and a temporary retreat occurred after March 1930. However, a renewed drive began later in the year. By 1931 over half of peasant households in the USSR had joined *kolkhozy* and large numbers of alleged kulaks had been deported to different parts of the country, sent to camps, or shot. The result of all these measures was the devastating famine of 1932–3.

For those peasants who joined *kolkhozy*, the new system seemed uncannily reminiscent of serfdom: in order to receive payments in the form of grain, they were required to work a certain number of 'labourdays' for the farm, which they perceived as similar to *barsh-china* (corvée, or a certain number of days of work for a landlord, which was required of serfs). The size of these payments depended on how much was left after the state had taken its (usually large) share. Many *kolkhozniki* simply left the farms and looked for work in the cities. The catastrophic decline in agricultural output jolted Stalin into adopting concessionary tactics, and a kind of modus vivendi was achieved in the mid-1930s. Almost complete collectivisa-tion was attained by 1937 and living conditions improved somewhat in the period from 1933 to 1937. Statistics for the entire USSR indicate that, whereas the peasant received 2.3 kg of grain per labourday in the famine year of 1932, this rose to 4 kg in 1937, the year of an exceptionally good harvest (the figures would have been lower in the relatively infertile Leningrad *oblast'*). The number of livestock and income from the free market also increased in the period to 1938, and there was a slight improvement in the acquisition of consumer goods. For example, from 1932–3 the purchase of shoes by peasants in Leningrad *oblast'* declined sharply, then began to rise again in 1935–6, reaching 85 per cent of its 1932 level in 1935–6 and 138 per cent in 1937–8. The picture is similar regarding cloth, consumption of which fell after 1932–3, but by 1937–8 had increased to 173 per cent of its 1932–3 level.[2] Despite these modest improve-ments, the fundamental peasant antipathy towards the *kolkhoz* remained throughout this period and was exacerbated by the crop failures of 1936–7 and the pre-war crackdown on their private plots.

The peasant voice is usually less audible than that of the worker in this period, perhaps because the regime found it more difficult to monitor opinion in the countryside. Alternatively, it may be that peasants preferred to express themselves through more covert, anonymous forms such as rumours and songs. It is clear that negative feelings towards the collective farm were sometimes articulated in the form of millenarian rumours anticipating the abolition of the *kolkhozy*, such as those which circulated at the time of the Constitutional discussion.[3] Also common were *chastushki*,[4] some of which have been preserved thanks to the endeavours of the party and NKVD. These subversive *chastushki* appear to have reached a wide audience, since similar versions can be found in different parts of the USSR.[5] The majority of them date from the period 1934–6, and are dominated by negative representations of the *kolkhoz*.

The *kolkhoz* was frequently portrayed as a prison, *kolkhoz* life as repressive, and the end of *kolkhozy* as a form of liberation: 'Iz mogily pishet Kirov / Dorogomu Stalinu, / Ne derzhi narod v kolkhozakh / Raspusti po staromu' ('Kirov writes from the grave / Dear Stalin, / Don't keep the people in the *kolkhozy* / disband them like it was before'); 'Ia riazanochku pliasala / I prodernula kolkhoz / Prinudilovki mne dali / Dve nedeli zhat' oves' ('I danced a riazan /And tore the *kolkhoz* to bits /I got forced labour /And had to cut oats for two weeks'); 'Kirova ubili, Skoro Stalina ub'iut / Vse kolkhozy razbegutsia / Nam svobodnei budet zhit'' ('Kirov's been killed / Soon Stalin will be killed / All the *kolkhozy* will break up / We will live more freely').

Kolkhoz existence was associated with hardship and privation. Labour was portrayed in a negative light: 'Nadoeli nam palatki / Nadoeli nam koechki / Nadoeli nam rebiata / Lesozagotovochki' ('We're sick of tents / We're sick of bunks / We're sick, boys, / of logging'). Not surprisingly, food (especially bread) and the shortage of it featured prominently: 'Piatiletka, piatiletka / Kak vashi delishki / Khleba netu, ni kusochka / Plachut rebiatishki' ('Five-year plan, five-year plan / How's things going / There's no bread, not a jot / The kids are crying'). Party leaders were often represented as personally responsible for the lack of bread: 'Kogda Kirov pomiral / Stalinu nakazyval / Khleba vvoliu ne davai / Masla ne pokazyvai' ('When Kirov died / He ordered Stalin / Not to give out bread freely / Not to show any butter'). Sometimes peasants were portrayed as having to eat horsemeat: 'Ia shla mimo kolkhoza / Tam kolkhozniki sidiat, / Zuby belye bol'shie / Kobyliatinu ediat' ('I went past the *kolkhoz* / The *kolkhozniki* are sitting there, / Big white teeth, / They're eating horsemeat').

Lack of clothes and shoes was attributed directly to the new system: 'Piatiletka, piatiletka / Piatiletka p'ianaia / Ne iz za tebia li

piatiletki / Rubashonka rvanaia' ('Five-year plan, five-year plan /
Drunken five-year plan / Isn't it because of you, five-year plan, /
That my shirt is torn'). The mere act of joining a *kolkhoz* was seen as
a guarantee of impoverishment, symbolised through the loss of
clothes or shoes: 'Ia v kolkhoz shla tikhon'ko, / a iz kolkhoza vse
begom / Ia v kolkhoz – to shla obuvshi, / a iz kolkhoza bosikom' ('I
went into the *kolkhoz* slowly, / and left it at top speed / I went into
the *kolkhoz* in shoes, / and left it barefoot'); 'V kolkhoz prishla /
Iubka novaia / Iz kolkhoza ushla / Sovsem golaia' ('I arrived at the
kolkhoz / With a new skirt / I left the *kolkhoz* / Completely naked').[6]

Chastushki deliberately undermined official propaganda about the
good life in the *kolkhoz*. For example, 'piatiletka, piatiletka' was a
parodic reference to the numerous official slogans and jingles which
employed this refrain. This subversion of official values is clearly
evident when official *chastushki* manufactured by the regime are
compared with their unofficial equivalents. The former used imagery
from the natural world to convey a happy, harmonious view of life in
the *kolkhoz*: 'Na gore solov'i / Pod goroi kukushki / Khorosho v
kolkhoze zhit' / Milye podruzhki' ('Above the hills are swallows /
Below the hills are cuckoos / It's great living in the *kolkhoz* / Dear
girls'). The latter presented a diametrically opposed view, also using
similar natural imagery: 'V nashe pole priletela / seraia kukushka. /
Khudo, khudo zhit' v kolkhoze, / milaia podruzhka' ('Into our field
there flew / a grey cuckoo. / It's bad, bad living in the *kolkhoz*, / my
darling girl').[7] Through the symbolic overturning of the official
order, *chastushki* thus provided a temporary emotional release from
the drudgery of *kolkhoz* existence.

The authorities were forced to reconcile themselves to the peasant
antipathy towards collectivised agriculture graphically illustrated in
these *chastushki*. A process of negotiation took place, in which
peasants carved out small concessions from the regime.[8] As early as
1932, it became legal for peasants to trade the surplus produce grown
on the small private plots of non-*kolkhoz* land which they retained
after collectivisation. At the Seventeenth Party Congress, Stalin
spoke of the need to accommodate peasant private interest, which
included actively encouraging them to keep more private livestock.
The increasing turn to the market and phasing out of rations,
although not intended specifically to placate the peasants, was
probably welcomed by them. After Kirov's death, a *edinolichnik* in
Tikhvinskii district said 'In the countryside they are saying that

Kirov was killed because he allowed free trade in bread. Here in the countryside we are sorry for Kirov and fear lest the free trade which he got is annulled.'[9]

The most significant concession was the new *kolkhoz* charter, introduced in February 1935. This recognised the peasants' right to keep a private plot and a small amount of livestock (cows, pigs, chickens). It also included other provisions such as maternity benefits for women. Some aspects of the charter, including these maternity benefits, appear to have been genuinely popular, and there was an influx of *edinolichniki* into the *kolkhozy* in this period. However, there were also complaints that the document did not go far enough. While the legalisation of the private plot was obviously welcomed, some *kolkhozniki* demanded that the best land from the *kolkhoz* be used for their plots. There was also widespread dissatisfaction that horses were to remain the property of the *kolkhoz*, since the horse had always played an indispensable role in Russian peasant economy and culture. The charter therefore only went some way to satisfying peasant aspirations. In addition, scepticism was expressed about its actual effectiveness, for peasants had no illusions about the implementation of laws in their country. As one *kolkhoz* chairman said, 'It's fine to write this, but try to do it. It's easiest for Stalin to say it, for he doesn't do anything, people do it for him.'[10]

The concessions ensured the relative acquiescence of the peasants, but failed to eliminate criticism of the *kolkhoz* system, and especially of the high compulsory procurement quotas demanded by the state. Throughout this period the constant complaint was that Soviet power or the state bought grain for an absurdly low price and sold it for a much higher one. Productivity remained low as peasants felt little incentive to work outside their plots:

We've worked so much in the *kolkhoz* that we are naked and barefoot. No one wants to work now, because you won't get anything anyway. Before peasants strived to get as much as possible from the land and work with all their strength on it, and now there isn't that striving, although we have enough land.

For some, even the tsarist regime seemed preferable to the present system: 'Before life was easier. Under the tsarist regime it was easier for the peasant to work ten years in his own farm than now for ten days in the *kolkhoz*.'[11]

The attempt to stimulate productivity by introducing Stakhanovite methods into the countryside seems to have been largely unsuccessful despite the intense propaganda of images of Stakhanovite *kolkhozniki*, such as tractor driver Pasha Angelina and sugar-beet harvester Maria Demchenko. Peasants tended to regard Stakhanovism as designed only for the workers and they associated it with factories and machines. Thus one candidate party member, when asked at the end of 1935 what Stakhanovites were, replied: 'They are those machines which are very productive.' In January 1936, the Leningrad NKVD claimed that Stakhanovite methods were taking off very slowly in the countryside, because peasants considered the methods inapplicable to the *kolkhoz*, and poured scorn on the idea that a person could be made to work like a machine.[12] At 'Stakhanovite rallies' in western Siberia in March 1936, the NKVD also reported a passive mood and scepticism about the proposal that sowing should be accomplished with Stakhanovite speed in ten days:

We have done enough fulfilling, our horses will all be dead by spring. We like taking all they throw at us. They come, phone up, and there is nothing with which to do the fulfilling, and so they think up some Stakhanovites, while we ourselves have nothing to eat.

A socialist competition agreement was also ridiculed: 'What's the point of the competing without bread or shoes? If there was bread, and the horses got better, we could compete.' Here too, as well as objecting to the movement on practical grounds, some were suspicious of a method associated with factories and therefore with machines, which were distrusted and held responsible for the bad harvests, since, it was claimed, before the introduction of tractors and other machines they had always had enough to eat. Others resented the fact that rare manufactured goods had been put on sale to coincide with the rallies as a visible stimulus to Stakhanovite work, because the prices were impossibly high for peasants. One tractor driver who had been selected to take part in a delegation to see Stalin complained bitterly about the prices, and was not excited by the proposed trip to Moscow, because 'there is no money and I'm hungry'.[13]

Far from there being an increase in productivity in connection with Stakhanovism, the harvest of 1936 actually failed, partly because of unfortunate climatic conditions,[14] and partly because of the unpreparedness of the *kolkhozy*. When the NKVD checked 290 *kolkhozy* in forty districts of Leningrad *oblast'* during the spring sowing in April 1936, they found that many lacked sufficient seeds and haulage (horses were exhausted), that machinery had not been repaired, that measures to improve the soil were not being undertaken, that many peasants had left the *kolkhozy* since they did not even have their own grain, and that there were not enough agricultural cadres. The NKVD 'dealt' with these problems by arresting 1,072 people for 'counter-revolutionary' crime in disrupting the sowing campaign. By 5 May, the plan for sowing had been fulfilled by only 7.4 per cent.[15]

The subsequent crop failures were followed by a winter of discontent for the peasantry in various parts of Russia, including Leningrad *oblast'*. Private letters intercepted by the censor reported dire shortages, from which the *kolkhozniki* suffered the most, as bread brought in to the countryside from outside was distributed to teachers and *sluzhashchie*.[16] Writers described how the *kolkhozy* had collapsed, how they were obliged to stand in queues of thousands for bread. Some arrived at 6 p.m. to await the shops' morning opening, bringing with them chairs and pillows so that they might get some sleep, but even then they had no guarantee of obtaining any bread. Shop windows were smashed, and there was an upsurge in crime, especially murder and theft. Many said 'the famine has arrived', and deaths were reported, both from starvation, and from people, including small children, getting crushed in queues. Parallels were drawn with the Ukrainian famine of 1932–3. Others wrote that the situation was worse than in 1918.[17] The hysteria was compounded by rumours about the census due to be carried out in early January:

From 1 December there'll be no bread, only *sluzhashchie* get a loaf, while the *kolkhoznik* gets nothing, even if he dies from hunger ... take a look at the countryside, everyone's selling their last things ... perhaps on 1 January we won't be alive, as a Bartholemew's night is organised ... everyone is worried – what's a census at night-time. If people come for me at night I'll faint ... people are worried, everyone's hungry, from 1 December all the bread was hidden – across from Kortsovo they've been dying from hunger, and by spring probably half the population will rot, if it's like that.

NKVD reports confirmed the information contained within these letters, and provided additional details about the spread of scarlatina, diphtheria, and typhus. The press, however, remained silent, causing some people to wonder 'whether the centre knows about this'. In the absence of any official instructions on how to deal with the crisis, the people themselves took spontaneous action, introducing unofficial rationing through the organisation of 'closed' shops and the distribution of bread directly to people's houses.[18]

In some cases, the acute discontent with the rapid economic deterioration took on a more political colour. There was talk of the need for an uprising (*bunt*) and rumours about *bunty* in other regions. Various notes and leaflets appeared in the *oblast'*. A boy wrote a note which read 'I, Aleksandr Ob'edkov, declare that in the USSR hunger reigns, there is no bread, people get up at 2 a.m. to get a piece of bread. Gather an army and attack the USSR.' In one district, a leaflet attached to a letter box appeared, entitled 'Give bread', and enjoining comrades to 'rise up for bread, comrade peasants', to rout the shops and village soviets. School-children went on strike in some areas. In Shol'skii district pupils standing in queues shouted 'If you do not give us bread, we will not go to school', and many carried out their word. Others were less militant – for example, pioneers of Mginskii district who wrote to the Leningrad radio committee, explaining how they were late for school as a result of queuing, and asking if they might be permitted to get bread without queuing. They added that as pioneers they were ashamed because their parents were blaming Soviet power for the crisis.[19]

The crisis lasted until March or April in most areas, and even until May in some. A good harvest in 1937 alleviated matters somewhat; however, the fundamental problems of the *kolkhoz* system remained. The government tried to tackle them with a succession of decrees aimed at boosting productivity. These were treated with disdain by peasants, who had little faith that they would be implemented. In April 1938, an NKVD report noted many departures from the farms and the collapse of labour discipline. This was explained partly as the result of instability generated by rapid changes of leadership, which occurred every month in some cases (presumably in connection with the purges). It was also because *kolkhozniki* were not being paid enough for their labour.[20] In order to combat this problem, which deprived peasants of almost all incentive to work, the government issued a decree on 19 April 1938 'On the incorrect distribution of income in the *kolkhozy*'. This ordered that the *kolkhoz* administration should follow the charter by spending no less than 60–70 per cent of farm income on labourdays, and no more than 10 per cent on capital costs. The decree had little effect, and the *kolkhozy* continued to malfunction, with able-bodied men finding alternative sources of income, and leaving the *kolkhoz* work to their wives, fathers, and children. In Krasnogvardeiskii district, of 14,572 able-bodied people, 4,024 had worked less than one labourday in 1938, and 3,081 less than fifty.[21] Rises in the compulsory delivery quotas of some produce merely exacerbated the problem. For example, when new hay quotas were introduced in July 1938, *kolkhozniki* at one village in Borovicheskii district announced 'We do not want to work for Soviet power and will not allow ourselves to be robbed. We call on everyone not to go to work.'[22]

Peasants continued to devote most of their energy to their private plots, which had been steadily expanding in this period. Whereas in 1934, 3.6 per cent of the sown area of the *kolkhoz* in Leningrad *oblast'* was taken up by the plots, by May 1939, this figure had risen to 5.7 per cent.[23] The government decided to crack down on these, issuing the decree 'On measures to protect the communal land of the *kolkhozy* from squander' (27 May 1939). Designed to reduce the size of private plots, it inevitably exacerbated friction between the peasants and the state. Peasants felt deprived of what was theirs by right: 'we fought for the land, but the land is not ours'.[24] The official discourse on wrecking was invoked: 'This decree has been put out by enemies of the people'; 'To take away the plots is wrecking. Did Stalin sign the decree?' There was a prevailing sense that the regime's decrees were in any case ineffective: 'All the same by issuing this decree Soviet power won't achieve anything. If someone did not work in the *kolkhoz* until now, then he never will'; 'Soviet power makes enough decisions and none of them are fulfilled.'[25]

The implementation of the decree did encounter special problems in Leningrad *oblast'*, because of its large number of *khutora*, individual enclosed farms, many of which now nominally belonged to *kolkhozy*. According to the decree, *khutoriane* were supposed to be resettled in villages by 1 September 1940. By 25 July 1939 about a third had been moved. They were very reluctant to do so, and some committed suicide. Many felt that if they simply ignored the decree for a while, the authorities would eventually forget about it. Delaying tactics were adopted; for example, complaints were made that they were being resettled well before the deadline, and in one *kolkhoz* an official was told 'It's a disgrace. It's a clear infraction of Soviet laws. In the TsK VKP(b) and SNK decree it clearly says that the resettlement of *khutora* should take place before 1940.'[26]

As peasants had anticipated, the decree had no discernible effect upon enthusiasm for work on the *kolkhoz*, for a report of March 1940 noted the persistence of the usual problems. The charter was not observed, horses and cattle were being used for personal rather than *kolkhoz* purposes, and men continued to work on private plots or in other more lucrative jobs.[27] In 1940, the USSR was struck by another particularly bad harvest. The average grain payment per labourday in the country this year was 1.3 kg compared to 4 kg in 1937. This engendered what were described as 'unhealthy' feelings among the leadership of the *kolkhoz* in some regions. Thus, the president of one *kolkhoz* declared that the *kolkhozniki* could not work because they were hungry and added, 'It's better to be in a [prison] camp, there at least you get 200 g of bread, while in the *kolkhoz* there isn't even that.'[28]

With the continuing failure to stimulate work on the collective land, the government issued a new decree on 5 March 1941, 'On additional pay for the labour of *kolkhozniki* for raising the yields in agriculture and the productivity of animal husbandry in Leningrad *oblast*".[29] It encountered particular irony amongst peasants, who accused officials of telling them 'fairy-tales', and remained adamant that the decree would alter nothing.[30]

The response to the state loan of 1941 was especially poor amongst the peasants. In Siatskii district state farm, for example, almost all cadre workers refused to subscribe. Most people justified their reluctance in terms of lack of bread because of the previous year's poor harvest. There may also have been a deliberate reluctance to subscribe to the country's defence needs. This would have corresponded with the quite common desire for war among peasants. One person said 'For me, it's all the same what kind of power – let Hitler come, but I do not think it necessary to subscribe.'[31] The discontent accumulated during these years left much of the peasantry ill-disposed towards the regime on the eve of the war. A report of 18 June 1941 noted an increase in anti-Soviet activity in the countryside. Communists not only were failing to fight it, but were even falling under its influence.[32] Against this backdrop of disaffection, Hitler invaded the Soviet Union on 22 June, no doubt to the satisfaction of at least some peasants, who hoped that war would cause the collapse of the hated *kolkhoz* system.[33]

CHAPTER 3

Women, family policy, education

WOMEN AND POPULAR OPINION

In the mid-1930s, the Soviet regime abandoned its earlier ambivalent relationship with 'bourgeois' institutions such as marriage, resurrected the ideal of the stable family, and actively promoted motherhood, while simultaneously continuing to espouse sexual equality in the workplace.[1] Women entered the labour force in ever greater numbers in the 1930s. However, in many respects they remained disadvantaged. Gender stereotypes were perpetuated, and women continued to assume almost sole responsibility for the home and family, even when working full-time. How did these circumstances affect women's attitudes? It is often difficult to differentiate the opinions of men and women workers or peasants – a poor working man and a poor working woman shared similar concerns, and many of the opinions discussed in this study were articulated by both sexes.[2] However, the particular burdens of women did shape their discourse, and for this reason it is worthwhile considering in more detail their views, which tended to be oriented more towards questions of *byt* (everyday life): the home, family, and consumption. Yet it is also important to note that working-class women do not seem to have experienced a solidarity based on gender which might have transcended 'class' loyalties, for resentment was expressed towards the 'middle-class' housewives feted in the media.

The analysis will concentrate on the views of women workers in Leningrad, since those of peasants are less well represented in the sources.[3] A significant share of the Leningrad labour force was female. On 1 January 1935 women constituted 44.3 per cent of workers and *sluzhashchie* in all branches of labour, and 44.7 per cent in industry alone (25.7 per cent in the metal and electrical industry, 55.0 per cent in the chemical industry, 78.5 per cent in the textile industry, 83.8 per cent in the sewing industry, and 66.6 per cent in the food industry). Many of these women had joined the labour force during the first five-year plan. For example, the overall proportion of women in the metal and electrical industry expanded from 11.1 per cent in 1930 to 26.6 per cent in 1934. Despite near equality with men in terms of representation, women were nevertheless disadvantaged. They sometimes earned less than men with identical qualifications and experience. Literacy levels were much lower among women workers. In 1935, more than half of all female workers at textile factories were semi-literate. Few women were involved in political study and female party activists were concentrated in textile factories. Few attained high positions: of 328 factory directors in Leningrad in 1935, only twenty were women, seventeen of whom worked at textile and sewing factories. Fifty to sixty per cent of doctors were female, but there were only four women head doctors at hospitals.[4] In the second half of the 1930s, the party launched prominent campaigns to try to promote more women in the party and workplace, but their effects were limited.[5] The numbers of working women did continue to rise, however. By 1937 women made up 49.6 per cent of Leningrad workers, 21.4 per cent of the ITR, and 66.1 per cent of the *sluzhashchie*. By 1940, after the introduction of universal military conscription for men, women took on men's jobs, and constituted almost 60 per cent of the factory labour force.

Gender stereotypes at the workplace persisted during this period. Sometimes these were reinforced by women themselves, but men who engaged in harassment and discrimination also perpetuated them.[6] Stereotypes about gender and politics also continued, although these rarely featured in opinion reports, perhaps because this subject was not deemed sufficiently important. The few comments which were recorded are indicative of the tenacity of traditional patriarchal attitudes. The 1936 Constitution was explicit about guaranteeing equal rights to women, which provoked one male worker to comment that 'Soviet power is bad to confirm the Constitution and thereby give women lots of rights. Now you can't do anything at home, the wife drives you out of the flat.' Misogynist feelings also emerged during the 1937 elections, when a worker from the Kirov works said that he would not vote for women, since they were 'useless', while another protested against women being allowed to participate in elections: 'In the old days women were not allowed anywhere and that was right because women are beneath men.' A few women also used stereotypical language in relation to female electoral candidates. One, significantly a peasant, agitated against a woman standing in local soviet elections, arguing that she had been chosen as a candidate because 'she is a girl. Previously they chose women so they could go out with them, and now it's the same, not to decide questions, but to go out.'[7]

With the perpetuation of long-established attitudes and practices amongst both men and women, the average Leningrad woman worker was likely to be less well paid, less literate, and less involved in political and technical education than her male counterpart. For these reasons, women may have been less inclined than men to hold and express the sort of opinions with which this study is concerned. Party and especially NKVD opinion reports give the impression that men were more vociferous than women, although it is also possible that informants were primed to pick up on and take more seriously the views of men. Some party activists certainly believed that women did not have any serious opinions. At one party meeting it was observed that 'many women are *meshchanskie* [bourgeois, philistine]; they love their comfort, are not interested in social life, don't worry about production'.[8] This stereotype may have influenced the reporting of women's opinions by the party and NKVD. Nevertheless, the reports reveal that some women did express views on political, economic, and social questions, although their interests were not always identical to those of men. Despite its condescending tone, the observation about women's indifference to 'social life' contained some truth, in that women's attention was indeed focused on the home and family. This was hardly the result of a love of 'comfort', however. Women were simply obliged to deal with domestic matters because of the enduring assumption that the wife should take on the bulk of the responsibility for shopping, child care, and housework, despite the fact that she was now often also involved in full-time work.[9] This double burden inevitably meant she had less leisure for reading, political education, and discussion than her more carefree husband.[10]

So, while men were more likely to debate the merits of Trotsky and Stalin, or discuss the implications of party congresses, women tended to talk about their children's needs, queues, or fluctuating prices, and to protest against policies which threatened the economic well-being of the family.[11] This is, of course, a generalisation – some women discussed theoretical political questions avidly; many men also talked about prices. During the period of mandates to soviets in December 1934, questions of *byt* featured prominently in the suggestions of both sexes. However, women in particular stressed the need to improve material provision for children. The following is an example of many such speeches made by women:

We must struggle decisively with children who stand and beg at bread shops. We must improve children's food. Children's shoes are too expensive. We must, along with our achievements, eliminate our weaknesses.[12]

Likewise, at a meeting on 9 December 1934 of a department of the Khalturin textile factory, where women formed the majority of employees, a very lively discussion took place amongst women workers, who also demanded better food and clothing for their children. One, Smirnova, stated that it was impossible to look after children on their wages: 'a child goes to school hungry and doesn't eat there either. Children do without boots, and they're impossible to buy.' The women also requested better accommodation for themselves and their families. Korotkova said 'I have seven people in my family, we live in a small room, we can't get accommodation.' As their requests were enunciated in fairly critical terms, another worker, Gudkova, retorted:

It's good that the workers are making suggestions. We ought to speak about our achievements, in particular, about what we have achieved at our factory, for example: the surgery has grown into a strong medical department, and our canteen has also expanded and improved. Wages have gone up recently, supplies for workers have improved, life has become easier.

Other women did not agree with this attempt to gloss over problems and argued that on the contrary all was not well. Savel'eva maintained strongly:

We are in a crisis, and we know it, and it's fine for Gudkova to talk, she has an easy life, but I have a sick child, he's in hospital, they give him porridge without butter, and pay no attention to my comments. There are many injustices, for example, the hospital is supposed to give the children butter, but they do not get it.[13]

The overriding priority throughout this discussion was the welfare of children. This tended to colour women's opinions about a variety of issues. Thus, whereas some men discussed the issue of Soviet support for the communists in Spain in ideological terms, women raised the question of children. At Krasnaia Znamia Seregina said to other female workers: 'Your children don't see chocolate and butter, while we're sending it to Spanish workers.'[14] The mother's perpetual struggle to defend and provide for her family is summed up in a poem entitled 'A Mother's Cares', written by school-children in 1935 in their wall newspaper:

Segodnia den' iasnyi	Today is a clear day
Veselye deti	Merry children
Igraiut i plashut	Play and dance
Ne znaiut zabot	Know no cares
A doma mamasha	But at home mummy
Khlopochet ne znaet	Toils and knows not
Chego na obed	What to cook them
Im svarit'	For dinner
Odet' i obut'	How to clothe and shoe
Svoikh detok rodimykh	Her own children
Ne znaet mamasha	Mummy doesn't know
Gde obuvi vziat'	Where to get shoes
Im nado pal'tushki	They need coats
Im nado sapozhki	They need boots
Zabotitsia	Worries
Bednaia mat'	Poor mother.[15]

As well as being concerned about the welfare of their children, women also seem to have been aroused by food prices, since it was they who did most of the shopping. As Trotsky observed: 'the worker-mother has her view of the social regime, and her "consumer's" criterion, as the functionary . . . scornfully expresses it, is in the last analysis decisive'.[16] The news about the end of bread rations met with particular consternation from women, especially those with large families. One housewife spoke up at a soviet electoral meeting: 'Our children do not get any fats, they are hungry and weak, get tuberculosis. My husband earns 150 r. and we have two children. After the end of rations, poor workers and their children will get neither butter nor bread.' Other housewives greeted this speech with applause, prevented a woman from rebuking her, and sent up notes to the chair asking why their children were so badly provided for. In general, women were much more opposed to the measure than men – at the Voroshilov works it was noted that while the men wholeheartedly accepted the policy, amongst women the mood was 'passive'. Similar responses were reported at other factories staffed mainly by females. Likewise, a report on reactions to the end of

rations on meat and other food in September 1935 recorded
dissatisfaction mainly amongst female workers and housewives that
only the highest quality, most expensive meat was on sale.[17]

Since women tended to be paid less than men, they were
especially reluctant to subscribe to loans. In 1935, many of those
who refused to subscribe to the loan were low-paid women workers
at textile and sewing factories, especially those whose material
circumstances were difficult because they had several children or
because their husbands had left them. For example, at the Khalturin factory, a woman earning 128 r. refused to subscribe. Her
husband had died in the civil war and she had a fourteen-year-old
son. Women workers often showed solidarity during loan campaigns. During the 1936 campaign all those on the third floor of a
shop at the Veretano textile factory (with wages of 250–80 r.)
refused to subscribe more than 50 r.[18]

This type of female solidarity probably did not extend beyond
the factory. To a certain extent *all* women shared similar concerns
about families, food shortages, and so on. However, it is unlikely
that factory workers felt much solidarity with the wives of engineers,
who, as Fitzpatrick has illustrated, were exalted in official Soviet
discourse for the first time in this period.[19] The *obshchestvennitsa*
(women's volunteer) movement promoted the idea of engineers'
wives doing useful charity work, as well as supporting their
husbands and model families. The 'bourgeois' connotations of this
were all too obvious to some women workers. Their resentment
emerged especially in 1936, when the 'wives' movement received
intense publicity. In May, an agitator reported that after the award
of the order of the Red Banner of Labour and the honour badge to
wives of captains of industry, several women workers had complained that 'So they're being given orders. What have they done
especially?' Likewise, factory women had little sympathy for the rich
housewives' practice of keeping servants. In July 1936 workers asked
what ought to be done in the case of housewives who had a servant,
but no children: 'We don't have non-workers, but why are there
wives of ITR and other responsible workers who have a servant and
don't themselves work?' Also in July 1936, low-paid housekeepers
wrote to the Leningrad Soviet to complain about their employers,
the wives of engineers, some of whom even kept cooks and maids.
According to these women, the wives were worse than the former
'ladies'.[20]

Table 3 *Abortions in Leningrad, 1930–1934 (per 1,000 population)*

Year	Births	Abortions
1930	21.3	33.9
1931	21.3	36.3
1932	20.7	34.0
1933	17.0	36.7
1934	15.9	42.0

Source and note: 24/2v/1180/54, 62. Abortion statistics, especially those for illegal abortions, are notoriously unreliable.

FAMILY POLICY

The resurrection of the ideal of the bourgeois housewife was only one aspect of the propaganda campaign to promote traditional family values which emerged in 1934–5. The new official line was in part a reaction to the demographic havoc wrought by crash industrialisation, manifested in a great rise in abortion and a decline in the birth rate. The abolition of the party's *zhenotdely* (women's departments) had not helped, since these had been active in the struggle against abortion. Abortions were comparatively cheap – about 28–32 r. – and in the first half of the 1930s they far outstripped births in Leningrad (see table 3). Similarly, after the introduction of 'postcard divorces' in 1926, the number of divorces had escalated. In Leningrad in 1926 there were 3.6 divorces per 1,000 people. In 1927 this nearly trebled to 9.8, and reached a peak of 11.5 in 1928. After this the rate declined a little, but was still at an unacceptably high level in 1934, when there were 5.0 divorces per thousand people (compared with 15.5 marriages).[21]

Pro-family propaganda on its own was unable to combat these trends and in 1936 more drastic measures were adopted. A bill on abortion and divorce was published on 26 May 1936. As well as outlawing abortion in all except potentially life-threatening cases, it envisaged allowances for mothers with more than seven children, greater maternity and nursery provision, more difficult and expensive divorce, and a crackdown on fathers evading alimony payments. The publication of the bill was followed by a public 'discussion', some of which was printed in the newspapers.[22] This was probably the most genuinely free public discussion in the period 1934–41 since, as well as the usual enthusiastic endorsements, the papers also printed negative views, albeit in small numbers.

The divorce proposals seem to have elicited much support, especially among women, who usually suffered most from the breakdown of marriages, since they were left with children to support on a low or non-existent income: one survey of broken marriages from the end of the 1920s indicated that, in 70 per cent of cases, divorce proceedings had been initiated by the man, and only 7 per cent by mutual consent.[23] The new bill proposed to increase the cost of divorce to 50 r. for a first divorce, 150 r. for a second, and 300 r. for subsequent ones. It also required both partners to appear at the registry for the dissolution of their marriage and laid down strict rules on alimony payments. The reports on the discussion indicate that the clause on alimony was welcomed, with most suggestions focusing on the need to make it effective – it was one thing to make a law, and quite another to chase up all the errant fathers. Predictably, some men seem to have objected to aspects of the bill, arguing that women could abuse it by demanding alimony from several 'fathers'.[24] However, in general, the legislation appears to have reflected popular aspirations, particularly those of women.[25] As a result of the new regulations, divorce declined in Leningrad, but so too did marriage, and by 1939 the marriage/divorce ratio was not much better than that of 1934 – about 3.5 marriages for every divorce.[26] The price of divorce was clearly not a sufficient deterrent and, in 1944, new legislation was introduced to make the process more complicated and prohibitively expensive.

The criminalisation of abortion seems to have been more controversial than the divorce proposals. Women were driven to abortion in ever increasing numbers mainly because of low wages and inadequate housing. The end of bread rations was an added disincentive to bear large families. One woman worker from Krasnyi Treugol'nik objected to the bill saying 'I have four children and they are hungry. I've had abortions and will carry on having them by some means or other regardless of any bans.' Another, from Bol'shevichka, argued 'How can you say no to an abortion when your family consists of five people and you have fourteen metres' living space?' Some women considered abortions positively beneficial, for example, Nazarova from Krasnyi Treugol'nik, who said: 'I think abortions even bring some benefit: 'I've had six abortions, don't have any children, my husband and I earn enough and we live in clover.' Others suggested amending the bill to allow abortions in certain cases: after the fourth child, when a woman conceived again immediately after giving birth, and in the case of insufficient living space or low wages. One woman advocated giving workers longer maternity leave than *sluzhashchie*, in view of the arduous nature of the former's work.

These women workers all approached the question pragmatically, citing material conditions in support of their argument. Such an approach contrasted with that of some women members of the intelligentsia, who regarded the matter rather as one of principle. According to one, the bill 'enserfed women', for a big family would demand all the woman's time and deny her the chance to work like a man. It is striking too that many of the critical letters published in the newspapers were from female students and members of the intelligentsia, who thought the criminalisation of abortion would prevent women from entering the world of work, and thus impede their liberation.[27] These opinions seem to be class-specific – it is unlikely that working-class women viewed their work as anything more than a source of income.

Despite the protest, the abortion legislation was enacted with only minor modifications. The number of both legal and illegal abortions declined immediately afterwards, but started to rise again later as the situation of women deteriorated, partly because of the shortages and preparations for war, but also because the new labour legislation of the pre-war period curtailed the rights of mothers. The labour decree of 1938 specifically reduced maternity leave from sixteen weeks to nine, and made it contingent on a prior period of seven consecutive months of employment. This seemed to fly in the face of all the pro-family propaganda and was resented by women workers, some of whom reacted by stating that they would not have any more children. One woman declared that Stalin must have gone mad to issue such a decree. Two female engineers expressed this general astonishment more eloquently: 'How disgraceful it is, after all the fuss that was made about the abortion law. Now thousands of women will mutilate themselves, deform themselves, as they are unwilling to give birth. What will happen now after this decree? Of course the birth rate will fall sharply and there will be more torture for women.'[28] This prediction proved accurate.

Table 4 *Abortions in Leningrad, 1936–1938*

	1936	1937	1938
Total	62,072	25,738	31,630
Of which, completed	43,999	1,879	3,728
Of which, incomplete[a]	18,073	23,859	27,902
Died from abortion	114	160	238

Source and note: 24/2v/3538/107.
[a] An incomplete abortion refers to one begun outside the hospital, i.e. in the majority of cases an illegal abortion.

The law on mobilisation of 1 September 1939 obliged many women to take over men's places in the factory. However, little extra provision was made for children and the lack of nursery places caused dissatisfaction.[29] The decree of June 1940 also made few allowances for women with children. Appalling cases were reported of women, who, unable to find places for their babies in creches, or with sick children, were forced to leave work, sentenced for doing so, and sometimes even sent to prison together with their children.[30] In these unfavourable circumstances, abortions continued in the back streets. The figures vary a little from source to source, but provide a general impression of the dynamics of abortion in Leningrad in this period (see table 4). Other statistics give slightly higher figures for the same years. They also show that the number of abortions, including those performed legally (there was a tendency to define the medical criteria necessitating abortion more broadly) continued to rise to 39,598 in 1939, falling slightly to 37,880 in 1940. The number of deaths from illegal abortions also increased, and in 1940 the press began to publicise the problem of back-street abortions.[31] From 1938, the birthrate began to fall, and by 1940 it had reached its 1935 level again.[32] Like the other so-called 'totalitarian' regimes of Nazi Germany and Fascist Italy, the Soviet regime was never able fully to control reproduction when its policies ran counter to popular opinion.

EDUCATION AND SOCIAL MOBILITY

Education was held in high esteem in both Bolshevik propaganda and in the minds of ordinary people. According to Fitzpatrick, support of the right to education was one of the rare examples of the adoption of Soviet values by peasants.[33] One of the party's greatest achievements lay in the widening of access to education. Particularly after 1927, there was a huge expansion in the numbers benefiting from primary, secondary, and tertiary education. The period of Cultural Revolution witnessed an attempt to encourage those from proletarian backgrounds, at the expense of people with 'class-alien' origins.[34] However, as part of the Great Retreat, this policy was modified for a combination of ideological and economic reasons. A decree of 29 December 1935 abolished social criteria for access to higher education. Henceforth ability alone determined who entered the *vuzy* (higher education institutions). The special schools which prepared workers for higher education, the *rabfaki*, were also phased out during the third five-year plan. Finally, a decree of 2 October 1940 introduced tuition fees for higher education and the top forms of schools, while making the award of stipends dependent on merit rather than need. Simultaneously the 'special labour reserve' scheme was developed to siphon off large numbers of youths aged fourteen to seventeen into production. All these measures were *perceived* as restricting social mobility, and they incited protest, which was articulated in the language of Constitutional rights and the rights of women, workers, and the poor.

The decree of 29 December 1935 abolishing social criteria for entrance to higher education was issued as part of a package of measures launched in the second half of 1935, including the Stakhanovite movement, and, on a more trivial level, the legalisation of Christmas trees. These policies were regarded as a 'retreat', stimulating hostile comments from some quarters that 'everything is going back to the past'. Stalin's new line that 'a son does not answer for his father' was thus regarded as part of this general strategy: 'In 1936 we won't recognise the USSR. They've started Christmas trees. Now they're burying the social past. They're wearing epaulettes. Soon we'll get to the "tsar-*batiushka*".' There was some confusion as to why such a 'liberal' line was being pursued towards those from class-alien backgrounds, at a time when people were also being urged to exercise vigilance against class enemies. A few people tried to explain the retreat in terms of impending war, which was forcing the Soviet regime to make concessions to 'aliens' and *lishentsy* (the disenfranchised). The policy of allowing the children of the latter equal access to higher education was opposed on the grounds that 'an apple does not fall far from the apple-tree'. Distrust of these groups and a feeling that they continued to represent a danger was expressed by one worker, who, employing the right/left terminology of the time, regarded the policy as a turn to the right:

That policy which was conducted in relation to the children of aliens was the policy of the left. Now when they have equalised the rights of those entering higher education – it is the policy of the right. They think that we will reeducate the child of a noble or a count. Noble blood will flow in these people's veins for several more generations.

The decree also elicited opposition from those who feared it would reduce the opportunities for workers to gain higher education, since 'the children of *lishentsy* will create competition, as they will study well and get high marks, while the factory worker will lag behind'.[35]

The tone of many of these comments echoed that of evaluations of other measures, such as the new Constitution with its guarantee of rights for all (see chapter 6). It reflected anxiety that, without positive discrimination, the working class would once again be relegated to its former lowly social position. These concerns had some validity. Although the absolute number of workers and peasants gaining education increased in this period, with the numbers of those in secondary and tertiary education doubling from nearly 6 million in 1933–4 to just about 12 million in 1938–9, a survey published in January 1938 revealed that since the first five-year plan, the proportion of working-class students had fallen, while that of students from white-collar and professional backgrounds had risen significantly. Workers and their children were still over-represented in relation to their numbers in the population – they comprised 33.9 per cent of students and only 26 per cent of the population as a whole; however, white-collar and professionals who made up 17 per cent of the population provided 42.2 per cent of students. Peasants continued to be under-represented.[36]

The decree of October 1940 seemed to restrict the opportunities of workers and peasants even further by introducing annual tuition fees of 300–500 r. for higher education and 150–200 r. for the three top forms of schools. The decree also inaugurated the State Labour Reserves to be formed from the annual call-up of 800,000 to one million youths aged fourteen to seventeen for training in special production-oriented schools. This decree, aimed partly at over-coming labour shortages, crudely symbolised a return to the notion of manual work for the poor and education for the rich, since the entrance requirements for the training schools were to be very low or non-existent, ensuring that already disadvantaged children from poorer families would follow this route. It was also designed to reinforce gender roles, since those to be called up were young males.[37]

Not surprisingly, the decree provoked protest. It blatantly contradicted the article in the Constitution guaranteeing the right to free education, a point which was not lost on many, who questioned the anomaly. There was commotion at student meetings and anonymous notes were sent up to praesidia with questions such as 'Under communism will education also cost money?' Signs appeared 'Down with integrals, boys into the army, and girls get married', 'I'm looking for a husband who earns not less than 1,000 r. Eighteen-year-old girl', and, in the eleventh class of a school, 'Wanted – parents with good wages, able to pay for education'. It was felt that the decrees would affect girls in particular. As one student put it:

Now we have not a dictatorship of the proletariat, but a dictatorship of Sovnarkom and Molotov. Under capitalism my brother studied for free, while under socialism, I pay for my studies. The decree is designed to make girls take up prostitution rather than studying.

Unfavourable comparisons were drawn with the tsarist period: 'Again we're going backwards. Before a boss wouldn't let a worker squeak, and now workers are repressed. Before children of capitalists studied in universities and now workers' children have only one route – to die at the bench like their parents.'[38]

Many spoke of regression to the past, and of greater inequality between rich and poor. At the timber-processing academy it was suggested that 'it'll be those with a lot of money who'll study, i.e. the rich, and not the children of workers and peasants. That will once more lead to the differentiation of rich and poor.' Complaints were heard that the fees were to be the same regardless of income (except for the very poor whose fees were to be waived completely). A communist from the Oktiabr' factory asked 'How can it be – an engineer earns 1,000 r. with one child and a woman worker gets 300 and has three children. On what means will she pay for school, her children want to study too.' This comment encountered much sympathy from fellow female workers. Some workers feared they would be forced to abandon their studies altogether, including a student at the shipbuilding institute, who wrote the following letter to his teacher:

I worked at a factory for five years. Now I'll have to leave my studies at the institute. Who will study? Very talented Lomonosovs and the sons of Soviet rulers, since they have the highest posts and are the best paid. In this way education will be available only to the highest strata (a sort of nobility), while for the lowest strata, the labouring people, the doors will be closed.

Even party officials were disconcerted by the decree, and unsure of how to justify it. The secretary of the party bureau of the Radist factory stated at a *raikom* meeting that the decree was wrong and asked how he was to explain to workers that the children of unqualified workers and cleaners could not receive a higher education.[39]

The new measure proved rather difficult to implement. The waiver on fees for very poor students seems to have applied to up to 10 per cent of students. For example, of 5,680 students at the industrial institute, 526 were exempt. Despite this concession, on 1 November, the day by which fees were due, it transpired that significant numbers had not yet paid, including many Komsomol members. At the engineering-economics institute, of 132 who had not paid, 105 were Komsomol members.[40] The State Labour Reserve also encountered obstacles, with a shortfall in volunteers. Only 600,000 young people were found to participate in the scheme in October–November 1940, and of these only 71 per cent were actually volunteers.[41] The conditions in which the young people were required to work were far from ideal and in many cases they were simply used as unpaid labour. In a letter to Stalin from the end of 1940, pupils at one school expressed their sense of betrayal, relating how they had applied to the school on the understanding that they would be studying under good specialists, when in fact it turned out that they were not studying at all, but being used to build and dig trenches. They complained bitterly that the 'bosses [*nachal'stvo*]' had deceived them and that they were being kept there under lock and key, concluding 'We have reached an autocratic regime, like under Nikolai Palkin.'[42] Thus, despite great social mobility in this period, for these young men, and other ordinary people, the new education policies certainly represented a Great Retreat.

CHAPTER 4

Religion and the nationalities question

The Bolsheviks were ideologically opposed to religion and nationalism, which conflicted with their own materialist, internationalist worldview, and which they wrongly assumed would eventually wither away under socialism. This chapter will show that, far from withering away, both religion and some manifestations of national sentiment remained quite prevalent into the 1930s. When this became apparent to the regime, there seems to have been a pragmatic acceptance of the need to mobilise rather than repress these feelings. Contrary to Timasheff's assertions, no outright 'retreat' took place, but it is clear that Russian national motifs became prominent in the propaganda of the late 1930s, with the exaltation of Pushkin, Suvorov, and other Russian heroes, and that the Orthodox church was harnessed to the Soviet cause during the 'Great Patriotic War'.

RELIGION

Despite the propaganda of atheism and concerted attacks on the church, particularly the Russian Orthodox church – a bulwark of the tsarist regime – the party failed to wean people from the 'opiate' of religion, and throughout the 1920s most peasants and many workers continued to consider themselves believers. During the Cultural Revolution, a fresh onslaught against religion was launched. Religious activity was limited to registered congregations within the walls of the church, and many churches were closed. This destructive phase was followed by a new period of 'calmer hostility' (Hough) or even 'ironical neutrality' (Trotsky),[1] as the party adopted a less aggressive stance from 1934 as part of its general policy of internal and external detente.[2] Churches of various denominations continued to function and were attended by significant numbers. Traditional

73

rituals and beliefs persisted and were not countered particularly
effectively by anti-religious propaganda, which suffered a decline in
this period. Believers were vocal in asserting their rights, and a
process of negotiation occurred between state and church. In 1937–8
the regime responded with severity to what it perceived as the
churches' over-assertiveness. However, predictably, this crackdown
failed to eradicate belief, and in the immediate pre-war period, the
regime was forced to recognise the importance of the Russian
Orthodox church.

Until 1938, the various churches maintained quite an extensive
network in Leningrad and the *oblast'*. At the beginning of 1936, there
were 958 active 'buildings of religious cults' in the *oblast'*, and 61 in
Leningrad itself, and 1,800–2,000 priests and ministers. By 1937 there
were 846 working churches in the *oblast'*, of which 50 were in
Leningrad, and more than 2,000 priests.[3] Each of these churches had
a *dvadtsatka* (registered congregation) of at least twenty activists. Some
churches successfully financed themselves by collecting money. For
example, one Leningrad church had capital of 100,000 r., its own
accountant, engineer, and so on, while even a little village church
managed to collect 16,000 r. in a few months for repairs – quite an
achievement at a time when many were desperately short of money.[4]
The Orthodox church was the most powerful and widespread form
of organised religion; however, there were many other denominations, including Baptists, Catholics, and Lutherans. The Old
Believers were also strong in certain areas, winning over converts
disillusioned with the compromises of the Orthodox church.[5]

Although it is obviously difficult to assess the extent of religious
faith, it appears that there were large numbers of believers in this
period. According to one study from the 1930s, a third of those in
Leningrad itself professed a faith. However, religion was much more
common in the countryside and a survey of *kolkhozy* in the *oblast'* at
the beginning of 1935 revealed that from 40 to 80 per cent of
kolkhozniki were believers. The abortive 1937 census indicated that
over half of the Soviet Union's adult population considered themselves believers.[6] The social composition of believers was quite
heterogeneous – they were certainly not all old peasant women,
although women and the elderly probably formed a majority. Some
indication can be derived from the regime's own information about
attendance at church festivals in Leningrad, although the figures are
clearly approximate. In Leningrad 132,953 people apparently

attended morning services at Easter 1934. Of these, 65,500 were women and 31,057 men; 11,470 were young males and 18,875 young females, and there were 6,015 children and 35 military men in uniform. In 1935, 15,000 people celebrated the western Christmas, including 4,725 men and 10,275 women, 1,749 of whom were under twenty-five, and 833 under sixteen. The Orthodox Christmas service on 6 January 1936 attracted 21,047 men, 46,312 women, and that of 7 January 8,321 men and 31,718 women. At Easter 1937, thirty churches held services on the evening of 1 May; 81,500 people were actually inside the churches, and another 100,000 outside. Most (60–90 per cent) were women and aged over thirty-five. However, in some churches about a third were under twenty-five. The majority were housewives, people recently from the countryside, invalids, and the elderly, although there were also some groups of young workers, including girls dressed up for the occasion.[7]

The older generation clung to their beliefs, which they transmitted to their children. In some parts of the *oblast'*, large numbers of children attended church. In Kingisepp *okrug* 50 per cent of pre-school age children and 25 per cent of those of school-age were churchgoers. These children simply accepted their parents' beliefs without much questioning. Surveys of school-children in Starorusskii district revealed that from 30–80 per cent believed in God. Characteristic explanations for their faith were 'I believe in God because my parents believe. I don't know if religion is harmful or helpful'; 'We have icons at home, I believe in God, I don't wear a cross. I don't know if religion is harmful or useful.'[8]

The anti-religious propagandists, the members of the League of the Godless (*bezbozhniki*) were ineffective in their attempts to combat religion. Membership of the league declined by almost three times between 1932 and 1938. In 1936 it was noted that in Leningrad the organisation had collapsed, and that no one was now engaged in anti-religious work.[9] The new Soviet 'religion' with its festivals, rites, leader cult, and so on was not always a sufficiently alluring alternative to established religion, partly because of the strength of tradition. Religious rites, particularly those associated with the life-cycle, were deeply embedded in the fabric of everyday life, and continued to be celebrated in this period, albeit less frequently than in the 1920s.[10] In Pskov, 54 per cent of those born during six months of 1935 were christened in church and 40 per cent of the dead were given religious funerals. In Kingisepp *okrug*, 95 per cent of the dead had religious funerals, while 30 per cent of those marrying did so in church.[11]

The church was very skilled at organising festivals (*prazdniki*). As the statistics cited above reveal, large numbers of urban dwellers continued to attend church for important festivals, such as Easter. Probably the sheer aesthetic qualities of the services attracted some people. Not surprisingly, it was this aspect which was emphasised in the regime's own reports – for example, the report on Easter services in 1934 stressed that many were attending just for the spectacle. It stated that half of the congregation were simply curious, and that even at important moments in the service loud talking, laughter, and cursing could be heard. It also noted that the churches and cathedrals with the largest congregations were those whose clergy were most educated and wore the most luxurious vestments, whose decorations were the most theatrical, and whose choirs and artists were good. The *bezbozhniki* countered such spectacles with old films and dry literature.[12]

Easter 1937 illustrates vividly the conflict between church and state, religious and Soviet festivals, for in this year Easter fell on 1 May, Labour Day. Agitators in Leningrad attempted to distract workers from the church's celebrations, but their alternative festivities proved unattractive. A representative of the factory committee of Krasnogvardeets informed workers that on 2 May there would be a cultural excursion, to be paid for by the workers themselves. Many were indignant and retorted, 'We won't go the demonstration, better to celebrate Easter.' Another worker from the 2-ia Piatiletka factory maintained that 'Many will go to church with pleasure, because you can hear a good choir there, and it's free, while to go to the theatre you need money. In the church good artists sing.'[13] A report on the Easter services noted that they were indeed luxurious and bright with good choirs, in stark contrast to the drab atheist alternatives. It was estimated that about 15–20 per cent came just to look, not to pray, and that some were drunk.[14]

In the countryside, church holidays played an even more important social role.[15] They were a form of popular culture, a temporary liberation from everyday norms. Numerous saint's days continued to be celebrated, sometimes for several days at a time. For example, in Berezovskii village, twenty-eight saint's days were celebrated, usually accompanied by much drink, revelry, and violence. On St Michael's Day 1936, which was celebrated for three days, seventy boxes of vodka were sold, and fights broke out during which four people were killed. According to a party official, 'religious holidays are celebrated more out of a tradition which is strongly engrained in everyday life than from religious convictions'. He quoted one *kolkhoznik*: 'the point isn't to go to church ... you want to rest, drink, and eat party food'. Young people especially enjoyed saint's days because it gave them an opportunity to organise the traditional *gulian'ia* (outdoor parties). Church holidays seem to have been treated differently from Soviet holidays, for agitators who visited a distant part of Dedovicheskii district during the four-day long Pokrov holiday noted that while everyone prepared enthusiastically for Pokrov, they were not interested in the subsequent 7 November celebrations, stating 'It's a Soviet holiday.'[16]

For many, especially in the countryside, where there were few cultural attractions to compare with those in Leningrad, the church was explicitly associated with entertainment. As one *kolkhoznitsa* from Valdaiskii district put it 'I go to church like I go to the club – for entertainment. If you go to the club to see a film you have to pay, while to go to church is free.' In another district *kolkhozniki* also explained 'you want some variety in life. So you either go to church and are in different surroundings or else you buy some vodka, have a drink, and play the fool for a few hours and also get some variety.'[17] However, although the regime naturally tried to accentuate the recreational, social, and aesthetic functions of religion and to downplay the significance of genuine spiritual feelings, it is clear that the latter were also important for some people, such as the worker from the Samoilov factory who told party agitators, 'You demonstrate that God does not exist, but we do not believe in God, but in that high thing which we cannot reach. Perhaps it isn't God, but you don't have to demonstrate that it isn't.'[18] The regime, despite its Soviet festivals and leader cults, was impotent in the face of such feelings.

The more conciliatory line pursued by the regime in relation to religion from about 1934 seems to have encouraged the assertiveness of believers and clergy. Although some of the former apparently rejected the policy of rapprochement between church and state and were unable to trust the bishops because of their collaboration, others used the opportunity to negotiate with the regime, to stand up for and extend their rights. In 1934 it was felt that 'in 1933 big concessions were made to Soviet power because they listened to the Metropolitans; in this year we must not only stick to our position, but also restore some of the rights illegally taken away from the church'. In this year believers took a stand against the closure of churches and persecution of priests, arguing that 'churches are being closed and nothing is being given in return. We never went to the red clubs and never will go', and citing official policies: 'Litvinov told Roosevelt that there is no persecution of the clergy in the USSR, while the GPU arrests the best priests simply because they have conscientiously fulfilled their pastoral duty and worked on the spiritual development of believers.' A demonstration was arranged by a group at the St Nicholas cathedral during the funeral of one priest, Rybakov, who had died shortly after being let out of prison. Rumours spread that he had been tortured, and during the funeral the group asked that his face be uncovered so that they could see if this was really the case.[19]

This assertiveness grew following the publication of the draft Constitution in 1935. Priests were no longer disenfranchised and article 124 granted freedom of religious worship to all believers. During the public discussion of the draft, much publicity was given to the fact that some ordinary workers objected to article 124. However, there were many others, especially peasants, who welcomed it. Suggested amendments to the Constitution included the opening of churches and the prohibition of anti-religious propaganda. There was a generally positive reaction from priests, although some were more sceptical.[20]

The adoption of the Constitution was followed by a spate of religious activity in 1936–7, when attempts were made to establish some kind of harmony between church and state. At the February–March (1937) plenum of the party, Kosior scathingly described this attempt at peaceful coexistence:

We had meetings of believers, where they adopted greetings, curious greetings, very restrained, where it was cunningly shown that religion does not contradict socialism, that they will build socialism together with us, that comrade Stalin, as a most sympathetic person, understood this. These greetings end with oaths of loyalty to the Soviet system.[21]

There were many examples of this phenomenon in Leningrad and the *oblast'*. Lutheran pastors preached sermons in 1936 on the Stakhanovite movement, which ended with the words 'We should become Stakhanovites of our belief and religion.' Clergymen equated the languages of socialism and Christianity, criticising the kulaks because in the gospels it was written 'Woe to you, the rich' and, similarly, linked Stalin's words and Christianity: 'Stalin, working out the Constitution, took most of the statements from the gospels because the principle "He who does not work shall not eat" (article 12) is similar to that of the gospels.' A Baptist pledged loyalty to Stalin on religious grounds: 'Stalin – we respect him, because he was put in place by the Lord God.' Many of those who attended the 1937 Easter service at the Izmailovo-Troitskii cathedral were allegedly wearing official badges including those bearing portraits of Stalin.[22]

People began actively to defend their rights to free worship, justifying their demands in terms of the official language. One church sent a request to the village soviet, stating 'On the basis of article 124 of the Constitution we ask to be allowed to have a procession on St Antony's Day', while villagers in Lychkovskii district organised a delegation of 200 people to the village soviet to agitate for the reopening of their church on the basis of their Constitutional rights. When the soviet refused their request, the *kolkhozniki* did not go to work the following day.[23]

The mood in this period was generally positive. Believers felt that they had won an important battle and that matters could only improve. Large numbers attended the Easter services in 1937 (see above, p. 75) and comments were heard 'Last year they fined us for lighting candles on the street but this year, thank God, there aren't any militia men'; 'This year there's no procession, but next year they'll definitely allow one because we believers are more than half the population'; 'Ah, the Constitution! ... they couldn't prevent people praying to God, it's written clearly in the Constitution.'[24] Such optimism was premature. The regime's tolerance of religion crumbled rapidly when the 1937 census revealed a high incidence of religious belief amongst the population and the 1937 election campaign indicated that believers were becoming ever more involved in political affairs.

The 'sabotage' of the 1937 census was blamed partly on the church.[25] Not only did the census contain the notorious question on religious faith, but it was also carried out on 6/7 January, Orthodox Christmas. This coincidence generated a spate of rumours, the majority related to the question on religion. It was feared that a 'Bartholemew's Night massacre' of all those who declared themselves believers would take place, that believers would be excluded from the *kolkhoz*, tied to the *kolkhoz*, have a stamp in their passport, be resettled, refused bread, not obliged to go to war, and so on. Many felt that the Antichrist would come that night. Some of these rumours were allegedly encouraged by the clergy, who also tried to persuade people to declare themselves believers. People had difficulty answering the question on belief, especially young people who often prearranged with the census-taker to register themselves as non-believers, when in the presence of their parents they had said the opposite. One church warden asked the census-taker that he be registered as 'a bit of a believer' (*maloveruiushchii*), since he did not believe much in the existence of God, but was uncomfortable about registering as a non-believer. A priest in Luga declared that he was a non-believer, justifying this with the words 'a profession is one thing, and convictions another'. Others simply refused to answer the question.[26] The 1937 census was declared void by the regime, and a new census taken in 1939, this time without the question on belief.

During the election campaign of 1937 the church apparently took an active stance, which did not endear it to the authorities. Attempts were made to propose priests as candidates and priests sometimes organised their own agitation work, particularly in areas where the party's forces were weak. Some party members even tried to emulate their example: 'why do priests win people round quickly? Because he works with each person individually and quickly reacts to their requests.'[27] Priests were trusted because they were actively involved in community life, unlike many official agitators. At a time when criticism of soviet and party workers was being actively promulgated by the regime, and when leading party figures were being put on trial, popular respect for official figures was minimal. Priests, however, were sometimes able to deal with practical problems in a way in which state representatives could not. For example, in Dedovicheskii district during the terrible bread shortages, the priest gathered people on Sunday and organised an unofficial form of rationing using tickets. People naturally asked why Soviet workers were unable to organise what their Orthodox priest had done.[28]

Another characteristic phenomenon of this period which concerned the regime was the spread of a plethora of apocalyptic rumours particularly focusing on the Antichrist.[29] As Viola has shown in her study of the collectivisation period, these rumours had a long tradition in Russian culture, and seem to have emerged strongly during times of acute insecurity. The year 1937 was just such a period. Predictions and prophecies flourished, of which the following are just some examples:

I've read old printed books where it's written that the time of truth will come, Tsar Mikhail will rule on earth, and the dead will arise from their graves. The power will change.

The prophecies of the sacred writings say that when the time of Antichrist comes people will destroy each other; Zinoviev and the others were *vozhdi* not long ago, judged and shot people themselves and today they are being judged and shot; it's God's punishment for the fact that people have forgotten God and the church.

They [those on trial] are all bastards, I believe in God alone. In the gospels published in 1917, it is written that the time will come when the three roots of Nicholas II, Wilhelm, and Karl of Austria will break through and the so-called destroying star will rise up. That is Soviet power. The star triumphs in one-quarter of the land. The time will come when people will fight again under this star, a rebellion will flare up, and Mikhail will come to the throne. But then the sun will go pale and the end of the world will come. All this will come to pass in the 25th year of the appearance of the destroying star. Only the illiterate can be believers, the literate do not comprehend belief in God. He who does not work shall not eat: these are words taken from the bible. I will not subscribe to the loan because the government which has released it persecutes religion. I hate that government and will not subscribe.[30]

The upsurge in religious activity in 1936–7 was followed by yet another wave of persecution. Priests and believers formed a large contingent of the terror victims at the end of 1937, and churches were closed en masse. By Easter 1938, only five working churches remained in Leningrad (compared with thirty-three the previous year). Nevertheless, believers still continued to uphold what they considered to be their Constitutional rights and wrote letters to party leaders asking for churches to be reopened or left open, ensuring that these letters were couched in terms of the official language. One, from workers in the Vyborg side of Leningrad, complained that the Constitution was not being observed because churches were being closed so rapidly. In the previous two months, dozens of churches had been closed, and priests and believers arrested. The writers argued that the church had no connection with counter-revolution: 'All that is at the top – Bukharins, Rykovs, and so on.' The church was loyal to the state: 'When you are at church you hear only good admonitions to love your neighbours and respect the authorities and so on.' The letter ended with the assurance that 'We are not your enemies because we and you are one whole', and implored 'Do not offend your class brothers.'[31] Another letter begged Kalinin for assistance to keep open the church of John the Baptist:

> where we can pray for our great Motherland and for you our rulers. We gave up our children to you, they are honestly serving our great Socialist Motherland and guarding our borders from the enemies. Our great Stalinist Constitution gives us freedom of belief and does not shut our churches, but the enemy is whispering out from behind the corner 'look, the Constitution is a sham'.[32]

The writers suggested that the closure of the churches was inspired by enemies, who were hoping to benefit from subsequent popular dissatisfaction towards the government. Thus, despite terror and persecution, believers continued to fight for their faith and attempt to effect some compromise with the regime. The five churches remaining in operation at Easter 1938 were well attended. For example the Church of the Transfiguration in Dzherzhinskii district and St Andrew's Church on Vasilievskii ostrov were both full, with another 1,500 to 2,000 people standing outside.[33]

The regime was forced to recognise the strength of popular belief. During the pre-war 'thaw' of 1939 to June 1941, the persecution of believers diminished. The official tone now echoed that of the two letters just cited: believers could also be supporters of the regime. The journal *Bol'shevik* admitted in 1939 that 'the majority of believers are our people, backward workers and collective farmers', while in March 1941, Iaroslavskii confirmed this: 'There are many completely loyal Soviet citizens still maintaining religious beliefs and superstitions.'[34] Aware of the strength of popular religiosity, the regime turned to the church in its hour of need. On the day of the German invasion on 22 June 1941, the head of the Orthodox church, Metropolitan Sergei, made a public appeal to believers to defend the motherland.

NATIONALISM AND ETHNICITY

Like religion, national sentiments proved difficult to eradicate, as Stalin himself admitted in his speech to the Seventeenth Party Congress, when he declared that 'survivals of capitalism in the consciousness of the people' were far more tenacious in the area of the nationalities question than in any other sphere.[35] The proletarian internationalism espoused by the Soviet regime after 1917 clearly failed to extinguish national and ethnic tension within the multi-ethnic USSR. In Leningrad this tension often assumed the form of anti-semitism. Anti-semitism and other forms of ethnic tension appear to have been exacerbated by crises and periods of instability such as the murder of Kirov, the terror of 1937, and war scares. In these situations, the inclination to search for 'enemies' became pronounced, and ethnic minorities were soft targets. Ethnic tension seems also to have had overtones of class conflict. Although there is some evidence for the existence of Russian national sentiment, this appears not to have been particularly well articulated amongst ordinary people.

This analysis will refer mainly to feelings in Leningrad city. In the *oblast'* ethnic tension was not as rife as in the city, perhaps because rural communities tended to be more ethnically homogeneous and isolated from other groups, and also because they were less exposed to nationalist ideas.[36] When tension did emerge, it was usually expressed as conflict between Russians and the second most numerous nationality in the *oblast'*, the Finns (in 1939 Russians made up 90.6 per cent of the population of the *oblast'*, Finns 3.3 per cent, Estonians 1.4 per cent, and Ukrainians 1.1 per cent).[37] It is probably not coincidental that such conflict often erupted during economic crises. During the acute bread shortages of early 1937, an NKVD report noted fighting between Finns and Russians in Toksovskii district. Likewise, economic factors seem to have played a part in Russians' poor treatment of Finns who had been resettled in Babaevskii and Kaduskii districts in 1937. A report of April 1937 noted a typical comment by a Russian *kolkhoznik*: 'The devil's brought you here, without you life is difficult [enough].' War, as well as economic difficulties, generated strain, and the Winter War in particular obviously exacerbated Finnish–Russian relations.[38]

The city of Leningrad was ethnically homogeneous in comparison to some other regions of the USSR. According to 1933 figures, Russians constituted 85.8 per cent of the population, Jews 6.7 per cent, and Poles 1.4 per cent.[39] By 1939, Russians made up 87.0 per cent, Jews 6.3 per cent, and Ukrainians 1.7 per cent.[40] In the city, the percentage of Jews far outweighed that of any other minority group, almost equalling the total number of other minorities. In 1939, Leningrad contained the highest proportion of Jews in the RSFSR, exceeding even Moscow, where the proportion was 6.0 per cent. In the RSFSR as a whole, Jews were only the sixth most numerous group – 0.9 per cent or 956,599, and 854,334 of these lived in towns. Almost a quarter of Russia's urban Jews resided in Leningrad.[41] These figures, when combined with the legendary Russian animosity towards Jews, may explain why anti-semitism was the most common form of expression of ethnic hostility in Leningrad.

Anti-semitism, which was virulent in the Russian empire, did not evaporate after 1917. The Whites exploited it to mobilise support against their opponents in the civil war with calls to kill 'Yids' and communists. It continued during NEP,[42] reemerging with particular vehemence during the second half of the 1920s amongst workers, the intelligentsia, and party members, especially in Moscow and Leningrad, where the largest concentrations of Jews were located.[43] Contemporary observers linked the resurgence with the contradictions of NEP and the continuation of class struggle at a time of increasing unemployment and economic hardship. When Iurii Larin held a consultation on anti-semitism, the questions he was asked included: 'Why don't Jews stand in queues?'; 'Why are Jews rich, have their own bakers, shops and so on?'; 'Why do Jews drag each other in at work, set each other up, and Russians don't?'[44]

The party resolved to take a stronger line on the issue, and from 1926 party leaders published pamphlets and made speeches on the question. However, the official attitude towards the problem seems to have been ambivalent. Iaroslavskii, at a meeting of the TsKK in January 1929, spoke of the need to combat both Great Russian chauvinism and also Jewish nationalism. He mentioned cases when *sluzhashchie*, 'infected with nepotism and petty-bourgeois protectionism' would fix up all their relatives at their work, simply because they were of the same nationality. This only exacerbated anti-semitism.[45] Evidently the party was aware of a connection between hostility towards Jews and antipathy towards specialists and intellectuals. Certainly during the Cultural Revolution, when the latter groups were hounded, reported cases of violent and verbal attacks on Jews also increased. At the end of the 1920s, the newspapers were full of 'show' cases of anti-semitism. In the 1930s, articles attacking anti-semitism continued to appear periodically in the local and national press. After 1935, the number of public references to all forms of nationalism diminished; however, the archival material indicates that popular anti-semitism was deeply engrained, and was given an added impetus during the terror.

Hostility towards other ethnic groups, and especially Jews, was expressed in a number of ways. In its 'everyday' guise, it included joke-telling at the expense of other groups and the use of expressions such as 'Yid'. Young people seem to have been particularly prone to this and Komsomol reports on the mood of young people throughout the 1930s period reveal a high incidence of anti-semitic comments.[46] More serious cases involved persistent discrimination against and verbal abuse of other groups, and violence against them and their property. Although the 'stirring up of nationalist enmity' was a criminal offence, many of these cases were probably never brought to court; and when they were, the courts tended to underestimate their gravity.[47] It is significant that little attention was devoted to comments with purely nationalist overtones in NKVD opinion reports, in comparison with the reports produced by the party and Komsomol, who were theoretically responsible for eliminating such prejudices. Yet even the latter usually recorded only comments which also had political connotations, and for this reason political motifs predominate in the following discussion of ethnic stereotypes in popular discourse.

Jews and other minorities were associated with a range of stereotypes. Jews in particular were constantly identified with a ruling elite, which included party members, state servants, and the 'Soviet intelligentsia'. The stereotype derived some of its potency partly from the fact that few Jews worked in factories, and even fewer in agriculture. For example, in 1924, at nineteen Leningrad industrial enterprises only 16 of 600 non-Russian workers were Jews. In the 1930s, the proportion of workers remained small.[48] Likewise, a disproportionate number of Jews had always been leading members of the party, and, although this number declined somewhat in the 1930s, there remained a tendency to place Jews and party members in one camp, as in the civil war refrain 'Kill Jews and communists!' Jews also came to be identified with state power, since state service was one of the few opportunities open to them after NEP, when many had been engaged in trade and commerce. They also dominated the Leningrad intelligentsia: in 1939 they comprised 18 per cent of all scientists and teachers in *vuzy*; 20 per cent of engineers; one-third of writers, journalists, and editors; 31 per cent of store managers; 38 per cent of all physicians; 45 per cent of lawyers; and 70 per cent of dentists.[49]

Jewish stereotypes emerged after the murder of Kirov, when complaints were heard that 'as soon as a pure Russian *muzhik* comes to power then he is killed', and that 'the murder of Kirov was carried out with the intention of reducing the number of Russians in government and increasing the number of Jews'.[50] Jews were blamed for the murder, since according to the stereotype, they were power-loving and greedy for world domination.[51] A Leningrad party secretary, Irklis, received a letter implicating Jews in the assassination and declaring that 'the sacred revolutionary Smol'nii is full of the Jewish nation' (Smol'nii was the Leningrad headquarters of the party and soviet). According to the letter, this fact was well known to all workers and was causing unrest among them:

All the traders' sons have set themselves up well with you in Smol'nii and behave brutally towards the old party members and towards the masses in general ... They shelve valuable applications and arrange responsible jobs for Jews and Jewesses at a fast pace, and now you can meet people of all nations amongst the unemployed with the exception of Jews, as they are all sitting in the leading jobs.[52]

Another letter expressed similar feelings that Jews had taken over all the positions of power. The letter, signed by 'A Russian', referred to the party organisation of the Leningrad Industrial Institute, whose leader, Zakhar Zabludovskii, was apparently 'not indifferent to people of Jewish extraction'. The writer claimed that 80 per cent of the apparat was occupied by Jews 'with dark pasts', and that Jews were given priority for housing, stipends, and other privileges, and were never excluded from the party. Zabludovskii had allegedly in a state of inebriation once shouted 'For one Jew, we'll expel 1,000 Russians from the institute.'[53]

The alleged Jewish dream of world domination was the subject of a letter to Zhdanov, which argued that the Jews found Russia too small for them, and so advocated world revolution. Reflecting on the fall in the real standard of living since the revolution, the writer concluded that socialism and communism were unviable, and simply a mask for the Jews to gain equal rights. The Jews organised 1917; Russians and other nationalities were simply pawns. Stalin, Kirov, and other leaders had been bought up by the Jews, forced to subscribe to the doctrines of Comintern, the 'international Yiddish cabal'. Zhdanov was warned that he too would be sucked in, bought products from Torgsin, be given cars, be flattered, and have his speeches and portraits printed, all in order that the Jews realise their dream of world power.[54]

The idea that Jews had taken power in Russia also emerged during the Constitutional discussion, when Jews were blamed for Russia's woes, and it was suggested that their civil rights be removed: 'We should arrange it so that according to the new Constitution Jews are deprived of electoral rights. They should be wiped from the face of the earth, but as it is they are tormenting Russians. Before, Jews used to be killed, but now they have power.'[55] Similar extreme sentiments were expressed before the 1937 Supreme Soviet elections:

Why should we go to the elections, for without us they will elect the candidate for the Supreme Soviet, Bogdanov, for whom we are forced to vote – he's an absolutely pure Yid. Only Yids are elected to the Supreme Soviet, when they shouldn't be elected, but killed, as they used to kill them before. For it's because of them that our brothers live badly.[56]

During the elections of trade union organisations in 1937, one worker expressed her pleasure that they were taking place, since 'Yids would be driven out'.[57]

Many prominent defendants in the show trials happened to be Jewish, and this merely reinforced the stereotype of Jewishness= being in power=corruption. The leading role accorded to the 'Judas Trotsky' in the drama ensured that ordinary people equated the alleged 'traitors' with Jews. Party reports on reactions to the trial of the anti-Soviet Trotskyite centre at the beginning of 1937 noted observations such as 'There are many Jews in this trial, because the Jewish nation loves power, and so they struggled for power so strongly'; 'the Jews are responsible for everything, and Trotsky should have been killed long ago, Kaganovich should be checked to see what sort of person he is because he's Jewish too'.[58]

In chapter 8, it will be argued in more detail that this antipathy towards Jews represented to some extent a wider phenomenon of hostility on the part of subordinate groups towards all forms of power. Jews were identified with power-holders and represented as implicitly opposed to the interests of the *workers*. For example, workers felt that 'In Spain there are many Yids, and so the workers will lose, Yids will betray the workers'; 'Jews squeeze us, and we are silent. The head of the central construction bureau is a Jew, and the president of the factory committee. They squeeze us and there is no one to complain to.' Jews were portrayed as dishonest and parasitical partly because they did no real, i.e. manual, work: 'we know that all Jews are former petty traders'; 'The Jews are layabouts and deceivers. For example, you give in your watch for cleaning, and they take things out the middle.' A worker at the Ekonomaizer factory reacted to the Soviet occupation of Poland in 1939 with the recommendation 'Kill fewer Poles and more Jews ... Truly more Jews should be killed. What's the point of them? They will surge into Russia, won't work, and we have enough of our own parasites. We don't need any Jews.'[59]

Although the stereotype of the Jew dominated popular discourse, other groups were also singled out, and discussed in similar terms. Partly because of the high proportion of Caucasians in the Politburo (Stalin, Ordzhonikidze, Mikoian), Caucasians, particularly Georgians, like Jews, were made the target of criticisms that Russia was not being ruled by Russians: 'Look, we are Russians and we are led by Jews and others, just take comrade Stalin, he isn't Russian, he's Georgian.'[60] Like Jews, Caucasian candidates were treated with suspicion during elections. In the 1937 Supreme Soviet elections, one candidate, Tevosian, provoked anti-Georgian sentiments: 'I don't like Georgians and I won't vote for them ... I live among Georgians and I know what sort of people they are, I didn't respect Ordzhonikidze either.'[61]

Some confusion prevailed about the actual nationality of non-Russians, especially Stalin. After the Kirov murder, it was stated that 'Better if they had killed Stalin, he is an Armenian, and comrade Kirov was a pure Russian', and 'Better if they killed Stalin than Kirov because Kirov is ours [*nash*], and Stalin not ours [*ne nash*].' 'Ours' and 'not ours' were then explained: 'Kirov is Russian and Stalin is Jewish.'[62] The actual label – Jew, Georgian, Armenian – was clearly not as important as the defining characteristic of non-Russianness. Nevertheless, Caucasians were sometimes attributed particular qualities; for example, they were perceived as wild and violent, epithets never applied to Jews. In relation to Ordzhonikidze, it was asserted that 'Those Armenians were savages before, and now they are in power, so many good people have died because of that bastard, but they will not kill and shoot them all, the time will come when all our leaders will be killed.'[63]

Russian identity was defined in implicit opposition to other groups such as Jews and Armenians, but was usually not articulated in a more positive way in this period. Before 1917, the concept of a

Russian national identity was probably underdeveloped outside the elite. Russians had historically felt a sense of allegiance to the tsar and church, rather than to the nation.[64] It is unlikely that nineteenth-century Slavophile ideas percolated down from the intelligentsia to the people. For the mass of Russian peasants, local and regional loyalties were probably more meaningful than national ties, although this may have begun to change at the end of the nineteenth century with the spread of literacy and books disseminating images of Russia as an imperial power.[65] However, Russian national identity remained weakly defined by 1914. Hubertus Jahn suggests that, during the First World War, Russian patriotism was less clearly formulated and more diffuse than negative attitudes towards enemy figures, such as the kaiser. There were no unifying symbols with which to articulate a coherent identity.[66] After the revolution, ordinary people were encouraged to think of themselves as Soviet, rather than Russian, citizens. While in the 1920s the other Soviet republics were allowed to express their long-suppressed national feelings, any manifestation of Russian national consciousness was equated with 'Great Russian chauvinism' and condemned. Only in 1937 did the Soviet regime begin to employ Russian nationalist imagery overtly in its propaganda.

It is thus perhaps not surprising that ordinary workers and peasants rarely expressed a positive sense of Russian identity in the period after 1934. Some cases of hostility towards other ethnic groups were accompanied by pro-Russian feeling: 'The majority in the Soviet of Nationalities from the RSFSR will be national minorities, won't they keep the Russians down?';[67] 'I won't vote for Stalin because he isn't Russian and does not defend the interests of the Russian people. One should vote only for Russians'; 'Jews and Poles are capable of all kinds of tricks. Where there are non-Russians there are enemies and wreckers everywhere. As long as nationalities exist, there will be wreckers and enemies.'[68] Yet there was little notion of what Russianness meant for ordinary workers and peasants. The majority of explicit comment on Russia appears to have been penned by the ideologues of imagined communities, literate intellectuals, and it can be found in written sources such as letters, and leaflets, which frequently exploited Russian imagery in their attempts to rouse people.[69] The language of nationalism thus served as a potent weapon for attacking the state. Some of the language recalls that of the narodnik intellectuals of the nineteenth century. Russians were attributed qualities of patriotism, bravery, generosity, and patience. The Russian had 'a large and broad soul', according to one party member writing to Zhdanov. A leaflet noted that 'only workers in the USSR can bear such difficult torture, for the Russian can be patient for long'. Another, addressed to 'Russian Citizens', described the disastrous economic policy pursued by the Soviet regime, declaring that 'The Russian people have waited for a long time, but even the Russian patience has an end, and then they say "Enough".' It attacked the press filled with Stalin's name and 'Yiddish dirt', and ended, 'Every Russian must help us in our struggle against the oppression of our motherland.' Yet another began, 'To the Russian people, devoted to their motherland' and called on the people to rise up. Russians were sometimes also represented as easily manipulated, as in a leaflet discovered during the local soviet elections of December 1939, which attacked the electoral farce, and asked:

if there are Russians in the [electoral] commission, then isn't it time for you to remember and stop being fools. Isn't it time for you to put an end to this comedy? Look back, Russian sheep, at what has happened to Russia ... 1932 and 1933 with collectivisation in the Middle Volga and Ukraine, more than a million people starved to death. Now there is a war, Russians are killed and mutilated ... But the Russian *muzhik* has remembered, the rifle is in his hands, don't forget and wait.[70]

How far ordinary workers and peasants shared this view of the Russian people is hard to gauge. The mere expression of anti-semitic opinions by ordinary people does not in itself indicate that they were fiercely nationalistic. Such feelings also had strong class overtones. Did people feel greater allegiance to a class than to a nation? Did they view themselves as Soviet rather than Russian? Did they continue to regard Russian national identity as bound up with the Orthodox church? Certainly the regime's turn towards more overtly Russian nationalist propaganda during the war suggests that it viewed this as potentially capable of mobilising the population. But for what were people fighting in the Great Patriotic War – for Russia, for the Soviet Union, for Stalin, for socialism, for the working class, or for none of these? These are intriguing questions which invite further research.

II

Politics and terror

International relations

International relations would normally be considered a subject peripheral to the concerns of many ordinary people; however, in this period of acute international tension, the external relations of the USSR with other powers were at the centre of everyday interest. With Hitler's seizure of power in 1933, Soviet foreign policy underwent a metamorphosis, symbolised by the USSR's admission to the League of Nations in September 1934, the adoption of a policy of collective security, and increasingly amicable relationships with the non-fascist capitalist powers, including France with whom the USSR signed a pact in May 1935. At the same time, Comintern abandoned its isolationist stance, advocating instead a 'popular front'. While espousing anti-fascism, and backing the Republicans in the Spanish Civil War, the Soviet Union none the less continued to make overtures to Germany at the end of the 1930s, which culminated in a pact of non-aggression. For ordinary people, the tension in Europe and the Far East made this period one of constant preparation for and expectation of war. For those dissatisfied with the regime, war represented possible liberation from the Soviet yoke, and Hitler and fascist policies evidently had adherents. However, others were categorically opposed to the dictator, and the volte-face of the Molotov–Ribbentrop pact left them shocked and confused. The USSR's expansionist policies in Poland, the Baltic states, and Finland also met with less than universal approval, while some people objected to being used as cannon-fodder for the military adventures of those in power.

The threat of a war launched by the capitalist powers against the infant Soviet state had always loomed large over the USSR and, with the rise of Hitler, the menace appeared to grow. The media made frequent reference to external aggression, and this was compounded by the narrative on the internal 'war' being fought out within the

USSR. The language of enemies and traitors, victories and defeats, battles and fronts, dominated official Soviet discourse. In popular discourse, speculation about impending war was also rife. Rumours tended to arise with particular intensity during other crises. For example, the expulsion of Leningraders from the city (see p. 121 in chapter 7) at the beginning of 1935 was thought to be connected with war, while the trial of Kamenev and Zinoviev in August 1936 provoked remarks that 'We must buy sugar as there will be a war because of the shooting of the terrorists.' Likewise the bread shortages of 1936–7 spawned a spate of rumours about a war which was imminent or had even begun. A vicious circle was created, as shortages of bread sparked off war rumours, while these rumours in turn encouraged people to hoard, leading to yet more shortages and queues.[1]

The regime classified remarks hinting at the USSR's possible defeat in an eventual war as 'defeatist agitation', which was liable to prosecution. Such defeatism seems to have been quite common, especially amongst peasants, who hoped that a war would precipitate the end of the *kolkhozy*.[2] The idea of war as liberation featured prominently in subversive poems:

Kirova ubili – tuda emu doroga	Kirov's killed – he's got what he deserves
Ikh ne zhal' ugrobit' dazhe vsekh	I'm not sorry if they kill them all even
Tol'ko zhal', chto mnogo	I'm only sorry that many
Vampiry rasstreliali	Vampires were shot
Eto rasstreliali za nego	They were shot because of him
Skoro vlast' sovetov	Soon Soviet power
Vyletit, chto probka	Will fly out like a cork
Iz pivnoi butylki na panel'.	From a beer bottle onto the path.
Nam tak zhit' v nevole	The way we live in captivity
Zhit' uzhe nedolgo	We don't have long to live
Zhit' ostalos' tol'ko do voiny	We only have to live until the war.[3]

. . .

Ne nadolgo vse proidet	Not for long, all will pass
Protivnik Stalina ub'et	The enemy'll kill Stalin
Skoro budet ved' voina	For soon there'll be war
I togda, togda, togda	And then, then, then
Budet Stalin laskov navsegda	Stalin will be kind forever
Kogda ego ne budet – stikhnet navsegda.	When he's gone freedom forever.[4]

The sentiments expressed in these poems, which were echoed in numerous other comments, reveal the close connection between war

and revolutionary transformation in the minds of the ordinary people. The revolutions of 1905 and 1917 had both occurred in the midst of Russian defeat in war, and the idea of war as a catalyst for change clearly remained potent.[5]

While some people looked forward to war, others were less enthusiastic, regarding it as a policy perpetrated by those in power, as a consequence of which the ordinary people suffered. Such 'class' feelings emerged during anti-aircraft attack exercises in Leningrad in September 1934, when a worker refused to buy a gas mask on the grounds that 'Anyway workers will all die in the war, and only communists will remain alive because they will escape to cosy little corners.' Similarly, at the Stalin factory, workers complained that, when there was no danger of war, their leaders were prepared to organise such exercises, but if a real war actually were to occur, they would do nothing and workers would have to organise themselves. When war finally did break out, such feelings became more pronounced. In September 1939, a worker from the Voskov factory in Sestroretsk objected at the call-up point that 'You're sending off only workers, while the "white hands" are left at home.' During the Winter War, the many deaths of ordinary soldiers and the manifestly useless command provoked comments that 'On the Finnish front many innocent people are killed, and the scoundrelous leaders sit in the rear, and get 800 r. or more, while soldiers are paid only 8 r.'; 'the Bolsheviks send soldiers to fight in Finland and starve people. The soldiers should kill the Bolsheviks rather than the Finns'; 'Just think, our people are sitting in Moscow and drinking champagne.'[6]

Does this type of reaction suggest that workers had imbibed the rhetoric of socialist internationalism, and espoused proletarian solidarity? For some, this may indeed have been the case. After the Molotov–Ribbentrop pact, a worker and former party member from the Kirov works said:

This is what I think – in France at the Renault factory there are 35,000 workers and 6,000 communists, while at the Kirov works we have 36,000 workers and only 3,500 communists. The workers at the Renault factory doubtless think that we have betrayed them, and so our people have decided, let Hitler squeeze and rout France, Belgium, Holland, and the Baltic states, just leave us in peace, to hide our rear in the bushes, and when Hitler comes to power, then willy-nilly we'll have to show it.[7]

It is perhaps significant that this was the view of a former party member. The attitude of other workers is less clear. Official propaganda made much of the workers' alleged internationalist feelings during the Spanish Civil War, manifested in their willingness to donate money to the Republican cause. Doubtless many did share such feelings, and some even wanted to go further – volunteering to fight, or suggesting that the Soviet Union should send in its army. But others thought the USSR was meddling where it should not, and were more loath to help. There was particular reluctance to give money to Spanish workers when they themselves had so little, and also anxiety that the money would not actually reach its intended destination. According to agitators, this reluctance was quite widespread.[8] Assistance to Spain was being proffered at the time of acute bread shortages during winter 1936–7, which sparked off rumours connecting the two events – 'there's not enough bread because it's being sent to Spain'. Similar reactions greeted Soviet assistance to China, Mongolia, and, following the 1939 pact, Germany: 'Bread's being sent to Spain and China while we go hungry'; 'We throw money to the wind for nothing. Why are we helping Mongolia, Spain, China? Look, we helped Spain and nothing came of it. And nothing will come of our help to Mongolia and China, the capitalists will crush them'; 'A curse on this life. First it's the Spanish, then the Chinese, and now we're feeding and clothing Hitler.'[9]

Attitudes to fascism and Hitler were far from unequivocally negative throughout this period, despite, or perhaps because of, Soviet propaganda. Hitler represented dynamism, economic success, authoritarianism, anti-semitism, expansionism – all policies which found adherents in Russia. One student said 'The fascists are constructing socialism in a peaceful way. Hitler and the fascists are clever people.'[10] In the same breath, he praised Trotsky's military ability and proposed that women should be men's slaves. In a school in Petrogradskii district, two pupils tried to organise a strike against dinner. One said that he was bored by the pioneer organisation, whereas 'in Germany it's good. There at least life is in full swing, there are fascist organisations which shoot communists and Komsomols.' On being told that this was surely not a good thing, he answered: 'Although it's not good, there are strong feelings because of it.'[11] Hitler's cult of youth and violence and the idea of 'Kraft durch Freude' ('strength through joy') clearly had considerable appeal for the younger generation, which had not suffered the effects of German militarism in 1914–18. The Hitler Youth movement seemed to have more purpose and energy than the Komsomol, which concentrated on intellectual rather than physical education. One worker at the Sudomekh factory reported that

In Hitler's Germany there is an organisation of Hitler working youth, who are given free training to be pilots, they give them the military training and uniform free of charge, and it is good for them living there. If they allowed us to have such an organisation in the USSR, I swear that many young people would join it, even your Komsomols.[12]

Support for Hitler was fuelled to some extent by his treatment of the Jews. The standard of living was also believed to be higher in Germany. According to a joke circulating in 1939, 'In Germany there's one car for every worker, and here there are two – the "black raven" and the ambulance.'[13] Hitler's charisma and popularity amongst his own people were emphasised: 'We are sure that the fascists will win in Spain because they are led by Hitler, and Hitler is a brilliant man and the chief man in the world'; 'Soviet power will not last long. The fascists under Hitler's leadership will win, because he is behind the people.'[14] He was perceived by some as courageous and determined, a *muzhik*:[15] 'Hitler takes everything in hand, he's a *muzhik* with a head. He fears no one, recognises no one, and does as he pleases'; 'Hitler's great. For he fears no one, controls matters as he wants. Annuls the agreement and spits on everyone'; 'In his own way Hitler is correct in his politics. He bravely goes for everything, knows that other powers will not be brave enough to get in his way.'[16] Adulation for strong leaders in Russia was clearly not limited to the cult of Soviet *vozhdi*.

Throughout this period, the NKVD and party reported finding swastikas daubed on walls, although this in itself is not necessarily indicative of support for Hitler and fascism. Drawing a swastika may simply have been a subversive act, since the symbol was so obviously illegitimate and people may have drawn it without being fully aware of all its connotations.[17]

Although there was some support for Hitler, others were categorically opposed to Nazism. Amongst these people, the Molotov–Ribbentrop treaty of 23 August 1939 generated confusion, shock, and numerous questions of the type, 'Why before did they shout that fascists are enemies, and now they make a treaty with them?' Agitators were unable to answer such questions and reports noted uncomprehension and 'often direct dissatisfaction' on the part of some groups, even communists and activists. Negative reactions to the pact were so widespread that Molotov publicly acknowledged popular 'lack of understanding' in his speech of 31 August: 'People ask, with an air of innocence, how could the Soviet Union consent to improve its political relations with a state of the fascist type? Is that possible, they ask.'[18]

Distrust of Germany and its motives was the dominant reaction: 'The very fact of the non-aggression pact with Germany says that Germany is conducting a murky policy in relation to the USSR. One oughtn't overestimate the peace-loving intentions of the Germans'; 'We ought not have concluded a treaty with Germany because Germany will break it anyway. We're used to regarding Germany as an aggressive country. Surely it cannot conduct a peaceful policy.'[19] Some, regarding the pact as indicative of Soviet weakness, resurrected old stereotypes about German superiority and cunning:

Germany is trying to apply new methods to get more information about the USSR and to calm the Soviet government on the question of armaments. Hitler will not retreat from his plan to invade us in 1940–1 ... The Germans were always cleverer than the Russians. The popular front is weak now and won't help the USSR. The Kremlin leaders are following the wrong policy.[20]

For others, the treaty symbolised the growing similarity between fascism and communism. Someone joked how quickly the pact had come about: 'the two dictators have agreed simply that there should be no leaders of the opposition and no parliaments. Now all that is needed is for Hitler to transfer from fascism to socialism and Stalin from socialism to fascism.' Another person continued this line of thought: 'And there's no need for a transfer, in Germany they do not take away plots, and in the USSR they do.'[21] The unlikely combination of fascists and communists also led to jokes that Hitler and Ribbentrop had put in applications to join the communist party, and that Moscow was deciding whether to take them or not.[22]

With the eruption of war in Europe at the beginning of September and Hitler's invasion of Poland, suspicion and anxiety grew that the USSR would be dragged into a European war, that Hitler would not stop at Poland, would proceed to take the Baltic states and attack the USSR. It was suggested that the USSR should protect Poland.[23] Instead, on 17 September, the USSR invaded Poland and took western Ukraine and Belorussia under its protection, for which the latter were allegedly heartily grateful. The invasion caused much consternation, and fears that war between the USSR and Germany would ensue. However, others guessed that the Polish strategy was part of a pre-arranged plan according to which Germany and the USSR would each take their former territories. There was even talk of 'secret treaties'. Soviet policy was criticised on the grounds that Germany and the USSR were colluding in the destruction of Poland, when the USSR should be helping its fellow Slavic country, and Stalin's pledge that the USSR would not seek others' territory was cited ironically. The feeling that the USSR was pursuing just the same aggressive policy as Germany grew stronger: 'fascism and communism are the same concept. Confirmation of this is the agreed partition of Poland.' Sympathy was expressed for the Poles, and also for the Belorussians and Ukrainians to whom the USSR was offering its 'brotherly help', and who would now be subjected to what the Soviet people had already endured:

We haven't got it so good ourselves at the moment, but they're taking even more people under their wing. When these peoples find out how *kolkhozniki* really live here, then there'll be 'gratitude' to Soviet power for such 'help'. There they had their own little houses, cows, horses, and land, felt themselves to be the bosses, and now they'll go hungry just like our *kolkhozniki*.[24]

By 23 September a report noted that:

the general political and moral condition of the population is healthy. However, there are unhealthy and sometimes directly anti-Soviet feelings bordering on counter-revolutionary conversations. These feelings have become especially strong in the last few days, when Soviet forces took a number of Polish towns, and Germany's attitude towards this became known.

Fear spread among women that their husbands were being killed and rumours circulated that France and Britain had declared war on the USSR.[25]

Leningraders were close to the front line of war, and were thus particularly concerned by these events. This was even more true of the Winter War against Finland. Accurate official information on the course of this war was sparse, but it was impossible to prevent Leningraders discovering for themselves what appeared to be happening. As early as 19 November 1939, a black-out in Leningrad led to rumours about an impending conflict with Finland. Shooting had already been heard, and it was claimed that Voroshilov had arrived. By 26 November, a defeatist mood was reported, as rumours spread that war had already started (indeed, this was the day on which it subsequently became known that the Finns had allegedly provoked Soviet troops by firing at them). On 27 November, meetings were held to discuss the actual outbreak of hostilities.[26] At this stage, people were already analysing the situation. A *sluzhashchii* from Pskov claimed that:

The Soviet Union wants to undress Finland, to take from it the best, dearest, and most valuable and leave it with nothing. They think that Finland will immediately give up everything they demand without any trouble. The Soviet Union offered Finland Karelia, but who needs that. There is only marsh and forest there. For example if they took your smart new coat from you and offered you lots of rags instead, of course you would not take it; it's the same with Finland.[27]

Immediately after the publication of Molotov's speech of 29 November on the war between the two countries, reports were compiled every few hours on the mood of the population of the *oblast'*. This was alleged to be calm, despite the fact that in some areas shots had been heard.[28] On 1 December, some 'backward feelings' were noted. Large numbers of wounded soldiers were reportedly arriving at the Finland station. A worker suggested that the Finns had not provoked the Soviet troops after all, and that it was wrong to believe the radio. People asked why the USSR needed to invade Finland, when it already had enough land of its own, and it was argued that the USSR enjoyed conquering small countries.[29]

The continued losses in the war meant that by mid-December there was panic in Leningrad, and rumours of wrecking by Soviet commanders. The latter were alleged to be deliberately leading soldiers under the artillery fire of the enemy. Voroshilov had apparently come and replaced the command.[30] Many of these rumours were accurate and based on first-hand knowledge and observation. The unofficial news network functioned remarkably efficiently. For example, at one military hospital in Leningrad, as soon as the wounded were brought in, they were surrounded by crowds who extracted the latest information.[31] Soldiers returning to Leningrad from the front related graphic stories. One reported:

In the first days of our forces' attack (Petrozavodsk direction) there were numerous losses, as a result of wrecking on the part of the command. The commander of one regiment gave an order to attack and he himself fled. The regiment found itself in a dense forest and was surrounded by white [enemy] Finns and destroyed ... there are many abnormalities in the actions of our military units. The infantry goes in front and the tanks behind. Only after Voroshilov came to the front were some of these abnormalities eliminated ... Many of our fighters have frostbite in their feet and have left the formation. Only in the last few days have soldiers got warm footwear ... Our commanders organised a Finnish corps of 6,000 men to work to the rear of the white Finns. Only 3,000 of the corps remain; the rest deserted to the white Finns.[32]

The mood amongst the soldiers of the Leningrad military district was very bleak. In letters to Zhdanov, they complained of the lack of basic equipment, maps, gloves, and food. One letter of 14 December reported that even the commanders did not know what their tasks were supposed to be, not to speak of soldiers who marched blindly from one place to the next. Others reported wrecking in the command and asked that Zhdanov deal with this urgently.[33] Many soldiers deserted to the Finnish side.

As the war dragged on into the New Year rumours of treachery and the numbers killed continued to circulate. Not surprisingly, when a peace treaty was eventually concluded on 12 March 1940, some people claimed that the USSR had been forced into signing because the operation had reached a stalemate.[34] In a rare note of *glasnost'*, Molotov, in a speech to the Supreme Soviet on 29 March, openly admitted great Soviet losses in the war, although he downplayed the actual numbers of those dead and wounded.[35]

The USSR's performance in this war did little to inspire popular confidence in the armed forces and its leadership. Germany, by contrast, took over the continent of Europe in 1940–1 with its spectacular policy of *Blitzkrieg*. Some Soviet citizens assumed that Hitler's next target would be the USSR. Right up to the eve of war in June 1941, rumour-mongers predicted the imminent defeat (or liberation) of the USSR in a war against Germany.[36]

CHAPTER 6

The Constitution and elections

Like international relations, constitutions and elections might seem an area remote from the concerns of ordinary people struggling to survive. However, the regime's intense agitprop campaigns on subjects such as the Stalin Constitution of 1936 and the 'free and democratic' elections which it inaugurated alerted at least some of the population to these issues. Yet people did not always interpret the propaganda in the intended manner. The show of 'Soviet democracy' did in fact provide a genuine forum for the expression of popular opinion and stimulate consciousness of civil and political rights.

THE CONSTITUTION

In reference to the emergence of a civil society in the USSR in the Gorbachev period, Geoffrey Hosking writes that 'the first germ of civil society was contained in the Stalin Constitution of 1936'. He goes on to demonstrate how the rights it proclaimed were used by dissidents from the 1960s onwards.[1] The aim of the following discussion is to show how this 'germ' was already sprouting small and fragile shoots in the period after 1936.

The draft version of the Stalin Constitution, approved by a party plenum in June 1936, differed significantly from its predecessors of 1918 and 1924.[2] Whereas the latter provided for open elections and a class-based restricted franchise, the new Constitution introduced secret elections, open to all aged over eighteen, regardless of class background. It stressed the achievement of socialism and the harmony of classes, and that all power belonged to the workers and peasants. It also contained a long chapter of rights and duties which applied to all citizens. These included civil liberties (freedom of speech, belief, etc.) and socio-economic rights (rights to work, rest, etc.) Although superficially a triumph for democracy, the Constitution was limited from the outset. For example, article 125, which guaranteed the freedom of speech, press, assembly, and demonstrations, was prefaced with the words 'In conformity with the interests of the toilers and in order to strengthen the socialist system'.

Before the Constitution was officially adopted by an Extraordinary Congress of Soviets on 5 December, an all-peoples' discussion of the draft was held. The people were encouraged to suggest their own amendments, the least controversial of which were published in the press. The discussion itself and subsequent interpretation and use of the Constitution by ordinary people provide an insight into the popular understanding of the whole question of political and civil rights.

It has been suggested that Russian peasants and workers, before and after 1917, had little understanding of, or interest in such rights. Richard Pipes states that the 'Great Russian Peasant, with centuries of serfdom in his bones, not only did not crave for civil and political rights, but ... held such notions in contempt'.[3] This common picture of the Russian as inherently servile, with no concept of freedom, except an anarchic destructive urge, has been questioned by other historians, who argue that the notion of rights was not completely alien to ordinary people. The language of rights was certainly employed in 1905 by both workers and peasants, who appear to have had some sense of the inherent value of rights such as the freedom of speech and inviolability of the person. Yet it is undeniable that workers at least also appear to have regarded civil rights partly as an instrument with which to realise their 'class' aims.[4]

The social polarisation of Russia probably ensured that the liberal conception of universal civil and political rights had little appeal by 1917. According to Marc Ferro, workers and peasants did not mention such rights in February 1917, focusing their demands on economic issues (in the case of the workers) and on the disempowerment of the landlords (in the case of the peasants).[5] However, Diane Koenker notes that Moscow workers demanded a Constituent Assembly and freedom of the press at various moments in 1917.[6] On the eve of the revolution, as the acquisition of power became the only priority, the political demands of workers centred on the suppression of rights, such as the freedom of the bourgeois press, and in this period, the Bolshevik Party, not the workers themselves, supported the convening of a Constituent Assembly.[7] In the months after the revolution, political rights seem to have been secondary to socio-economic issues on the popular agenda, despite some political rhetoric in mid-1918. Anti-regime, anti-Bolshevik sentiments may have been running high, but party politics, western-style elections, and 'democracy' were not necessarily the cure in the eyes of ordinary people.[8]

After the revolution, those opposed to the regime emphasised the importance of rights in conjunction with other goals. Among the demands of striking workers in February 1921 were calls for the restoration of political and civil rights. In their Petropavlovsk resolution, the Kronstadt rebel sailors also demanded *inter alia* 'to give freedom of speech and press to workers and peasants, to anarchists and left socialist parties' and 'to secure freedom of assembly for trade unions and peasant organisations'. It is significant that, in their view, too, rights had a strictly class character. Likewise, their idea of democracy was not the bourgeois Constituent Assembly, but direct popular democracy through re-elected soviets: 'Power to the Soviets, and not to parties!'[9] The language of these protests of 1921 reveals the influence of their *intelligenty* organisers. It is difficult to know to what extent ordinary sailors and workers thought in these terms. Reports on the mood of workers in Petrograd note that in mid-March talk about the distribution of clothes and shoes taking place in the factories was much more widespread than conversations concerning Kronstadt, let alone discussion of the need for 'rights'.[10]

In the period 1934–41, advocacy of rights was often the preserve of the more literate. Thus a leaflet of 1934 entitled 'Vozzvanie' ('Appeal'), called for a number of changes, including the end of party leadership and prison camps; a return to individual farming; production to be based on use and reproduction, not the market; wages to correspond to the value of a product; and 'freedom of the press and speech, without which progress is unthinkable'.[11] Generally this type of language was restricted to the intelligentsia, although a few ordinary people did speak about freedoms: in 1935, a worker complained that 'nowadays freedom of speech is not what it used to be'.[12] However, the civil and political rights embodied in the 1936 Constitution clearly flew in the face of some popular conceptions. How, then, did the people respond?

Some simply rejected the whole idea of a constitution in the current economic climate, arguing that, before writing constitutions, it would be better to work out how to feed people. Constitutional rights meant little to those who were hungry. As a group of workers at the Third Tobacco Factory declared 'We don't need your Constitution, we need bread and cheap food.'[13] Likewise, the brigade-leader of one *kolkhoz* said 'We have a lot of talk about freedoms and democracy, but it's all chatter. What kind of freedom is it, when Soviet power takes everything and gives the peasants nothing, leaves them hungry?'[14] For many, the Constitution was an irrelevancy, confirming the traditional socialist critique of bourgeois conceptions of rights, that such freedoms mean nothing to people who lack basic economic and social rights.

Other workers criticised the rejection of a class-based conception of rights. A widespread reaction was that the whole project was 'bourgeois' and a threat to the privileged status of the worker. Reports note that the draft was greeted with suspicion by communists and workers, since the idea of full democracy seemed to contradict that of the dictatorship of the proletariat. Some interpreted the draft as a sign that the dictatorship of the proletariat had had its day, and that, correspondingly, the role of the party was no longer so important. The notion of universal rights was equated with capitalism in the words of one worker, who said 'I disagree with the policies of the party. We are going towards capitalism, since the new Constitution gives the right to vote to all.' There were many suggestions that the previously disenfranchised *lishentsy* should continue to be deprived of the vote. People advocated restricting the freedom of speech to toilers, and classifying as enemies of the people those who used the freedom of speech and press to harm the interests of the toilers.[15]

Peasants seem to have favoured the concept of equal rights for all *toilers*, since their suggested amendments almost invariably focused on the need to accord the peasantry the same status as workers. Suggested amendments from the Leningrad *oblast'* included fifty proposals that article 1, which stated that the USSR was a state of workers and peasants, should be replaced by the words *gosudarstvo trudiashchikhsia* (state of toilers), since the latter word was all-inclusive, and removed the distinction between peasants and workers.[16] The Constitution favoured workers over peasants on a number of points, including the right to holidays and to work a seven-hour day, and peasants suggested that these rights should apply to themselves too.[17] The discussion seems therefore to have activated peasant 'class' consciousness. The NKVD noted it had led to the 'stirring up of *kolkhoznik* dissatisfaction regarding the workers' which was reflected in envious statements drawing attention to the gap in living standards: '*Kolkhozniki* live worse than workers. The workers lived better even before the new Constitution' and to complaints that 'the Constitution is written not for us, but for workers and *sluzhashchie*'.[18]

J. Arch Getty argues that the popular agenda during the discussion was limited: 'although citizens were concerned with bread-and-butter issues and popular control of local affairs, they were not worried about individual rights or civil protection'.[19] The official reports on proposed amendments may give this impression, but opinion reports and letters reveal that these questions were in fact raised in private. The vast propaganda campaign around the Constitution and its wide discussion served to awaken a consciousness of political and civil rights amongst those who may have never even been aware of such concepts. Thus, paradoxically, the propaganda itself stimulated popular criticism of the real nature of the Soviet regime. The Constitution made explicit the contrast between the ideal (the Constitution) and the reality (everyday Soviet experience). It drew attention to concepts such as 'freedom of conscience' and 'the inviolability of the person', to which many people, brought up on a diet of revolutionary ethics, or excluded from agitprop altogether, may have never given much thought. Awareness of rights is not innate; it must be learned. In this period, many people acquired a whole new language, and began to reflect upon the absence of such rights in the Soviet Union.

Some concluded that the Constitutional rights in themselves were good, but that they would not be realised in the USSR. Freedom of speech in particular was thought to be desirable: 'According to the Constitution, everything is fine. All the freedoms are given, but try to use the freedom of speech and say something the Bolsheviks dislike, and you'll get five years in exile'; 'Workers are so terrified that they cannot say anything, everyone has fallen silent, but life's very difficult and there would be something to talk about. So in the new Constitution too, try to say something and they'll find a punishment straight away.' People began to discuss other freedoms, particularly the freedom to form alternative parties. Peasants suggested joining together in groups to fight for their rights. There was discussion of what was meant by freedom, with some concluding that freedom could only be attained by abolishing the NKVD. Some compared the freedom to which they were entitled with that experienced by convicts: 'the freedom to exist and toil'. Many peasants said they would willingly give up the right to work. Others took the phrase 'Who does not work will not eat' and asserted that the converse was true: 'He who does not work not only eats, but drinks wine too, while he who works eats chaff.'[20]

The Constitution spawned unofficial constitutions, such as that sent to Zhdanov by a 'Legion of Revolutionary Democracy' in 1937.[21] It also alerted some people to the rights and duties of individuals at the grassroots as well as the state level. For example, after the adoption of the official Constitution, pupils in the top forms of the Second Sestroretsk middle school worked out their own 'constitution and declaration of the rights of the pupil and citizen'. This document laid out the rights and duties of the pupils, envisaged elections of a class 'TsIK' and a 'Cabinet of Ministers' and divided the pupils into two 'classes': boy Komsomol members and girl Komsomol members. The actual document contained articles such as 'Study is the duty of every pupil'; 'Every pupil has the right to leave the ninth class'; 'Pupils are guaranteed freedom of speech, press, street demonstrations, singing, friendship, preparation of lessons.'[22] This independent and spontaneous initiative, testimony of a quite sophisticated mastery of the principles of the 'real' Constitution, was deemed counter-revolutionary behaviour.

The role of the Constitution as a catalyst for unanticipated distortion and misinterpretation of the regime's intentions can also be observed in the manner in which the various rights enshrined in the Constitution were understood and employed. While some people did not take the project seriously, seeing it as a smokescreen, a concession to the West, others chose to uphold their rights in battles with the regime. This was particularly evident in relation to the rights to the freedom of speech and religion. Many assumed that the freedom of speech would extend to those holding oppositionist and anti-Soviet views. One worker suggested that Trotsky should be allowed to return to the USSR if that was the case.[23] The right to the freedom of speech was used as justification by those brave enough to criticise the government. An example of this was I. Fursenko, who worked at the Pavlov biostation and who, in October 1937, condemned the terror in a letter to Zhdanov. He began the letter with a quote from Pushkin, 'Woe to the country where only slaves and flatterers are near to the throne', and continued:

We have the freedom of conscience and speech and if it is still possible to suspect a man who loudly and publicly criticises the actions of the powers, as if he were agitating against them, then this address containing such condemnations to you – a representative and leader of these powers – cannot be incriminated as anti-Soviet activity. It is our sacred duty to inform you of our doubts and protests against that with which we cannot agree, that which our reason cannot accept.[24]

The letter was remarkable for its honesty in attacking the terror and analysing its effects: cowardice, the paralysis of initiative, the irresponsibility of local leaders. Fursenko realised he was taking a risk in writing so openly to Zhdanov, and therefore shielded himself behind the rights proclaimed in the Constitution. Fursenko was not an ordinary worker, but the same tactics were used by ordinary people, especially in relation to the article 124 on the freedom of religion, which was often cited in petitions to keep churches open. The socio-economic rights enshrined in the Constitution were also actively defended. For example, the introduction of an eight-hour working day and the abolition of free education in 1940 were both held up as examples of infractions of the Constitution.[25]

The Constitutional discussion thus succeeded in raising the level of political awareness in ways which were probably unanticipated. The relative spontaneity of the debate in 1936 gave the regime plenty of food for thought. One of the main discussions at the February–March (1937) plenum centred on how to improve agitation work in connection with the forthcoming elections. As Popok noted, 'harmful' elements, including nationalist groups, had accelerated their activity after the adoption of the Constitution: 'The Constitution was a legal way, so to speak, for them to strengthen their activity.' The plenum repeatedly warned of the need to avoid spontaneity, what it termed 'surprises'.[26] However, despite these resolutions, the party was not entirely successful in controlling opinion in 1937, partly because ordinary people regarded the election campaign as a real possibility of airing political views.

ELECTIONS

The 1937 elections to the USSR Supreme Soviet evoked a similar range of popular response as the Constitution. On the one hand were those who poured scorn on the whole idea of elections as irrelevant to their actual lives. On the other were people who used the election process to express their views and make criticisms. Apathy was expressed by those who realised that the elections would change nothing, either because the same people would be re-elected, or because their own standard of living would not be affected. In a house inhabited by sixteen workers, which suffered from damp and had no form of lighting and a hole in the roof, the workers said 'What are the elections to us? We live worse than *kolkhoz* pigs.'[27] A janitor reported that a pre-election meeting due to convene on 17 October failed to take place because no one turned up, which he considered justified since at these meetings there was never anything but 'empty chat about how everything is good, when in fact it's quite different. I get 120 r. a month. How can I live well? With this kind of life, I'm not up to meetings.' He went on to state that people would only vote because they had to, knowing that the candidates were already appointed and that the votes would not be counted.[28]

The awareness that most of the candidates had been approved from above destroyed the faith of those who had hoped for real changes from the democratic process. A worker from Krasnaia Zaria declared:

I thought that we would elect a new government, which would improve the position of the toilers, when in fact we have once again proposed the old leaders. They could have appointed the current government, published it in the newspaper, and not have made a fuss. It's all the same to me, who's in power, as long as I live well.[29]

The mood of apathy grew more acute when it transpired that the seats would not be fought for, since previously it had been assumed that elections would be contested. Zhdanov had certainly implied this at the February–March plenum, and it appears that the decision to hold single-candidate elections was only taken at the October plenum.[30] A report of 20 November noted that, amongst many non-party electors, communists, and even activists of all constituencies, dismay and confusion about this matter reigned. At a meeting of communists in Vasilievskii ostrov, there was one general question: 'Is it correct that there will be only one name on the ballot paper, and is this not an infringement of democracy?' A party member since 1905 from Pushkinskii district asked 'How can one candidate stand? In practice will the elections be open? We must quickly propose some more candidates, because one candidate cannot stand alone.' Others echoed this suggestion.[31] These disgruntled communists probably conveyed their dismay to the ordinary people and aroused their indignation. An agitator from the *oblast'* recounted how everyone was wondering why there was only one candidate, not two, and asking if it was possible to cross out the name and add their own choice. He replied by explaining that those already chosen were the best people in the country, an argument which clearly failed to convince everyone.[32]

Alongside this disillusionment with the elections, there were also attempts to use the electoral system to air grievances. Stalin had intended that the elections would provide an opportunity for people to criticise the work of soviet organs. However, often this criticism took on a more serious 'anti-Soviet' colouring, as a report on agitation work reveals. This report concluded that the failure of the relevant bodies to fulfil the everyday needs of the population often led to dissatisfaction which impeded agitation work. It cited an example of a case on 21 October, when a worker complained during a discussion group that no one attended to his needs, concluding 'We do not know where to complain to; perhaps we should ask Germany?'[33] The main concern at meetings was usually the state of the economy. In Kaganovicheskii district of Novosibirsk *oblast'*, general questions were asked 'Why do *kolkhozniki* give up bread to the state, and have nothing left for themselves?', 'Why are there big queues?', 'Why do the buses not run?', and so on.[34]

Sometimes these pre-electoral meetings did not stop at listing grievances, but advocated the use of the electoral process to remove those perceived as responsible for the problems. This type of situation put the party leadership in a dilemma. At a meeting of propagandists at the Leningrad *obkom* in the autumn of 1937, one propagandist, Semenova, described a meeting of housewives during which one participant declared that they must actively prepare themselves for the elections and not re-elect people like those in the town soviet, because there were queues everywhere. Semenova considered this a politically incorrect speech, but a member of the *obkom*, Nikanorov, interjected with the point that 'we have to fight queues' and implied that with the attitude of Semenova 'you might stifle every type of criticism'.[35] The borderline between criticism and anti-Soviet sentiment was a fine one.

Criticism of the nominated candidates was quite vociferous and tended to focus on their personalities rather than their policies, partly because the candidates were all standing on essentially the same ticket. Smetanin was described as a hooligan, drunkard, and wife-batterer. Korchagina-Aleksandrovskaia was rumoured to be two-faced, praying at home but publicly denouncing religion. Aleksei Tolstoi was criticised for being 'really fat [*tolstyi*]', Kalinin for being too old. A worker in the city suggested removing Mikoian's candidature, since he led a dissipated personal life. One smith said he would vote only for Voroshilov, 'the old warrior', since he trusted him alone. Stalin he described rather unflatteringly as 'seemingly a good man', but one who did not personally get involved with *kolkhoz* questions, preferring to make speeches on the basis of others' reports. Some did not want to vote for women or Jews. There were also complaints that many of the *vozhdi* were standing in several constituencies, and calls for individual *vozhdi* to be rejected. Occasionally, what were perceived to be the candidates' policies were attacked. In Palkinskii district, a peasant said that they wanted to vote for Kalinin but not for Stalin, since the latter was 'torturing them with taxes'. Another declared that he would refuse to vote for Stalin, as the general secretary had not followed the path of Lenin.[36]

As well as verbal attacks on the existing candidates, there were suggestions that the elections should be sabotaged by proposing alternative candidates or by dropping the electoral bulletin into the urn unmarked. Suitable alternatives ranged from Bukharin and Rykov to Trotsky, whose names were often mentioned in the subversive leaflets which spread in numbers of anything from five to up to a hundred in this period.[37]

Occasionally the opinions of citizens actually had an impact upon the conduct of the campaign. The more politically active put forward their own choice of deputy, such as Vinogradova from the Lebedev factory in Leninskii district. At a meeting of the factory committee on 24 October, she proposed the factory's accountant, Lazareva, but this was rejected on the grounds that Lazareva had once been a guest at the house of a person now arrested. She concluded that *nashi* (our) candidates were deliberately made to fail.[38] At one meeting at a construction project, an engineer, Kovarskii, advised workers not to choose Ezhov as their candidate, since he might well turn out to be an enemy. He proposed instead an academic, Graftio, whom Lenin knew, and who was a conscientious and politically responsible figure. As a result of this suggestion, Graftio won 140 of the workers' votes (Ezhov received 170), after which it was suggested by Kovarskii and others that Graftio be put forward anyway, since Ezhov had only won a majority because of pressure from the party committee.[39] In Novosibirsk, a party member, Stakhanovite, and activist, Votintsev, spoke out against Stalin's candidature on the grounds that he was already standing in many places. He proposed instead Alekseev, the party secretary in Novosibirsk. In the voting, Stalin received 50 votes and Alekseev 150.[40]

Such incidents were clearly isolated, but they reveal how even in the conditions of Stalinist terror and despite the concerted efforts of the party leadership to direct and fix the elections and public opinion, some people, including those basically loyal to the regime, took Soviet 'democracy' at face value and used it to voice their real opinions. These opinions reveal that part of the electorate had a quite clear understanding what 'genuine' democracy should entail. Popular reservations about the electoral process did not ultimately deter the majority from coming out to vote on 12 December as was expected of them. Yet, even with coercion, a 100 per cent turn out was not achieved. Throughout the USSR 96.8 per cent of voters took part in the elections, with some of those participating deliberately spoiling their ballot papers.[41] In some regions the figure was as low as 90 per cent. In Dedovicheskii district, 33,064 of 36,808 voted, and of these, 32,231 selected the chosen candidate, Antselovich. There were 53 non-valid papers, and 658 crossed out his name. A part of the *oblast'* inhabited by a preponderance of Old Believers and *edinolichniki* only managed a turnout of under 83 per cent.[42] Voters took advantage of the secrecy of the elections to write hostile messages on their bulletins. A report noted that in Kargasoksii district, Novosibirsk *oblast'*, 'the name of the *oberbandit* [superbandit] Trotsky was written instead of the name of comrade Antoniuk' on one bulletin. Others were inscribed with statements such as 'I am voting for the heavenly tsar' or 'We are not voting.'[43]

The political activity of ordinary people in this period was quite unprecedented. Roused from their usual concern with the everyday issues of bread and work, they began to understand and use their political and civil rights, albeit on a small scale, and with limited effect. Subsequent elections (to the RSFSR Supreme Soviet in 1938, and to local soviets in 1939) generated much less activity, partly because the most active citizens had disappeared during the purges, partly because the novelty of 'democracy' had worn off, and partly because the 1937 experience had made it quite plain that Soviet 'elections' were to be used simply as a way of ratifying pre-selected candidates.

CHAPTER 7

The Great Terror

The Great Terror which engulfed the USSR in the second half of the 1930s at the cost of possibly millions of lives is shorthand for a complex and chaotic series of events involving party purges (*chistki*), attacks on engineers and administrative personnel, the persecution of the intelligentsia and church, the show trials of leading party figures, and the hounding of ordinary citizens. The number of victims is a matter of long-running historical controversy.[1] What does seem likely is that vulnerability to the terror was greatest amongst high-status groups, and that in *relative* terms ordinary workers and peasants suffered less than others.[2] Fitzpatrick suggests that the terror was probably not as traumatic for peasants as the famines of 1932–3 and 1936–7: 'the available sources give no indication that "the year 1937" ever possessed the sinister resonance for peasants that it had for the urban educated population'. Workers too were generally 'just part of the popular audience for the terror that Stalin unleashed against the elites in 1937–8',[3] and, as was suggested in chapter 1, they may have even been more adversely affected by the repercussions of the 1940 labour decree.

It seems plausible that the terror was in part a populist strategy designed to mobilise subordinate groups against those in positions of responsibility, thereby deflecting discontent away from the regime itself. The strategy appears to have enjoyed some success. The terror against what was perceived by many as the new elite in factories and *kolkhozy* certainly elicited a positive response, since it resonated with grassroots feelings about 'us' (the people) and 'them' (those in power). This 'dialogue' between official and popular discourse will be investigated more fully in the next chapter. This chapter will consider two different questions. A number of memoirs, usually written by members of the intelligentsia, imply that the propaganda relating to the terror was effective, that citizens believed in the existence of 'enemies of the people' and considered it justified.[4] So, firstly, did ordinary people question official propaganda concerning the Kirov murder and the show trials and, if so, what alternative explanations did they proffer? Secondly, were the harsh measures meted out to the 'enemies' deemed legitimate, or was there any opposition to the use of terror?

The murder of Leningrad party secretary Kirov on 1 December 1934 provides the most detail on the first of these questions, since hundreds of reports were compiled on popular reactions to the event in Leningrad – far more than for any other issue.[5] This case is particularly interesting because the party was caught off guard, unable to prepare and direct public opinion as much as usual. Official information about the murder was sparse, and as a result, numerous alternative versions circulated in the form of rumours. So, in this case, it was not so much that the propaganda was questioned, but that, in the absence of adequate propaganda, people had little choice but to rely on rumour. The first official announcement about the murder on 2 December stated merely that:

On 1 December at 16 hours 30 mins. in Leningrad in the building of the Leningrad Soviet (the former Smol'nii) comrade Sergei Mironovich Kirov, secretary of the Central and Leningrad Committees of the VKP(b) and member of the praesidium of TsIK SSSR, died at the hand of a murderer sent by enemies of the working class. The man who fired the shot has been arrested. His identity is being established.[6]

This terse statement failed to satisfy popular curiosity and unofficial, often wildly inaccurate stories and rumours began to spread at the grassroots. It was suggested that Kirov had committed suicide, had arranged the murder himself, or was still alive. On 2 December, he was reported to have been spotted leaving hospital in the direction of Smol'nii. As a result of this story a crowd of people allegedly rushed to Smol'nii to see him. Chudov, Kirov's deputy, was also rumoured to have died as a result of suicide or murder. Another very persistent story disseminated on 9–10 December revolved around the alleged death of the writer Gor'kii. There were also suggestions that attempts had been made on the lives of other leaders, especially Kaganovich, and that the German Communist leader, Thalmann, had died. This tendency appears to be common in such situations. After Kennedy's assassination, there was an unconfirmed report that Johnson had suffered a heart attack, while when Roosevelt died there were rumours about the deaths of General Marshall, Bing Crosby, and other notables.[7]

The identity of Kirov's assassin was not revealed until 3 December, but before then speculation was already rife. A report on the Khalturin factory noted:

The mood amongst the young workers is not very healthy. Young people are mainly interested in the formal side of the events. So they ask questions such as: Who killed Kirov, a worker or not? Where did they kill him? Where did he shoot? etc.[8]

Similar questions were posed all over Leningrad. Interest centred especially on whether the murderer belonged to the party. On 3 December the newspapers reported that his name was Leonid Vasil'evich Nikolaev, he was born in 1904, and he was a former employee of the Leningrad Workers' and Peasants' Inspectorate.[9] His party allegiance was not mentioned, although many deduced correctly from his former employment that he was a party member. Rumours still abounded, forcing the head of the Leningrad NKVD, Medved', to instruct party and soviet officials in Smol'nii to be discreet:

We inform you that, at the suggestion of the NKVD SSSR, on no account must any information of any sort about the identity of the murderer – Nikolaev, Leonid Vasil'evich – be given out to anyone, including institutions and correspondents, especially correspondents of foreign newspapers.

Should anyone ask for information, immediately inform the NKVD administration of Leningrad *oblast'* – com. Gorin ...

Take measures regarding any of your workers possessing any data concerning Nikolaev.[10]

Nevertheless, stories continued to proliferate. People who had lived or worked with Nikolaev or his relatives supplied factual details about his past. Others relied on their imagination. Nikolaev was portrayed variously as a disillusioned party worker, seeking revenge for previous wrongs, such as exclusion from the party, or an NKVD agent, or mentally ill, or Kirov's illegitimate son.[11] There was a tendency to romanticise him – he was assimilated to a traditional representation of the noble terrorist: 'I like brave men like Nikolaev who must have gone to a certain death'; 'That's a hero, a brave man, killed Kirov, well done'; 'the murderer was a hero, he didn't give anyone up'; 'You have to respect Nikolaev, for he never crept round attics, but came to the place and did what he had to.' Sometimes this representation was directly associated with that of populist terrorists:

'It's clear that not all the Zheliabovs have disappeared in Russia [*na Rusi*], the struggle for freedom goes on'; 'Nikolaev is brave, decisive, and courageous. In general Nikolaev is a hero for he acted like Sof'ia Perovskaia.'[12]

On 4 December, the press reported a few factual details about the circumstances of the murder. Kirov had been shot from behind by Nikolaev as he was going into his study, where he died shortly afterwards. The murderer was detained on the spot. After this announcement, two weeks elapsed before any new information was released. Only on 18 December was the involvement of a Zinovievite organisation made public. Before then, speculation about the motivation for the murder was intense. Little credence was given to the first official explanation that it had been accomplished by an assassin sent by enemies of the working class. A plethora of different versions emerged,[13] all of which tended to revolve around one of four motifs already part of everyday popular discourse: sex, political conflict, the economic situation, and the 'enemy' in various guises.[14]

The motif of sex appeared in the widespread allegation that 'Kirov has been murdered because he had many women'; 'Kirov was well known throughout the town as a great *iubochnik* [skirt-chaser]; he was having affairs with all the *obkom* workers.' Those with greater access to information produced more credible and detailed versions: Kirov had been having an affair with Milda Draule, Nikolaev's wife, who worked in Kirov's office.

Others represented the murder in terms of a political battle within the leadership. The most common version of this story was that Stalin had arranged for Kirov to be killed. There were also suggestions that the conflict was a more local one, for example, between the other party secretaries, Chudov or Ugarov, and Kirov. Related rumours also spread, including the story about the mysterious death of the office manager of Leningrad Soviet, Chudin, at the end of 1933. Rumours about political conflicts alleged to have taken place in the past also resurfaced, including stories about the *vozhdi* fighting: 'Once upon a time Stalin and Voroshilov knifed each other when they were drunk'; 'When Krupskaia was drunk she shot Stalin, who was also drunk, because he does not allow her to speak up for workers' children.'[15]

The decision to abolish bread rationing with effect from 1 January 1935 was publicised just before the murder. To many ordinary people, this seemed to be more than a coincidence and it led to a spate of rumours. Peasants suggested that Kirov had been killed by workers because he had cut back on their rations.[16] Workers made the connection too. At Krasnyi Putilovets, a rumour circulated that, when the decree on the end of bread rations was announced, strikes had broken out in some of the workshops and one worker went to Smol'nii and killed Kirov.[17]

The official version of the plot utilised the idea of an 'enemy'. However, other unofficial versions based on this motif also emerged. One worker claimed that Kirov had been killed by a German working in Leningrad, and that Germany would declare war against the USSR if he was not freed. Others alleged the involvement of foreign powers such as Finland, Turkey, and Poland.[18]

Some of these motifs can be discerned in a poem from this time found in a school in Kronstadt:

Kogda Kirova ubili, a Kalinin	When Kirov died, and
prikazal khleb bez kartochek	Kalinin said give bread
davaite, a tsenu podnabavlaite	unrationed, but put up the
Chtoby deneg nakopit'	price to save money
I Kirovoi plat'itse kupit'	and buy Mrs Kirov a dress
A rabochii ty vorochai	And you worker, move on!
Stalin v Smol'nom piroval,	Stalin feasts in Smol'nii
A rabochii golodal.	While the worker starves
Ne nadolgo vse proidet	Not for long, all will pass
Protivnik Stalina ub'et	The enemy'll kill Stalin
Skoro budet ved' voina	For soon there'll be war
I togda, togda, togda	And then, then, then
Budet Stalin laskov navsegda	Stalin will be kind forever
Kogda ego ne budet – stikhnet navsegda.	When he's gone freedom forever.[19]

While the majority of rumours related to Nikolaev and the motive for the murder, interest also focused on Stalin's behaviour during his visit to Leningrad after the murder, and on the role of the NKVD. Stalin was apparently very angry and rude to Leningrad party and NKVD workers, and he personally interrogated Nikolaev.[20] The mysterious death of Kirov's bodyguard, Borisov, while on the way to an interrogation with Stalin, soon became public knowledge. According to some sources, he had thrown himself from the car because he was so terrified of meeting Stalin. Others claimed that the NKVD had arranged the 'accident'.[21] The NKVD's role in the whole affair seemed rather suspicious. It was rumoured that the head of

Leningrad NKVD, Medved', had given Nikolaev a pass into Smol'nii or even that Medved' himself had killed Kirov. Such rumours were given added impetus by the sacking of Medved' on 3 December, which was followed by much speculation about his fate, and suggestions that he had killed himself, had a stroke, or run away.[22]

Rumours connected with the Kirov murder gradually abated after a few weeks as people lost interest in the case and attention began to focus on the involvement of Kamenev and Zinoviev. The regime had learned its lesson, however. The episode highlighted major deficiencies in its capacity to direct public opinion, and from 1935 new emphasis was placed on both agitprop and the surveillance of opinion. Although never able to quash the spread of rumour, the propaganda machine functioned more efficiently in relation to the next phase of terror against the party elite.

In January 1935, the trial took place of the Moscow and Leningrad 'centres' allegedly involved in the murder of Kirov. Zinoviev and Kamenev received terms of imprisonment. Following another trial in August 1936, they and others were sentenced to death for their part in a 'Trotskyite–Zinovievite bloc', responsible not only for Kirov's murder, but also for plots to kill Stalin and other leaders. A trial of the 'anti-Soviet Trotskyite parallel centre' in January 1937 found Piatakov, Radek, and others guilty of similarly improbable crimes. In February, Ordzhonikidze died, allegedly of a heart attack. In May–June 1937, Red Army leaders including Tukhachevskii and Iakir were arrested, tried, and shot. Finally, in the last act of this great tragedy in March 1938, a group which included Bukharin, Rykov, and Iagoda, was accused and sentenced to death.

These dramatic events encountered incredulous reactions. People expressed shock that such renowned revolutionaries had fallen so far. Some simply refused to believe that Lenin's close associates could be guilty.[23] Official information promulgated in the newspapers was treated sceptically. During the August 1936 trial, one person asked:

How could it happen that Zinoviev and Trotsky, who worked together with Lenin, became fascists? The accusation against them is false and you shouldn't believe the newspapers. The national relations between Stalin and the Jews play a large role in this affair – Georgians and Jews are perpetual enemies. The whole trial is really exaggerated; in fact it isn't like how the press informs us.

Another said: 'I don't believe that Trotsky really did what is written in the papers. You can't believe everything that's in the papers, especially in our country.' During the trial of the 'parallel centre', one person asked 'Why didn't the radio transmit the actual words of the accused? Our newspapers lie. In the Soviet Union there is no truth, everyone lies and deceives the workers', and someone else claimed: 'I know Piatakov personally, all the accusations made against him are a lie. He's not guilty, hundreds of innocent people will suffer. And they still say that Soviet power is the workers' and peasants' power.' Various alternative explanations for the trials were advanced. It was suggested that the case against Kamenev and Zinoviev had been fabricated in order to find an excuse for the arrest of former oppositionists. This trial, and that of Bukharin, Rykov, *et al.*, were also thought to have been designed to distract people from production difficulties, or to 'pull the wool over the workers' eyes'.[24]

The trials of 1937–8 generated spates of rumours about the guilt and arrest of other members of the ruling elite. The downfall of Piatakov cast suspicion on his close associates Ordzhonikidze and Kaganovich. The news of Tukhachevskii's arrest was followed by reports that Voroshilov would be the next to go and that Vyshinskii had shot himself. During the March 1938 trial, rumours spread that Litvinov, Egorov, Dybenko, Bliukher, Belov, and Tupolev had been arrested. People looked for conspiracies everywhere, and the official news that Ordzhonikidze had died from heart attack was rejected in favour of a version that he had been driven to suicide by the trial of Piatakov, or that he was the victim of a terrorist act or poisoning.[25]

While grassroots support for terror against these prominent enemies of the people seems to have been widespread, it was certainly not universal. Some ordinary people were indifferent – neither strongly for nor strongly against the terror. As chapter 8 will show, all these figures were regarded as rather remote 'high-ups' and according to Kravchenko 'the population at large ... were pretty indifferent to what seemed to them a family quarrel amongst their new masters'.[26] The agitprop campaigns during the trials failed to arouse everyone's interest. Cleaners at Proletarskaia Pobeda factory responded succinctly to the trial of the anti-Soviet Trotskyite parallel centre: 'We clean the floor; that doesn't concern us.' Workers and especially peasants were far more concerned by the bread shortages in 1936–7 than with show trials. As one *kolkhoznik* retorted to agitators in 1936, 'we don't particularly want to discuss this matter because we don't have any bread', and meetings held in the countryside to discuss the trial of the parallel centre often turned into occasions for people to complain about the shortages. In the city indifference at meetings was also observed, especially amongst young people.[27] The atmosphere at such meetings is captured by an albeit unsympathetic contemporary observer, Arzhilovskii, who described the meeting held at his factory to discuss Ordzhonikidze's death:

it was deadly dull, it dragged on and on, and the speakers had to be forced to go on-stage. They elect the praesidium for the meeting. The audience is restless and noisy, and at first you can't hear the speaker. He grimaces, trying to find the right words, but then warms up to the task and gives a fairly coherent speech. The speech ends. The director addresses the audience: 'Who will be speaking next, comrades?' Dead silence. 'No volunteers?', the director insists, and a threatening tone creeps into his voice. Eventually one party member, then another, forces out a few words proposing that the factory, to commemorate the death of the staunch Bolshevik, should increase its productivity, etc. They speak without emotion, without inspiration, following a memorised formula ... Well, what of it! Ordzhonikidze, in my view, was not such a big shot, and they'll find someone to replace him. In this case the country hasn't lost much, though it hasn't gained much either: one more, one less – the overall picture doesn't change.[28]

The death of Ordzhonikidze was rather different from the show trials; however, it seems likely that some of the meetings held in connection with the latter may have encountered a similarly unenthusiastic response.

A few people took a more active stance, and spoke out against the use of terror. While the majority of workers seem to have objected when Zinoviev and Kamenev were not sentenced to shooting in January 1935, others thought they should be spared: 'Zinoviev should not be shot because he was Lenin's pupil'; 'Zinoviev, Kamenev, and Evdokimov have served the proletarian revolution, and therefore the sentence is correct.' It was felt that rather than being shot, they should be isolated, as Trotsky had been.[29] Likewise when they were finally sentenced to be shot in August 1936, some people were horrified: 'How is it possible to shoot people who fought for an idea?'; 'Zinoviev and Kamenev worked with Lenin and Stalin for a long time. They should not be punished so severely.' Instead, they should be sent abroad because they 'carried the revolution on their shoulders'. Others compared their treatment with that meted out to revolutionaries under the tsars: 'Why are they shooting politicals? Before, under the tsar, they didn't shoot politicals.' Several party members refused to read out the judgement at workers' meetings.

The fate of Tukhachevskii was deplored too – he should not have been shot, since 'he was the best commander'. The sentencing of Bukharin, Rykov, *et al.* also sparked off protest from those who held them in high regard, and objected to the wave of death sentences: 'These people were valuable for a long time, belonged to the VKP(b) and now they are being shot. The NKVD's approach to certain people is wrong – arresting, exiling, and shooting.' At one meeting a worker said that Bukharin should not be killed because there had already been too many death penalties.[30]

Objections were also voiced to the campaigns of terror against less prominent citizens. The Kirov murder was followed by reprisals against all suspected Zinovievites, and also *byvshie* ('former people', the term for former aristocrats and so on), criminal elements, and those without passports, thousands of whom were expelled from Leningrad in the early months of 1935. Although many workers clearly welcomed this policy and questioned why undesirable groups had continued to live in the city for so long, there was also some compassion for those expelled. This was apparently more prevalent in institutes and departments than in factories; nevertheless, one report noted that:

Even at factories, amongst a small number of workers and *sluzhashchie* (partly people themselves from hostile strata, former kulaks, traders' sons, etc., partly workers with a blunted class sensitivity), there can be observed unhealthy notes of 'sympathy' for the expelled and lack of understanding of the need for exile.[31]

One worker from the Ravenstvo factory expressed sorrow that her neighbour had been exiled: 'A former kulak has been expelled from our house, but he's a good chap; he lived with us for thirty years and did no one any harm.'[32] Others argued that it was a waste of talent to expel so many potentially useful educated people. It was also felt that, since many were old (especially the former aristocrats), they did not represent any real danger, and that the suffering of the children was certainly unjustified, since the latter had done nothing wrong.[33] There were cases of attempts to raise money for the exiles: a Komsomol girl from the *artel'* Novaia Kniga organised a fund to which six or seven people contributed 15 r. to help a former White officer who had been working in the *artel'* for two years. A school collected money for another former White officer, and organised a send-off for him at the station.[34] As well as this compassionate reaction, there was also a feeling that 'today they take them, tomorrow it could be us'. Exaggerated rumours spread about the expulsions, that all *kustar'* workers would be expelled, as would workers who 'flitted' from factory to factory, and that the NKVD had a list of 750,000 people to expel.[35] These stories reflected the mood of insecurity in the city following the Kirov murder.

Ezhov's campaign of mass terror, the *ezhovshchina*, also encountered opposition. Some felt that it was the good, honest, free-thinking people who were being arrested: 'In the USSR honest, innocent people are being arrested in droves. The people are terrorised.' Grave doubts were expressed at to why such people were prepared to confess to crimes they had evidently not committed, and it was suggested that they did so because they were tired of being in prison.[36] The majority of mass arrests occurred in autumn 1937, during the lead-up to the Supreme Soviet elections. Many people noted this 'coincidence' and surmised that the arrests were being carried out with the aim of ensuring that the elections were not hampered in any way – it was simply a different way of disenfranchising undesirables, a 'pre-electoral terror'. Lyubov Shaporina records in her diary a child coming back from school in October and saying 'They told us there are mass arrests going on right now. We need to rid ourselves of undesirable elements before the election.' According to one worker:

Stalin is afraid in case the alien element [*chuzhdyi element*] gets into power, and therefore, just as Hitler in Germany safeguards the existence of the fascist regime by making arrests, so here too Soviet power safeguards the elections to the Supreme Soviet with mass arrests. After the elections, three-quarters of the arrested will be freed.[37]

Similar comparisons with Hitler's terror were made by others, although some concluded that Soviet power was worse, because it imprisoned more people.[38] Rumours spread about the numbers involved: according to one, the USSR's population had declined from 175 million to 135 million thanks to the terror.[39]

Much of the criticism seems to have emanated from non-workers. A report from Novosibirsk explicitly underlined that it was the intelligenstsia and *sluzhashchie* who were most active in protesting against the terror.[40] Several leaflets and anonymous letters from this period suggest intelligentsia authorship:

Comrades! Protest against the unheard-of terror. Demand real democracy, freedom of speech, inviolability of the person. At the elections put in clean bulletins, cross out all the names. Down with the bloody dictatorship! Long live a free USSR!

To the Russian people, devoted to the motherland. All around the popular masses are groaning under the yoke of Bolshevism. The bloody hangman of the soviets – the NKVD – is fulfilling its foul work. Unite in a powerful nucleus to achieve the right to freedom. It is near and belongs to us. Everyone is prepared for an armed uprising, but time is holding us back. Down with the soviets!

Comrades. The regime of unheard-of terror continues. Hundreds of thousands of new people are arrested, exiled, and killed. The 'inviolable' deputies have been arrested: Postyshev, Zakovskii, Egorov, Dybenko, Ushakov, and others. Dybenko, the hero of the civil war, has been killed. With a cruelty far outweighing that of the tsarist hangmen, the families of imaginary 'enemies of the people' are persecuted. Without any selection Germans, Poles, Latvians, and others are arrested ... The free Soviet people cannot and will not remain in slavery to a handful of violators and enemies of the people. The more arrests and violence, the more enemies of the bloody regime, defenders of freedom. Everywhere and in all places protest against terror. Demand real freedom of speech and inviolability of the person.

The most fanatical medieval persecution of dissent, intolerance like during the holy inquisition: the destruction of honest, brave, but dissenting people who are not in bandit Stalin's crib; Bolshevik fanaticism and barbarism under the mask of Bolshevik 'science', 'culture', and 'freedom' – that is the cruel, bloody regime of Bolshevik fascism ... Executions, exile and arrests – the Stalinist route! And the bloody rogue rules over the whole country. More executions! More exiles! ... The Kremlin hangmen and charlatans are cowards ... I know that only on the basis of deception and executions can the bloody suppressers remain in the Kremlin lair.[41]

Ordinary workers and peasants whose families and friends were directly affected by the *ezhovshchina* may have shared these sentiments, but more evidence is needed to prove this. Much of the available material points to popular indifference to, and even approval of, the terror, and the latter will be discussed at more length in the next chapter. What this chapter has shown is that the official propaganda was not universally believed, that numerous unofficial interpretations of the events circulated at the grassroots, and that *some* people did strongly object to aspects of the terror.

CHAPTER 8

'Us' and 'them': social identity and the terror

One theme in popular opinion emerges prominently in many of the previous chapters: a strong sense of social cleavage, of 'us' against 'them'. This chapter will focus specifically on this theme, exploring its various modes of articulation, and suggesting how it may have resonated with official discourse on the terror.

According to Stalin, by the mid-1930s the Soviet Union had evolved into a socialist society without private property or antagonistic classes, in which a united Soviet people (*edinyi sovetskii narod*) of workers, peasants, and intelligentsia shared common interests. Since then, much energy has been expended on debates over whether the USSR could be considered a class society in the Marxist sense.[1] This theoretical question will not be addressed directly here. Instead the focus will be upon the subjective perceptions of ordinary workers and peasants, and, in particular, on the language they employed to construct representations of their social identity.[2]

The chapter will consider only identities articulated as 'us against them' in the sense of the 'people' (in various guises) against those perceived as powerholders. This conflictual, dichotomous image of society was in stark contrast to the static, hierarchical image propagated by the regime.[3] It coexisted and competed with many other cleavages including those between new and cadre workers, between male and female workers, and between workers and peasants.[4] However, such divisions were not incompatible with broader solidarities based on identification with 'the people' against 'them', the powerholders. Simply, different identities were articulated on different occasions and for different purposes.

The dichotomous image of society is present in many cultures, as Dahrendorf shows. It is articulated as 'them' against 'us', 'die da oben' and 'wir hier unten', 'ceux qui sont en haut' and 'en bas'.[5] Ossowski maintains that the spatial metaphor of vertical stratification of people into two main groups – those above and those below – has an ancient lineage stretching back to biblical times.[6] In Russia, this image of social polarisation was acute in the pre-revolutionary period, partly because of the sharp division between state and society, 'official Russia' and the people, which gave rise to an image of 'dual Russia'.[7] As Haimson shows, it was felt strongly by workers during the revolutionary period.[8] According to Lenin, 'the whole world [of the workers] is divided into two camps: "us", the working people, and "them", the exploiters'.[9] This sense of polarisation did not vanish with 1917. It continued in a modified form throughout NEP, found an outlet during the Cultural Revolution, and re-emerged in the 1930s, when the social divide became pronounced and egalitarianism was officially denounced.

In this period, the categories used by ordinary people to define themselves were 'we', 'the workers', 'the people', 'the *nizy*' (those at the bottom), 'the peasants', 'the Russians', and 'the masses'. These categories tended to overlap and be used rather indiscriminately to identify the whole stratum of people excluded from power. They reveal the influence of SR, nationalist, and populist as well as Bolshevik language. Partly because the bonds uniting 'the oppressed' were not very strong, and were always being undermined by competing sources of identity, popular self-identification often had a rather negative quality, in that it appeared to rely on identification *against* more than identification *with*. The role played by the 'other', the 'enemy', in uniting the people/workers/peasants therefore assumed a disproportionate weight. The enemy was defined in a variety of ways. The most common labels were 'they', '*verkhi*', 'responsible workers', 'party members', 'the state', 'the rulers', 'the new bourgeoisie', 'bureaucrats', 'ITR', 'Jews', and, less commonly, 'rotten intelligentsia', 'academics', '*tsar'ki* [little tsars]'. The use of such terms reflected the influence of both pre- and post-revolutionary discourse.[10]

The fundamental dichotomy between elite and people, us and them, was represented and explained in different ways. These rarely involved Marxist criteria. One common interpretation of the conflict was that it lay in an unequal distribution of political power. This was articulated through the use of analogies such as slaves and masters. Another means of representing it was in terms of ethical criteria, of good versus evil. A different representation focused on economic division, the cleavage between rich and poor. Often representations of the dichotomy relied on more than one explanatory factor; however, the following analysis will examine each type of explanation in turn.

It seems likely that this sense of dichotomy did much to legitimise certain aspects of the terror in the eyes of the ordinary people, and that the regime may have to a certain extent deliberately manipulated and promoted the us/them thinking, particularly in 1936–7.[11] In official discourse, the terror was portrayed as a battle between the 'people [*narod*]' and the 'enemies of the people [*vragi naroda*]'. This opposition people/enemy of the people shared many similarities with the us/them dichotomy. Both were directed against those in positions of responsibility (although, of course, the terror targeted other groups as well, including ordinary workers and peasants), and both emphasised the political, economic, and moral corruption of those in power. However, it is also clear that popular understandings of the official representation of people versus enemies of the people could diverge from those intended by the regime. While the regime intended this language to mobilise support, subordinate groups could use it to indicate disaffection – to highlight inequality, the powerlessness of ordinary people, and distrust of *all* those in power, not simply the officially designated enemies.

THE POLITICAL DICHOTOMY

According to the propaganda, power in the USSR belonged to the people, namely the workers and peasants. The country's leaders were the representatives of the people: *vozhdi naroda*. In practice, and in the perceptions of many of the supposed powerholders, it actually rested in an elite of officials, Jews, and so on. Ordinary people felt strongly that they were excluded from power, and that those in power did not consult with the masses and ignored their opinions. This created indifference to politics amongst some, although others felt that it was necessary to take action, and to put 'their' own people in power. The predominance of 'high-ups' in the show trials encouraged people to conclude that all powerholders must be 'enemies' and 'wreckers' and that this state of affairs would only be remedied when the government contained a higher proportion of workers and peasants.

The imagery used by the people to represent the distribution of political power derived from the traditional language of power relationships: 'We non-party workers are slaves'; 'workers were slaves and remain slaves'; 'The communists have white bones, and the non-party people, black. If you look at in the old way: the communists are the nobility and the non-party people, the workers'; 'the masses are the manure of history'; 'The people are pawns, they understand nothing, you can do what you want with them'; 'the workers are lumps, drop them where you like'; 'workers are treated like dogs'. Those in power were bosses (*khoziaeva*), 'Soviet directors', 'our gentlemen Bolsheviks [*gospoda bol'sheviki*]'.[12]

A concerted propaganda campaign tried to portray the country's leaders in a populist guise as *vozhdi naroda*, an image which clearly had the potential to resonate with ordinary people's own representations of the 'ideal' leader.[13] Although this propaganda undoubtedly worked to some extent, as the popularity of the leader cult demonstrates, others questioned the veracity of the images. Leaders were perceived as being non-proletarian: 'Our leaders are not from the workers; Stalin is from an artisanal family. How could Kirov get an education if he was a *bedniak* [poor peasant]?' Kalinin, who had been a worker at Krasnyi Putilovets before his rise to power, was distrusted for having lost his proletarian roots: 'Kalinin has broken away from the masses and does not want to know the working class.' It was felt that most of the *vozhdi* were afraid of the people. Stalin and his colleagues 'are afraid of us, and do not trust us workers'. Zhdanov too was a *vozhd' bez naroda*, a leader without a people.

Kirov was sometimes represented as an ideal, and compared favourably with others, since he was perceived as being on the side of the workers: 'Kirov was close to us [*blizkii*], simple, completely one of us [*tselikom nash*].'[14] His behaviour was contrasted with that of his successor, Zhdanov. In a discussion circle at Krasnyi Treugol'nik at the end of 1935, workers complained that while Kirov often used to come to the factory, Zhdanov had not been once, and they asked that he rectify this.[15] A similar comparison between Kirov and Zhdanov was expressed in a letter of 1938 from a long-time worker, who maintained that Zhdanov only knew about affairs at the grass-roots from reports:

You do not hear stories about their [workers'] lives, or ask questions of thousands of ordinary communists, Komsomols, and non-party people which they could answer directly in their own words, and that is very bad. It's bad that you are never at factories and in the districts. In this you are not like the late Sergei Mironovich Kirov. He was close to the people. It was impossible for all the workers not to love him; it was impossible for his enemies to hate him. The party has always relied and relies on the working class. Therefore it was and is victorious. There is no other way. Therefore there's no need to fear the workers, but you must come to us at the factories. The tsar was afraid to come to the people – and they killed him ... You must come to the factories; that will be more useful than your presence at the academic theatre in Moscow ([for a celebration of the] decade of Azerbaidzhani art).[16]

It is indeed the case that, unlike Kirov, Zhdanov was heavily involved with work in Moscow and had little time to listen to ordinary factory workers in Leningrad.

This sense that the elites did not listen to grassroots opinions was quite widespread. A smith, speaking at a pre-electoral meeting in December 1934, denied that their suggestions and amendments to the soviet had any influence, because 'the bourgeoisie and land-owners [*pomeshchiki*] are in power ... poor peasants have been exiled, kulaks remain, and there are only Jews in power'.[17] This feeling emerged prominently when decisions were taken which seemed quite contrary to popular wishes, and it was accompanied by demands for ordinary people to be given a consultative role. For example, at the end of 1934, when the decision to abolish bread rations was announced, a worker asked why they could not have a plebiscite in order to find out about popular opinion as had been done in Germany. Another said that the party was a 'handful of people ruling not in "our" interests. They ought to first of all ask the workers' opinion, have a meeting and, only if we agreed, only then sign a government decree.' Similarly, after the publication of the labour decree of June 1940, supposedly at the workers' behest, there were complaints at several factories that in the USSR, in contrast to Britain and the United States, the government never *asked* the people for help in improving the national economy, they simply issued a decree.[18]

Despite the considerable social mobility of this period, the ruling elite was often represented as inaccessible to workers and peasants, perhaps because when any of their own people did move up the hierarchy, their life-style changed radically.[19] Elections were re-garded as a formality, since ordinary people were allegedly never elected. The 1937 elections to the Supreme Soviet were treated with particular irony, as the existing powerholders were thought to have already arranged things so that they would be re-elected: 'Whoever was in power will be again, we won't get in.'[20] This system was effective because it relied on fear, as one worker from Leningrad Water explained:

It's just talk that the people will take part in the Supreme Soviet elections. It's nothing like that. Some person suggests the candidacy of Stalin or Kalinin and everyone begins to vote for them. They are afraid not to vote for them, because those who don't want to get arrested. After the elections to the Supreme Soviet, the situation will not change because the same people will remain.[21]

In practice, relatively few workers and peasants were elected in party or soviet elections. For example, in the elections to the PPOs in Leningrad in 1938 only 19.1 per cent of those elected by 23 April were workers, prompting one old worker to ask 'Why do they not elect us, and only engineers?'[22]

While this worker identified the 'other' as 'engineers', the feeling that power was in the hands of an alien group led some to insist that it had been taken over by the 'Jews', as many of the letters and comments in chapter 4 reveal. Although these referred specifically to Jews, the sentiments they profess indicate a more general hostility towards the existing power structure, an anxiety that power was in the hands of a self-seeking alien group with its own interests and rules. Similar sentiments were expressed about other powerholders, although without the particular language associated with anti-semitism. The more politically aware argued that the party had become bureaucratised. These claims echoed the complaints of the opposition movement of the 1920s. For example, at the height of the 'self-criticism' campaign in 1937, the non-party secretary of the foreign department of the newspaper *Smena* declared:

The party has become bureaucratised, TsK directives are either completely distorted or do not reach the *nizy* at all, the party has become cut off from the mass. With us it is enough to have a party ticket to make a career for life, even if you are a fool, and vice versa, being non-party is alone sufficient to make people not trust you at all, not value you etc. ... that is why in Sovnarkom there is not one non-party person, in general why are there no non-party people in responsible positions? With us the external, formal sign is given much attention. So if a person makes a good show, if he was in the Red Army, for example, if he had a long period in the party underground, then that is already enough for him to have access to every advantage. Take, for example, Andreev, a totally talentless figure, lacking any qualities, messed up work with transport, made a fuss, and imprisoned everywhere enemies of the people, and instead of putting him on trial, they made him a TsK secretary.[23]

Likewise, in 1937, a party member wrote to Zhdanov for help, complaining that the party, in Lenin's words, had become conceited (*zaznalsia*), had created a 'caste'.[24] These people were only expressing in a more intellectualised way what ordinary people were saying and writing incoherently with the use of anti-semitic and other language.

The sense of being totally superfluous to the workings of power resulted in some apathy and alienation from politics on the part of workers. During the show trials, the following comments were heard: 'The working class never fought for political rights. Only unconscious workers took part in the October revolution. For the worker it is all the same who is in power, as long as he lives well. Each lives only for himself, and is not bothered about the rest'; 'Workers were slaves and remain slaves. For us it makes no difference what kind of power there is, Soviet or fascist.' The traditionally indifferent peasant also took the line of least resistance: 'It's all the same to us, who's for Stalin, who's for Trotsky; better if they demanded fewer deliveries after the trials, but as it is they hurt each other, and the *muzhik* takes the rap.'[25]

While these people professed indifference to the machinations at the top, others appear to have perceived the show trials and purges as a chance to express their disaffection with the 'other'. The officially sanctioned punishment of authority figures merely accentuated pre-existing popular hostility towards powerholders. The scapegoating intention and/or effect of the terror against officialdom is clear and has often been commented upon.[26] Like the Cultural Revolution, the terror served as an outlet for popular hostility and hitherto thwarted social mobility. It represented the violent overturning of the status quo, the fulfilment of the utopian dreams expressed symbolically in the numerous *chastushki* depicting the destruction of authority figures: 'Kommunistov stalo mnogo, / My verevochek nav'em / eto pravo peremenitsia / Davit' ikh povedem' ('There are many communists / We will wind up some strings / this rule will change / We will strangle them'); 'Ia riazanochku pliasala / Na kamennoi plitke / Komsomol'tsa zadavil i na surovoi nitke' ('I danced a riazan / On the stone tiles / I strangled a Komsomol boy / with strong thread'); 'Predsedatelia kolkhoza / Nado golovu slomat', / Chtob moloden'kikh devchenok / Ne zaderzhivat' guliat'' ('The *kolkhoz* chairman / Must have his head broken, / So he doesn't stop / Young girls going out').[27]

The regime doubtless intended the purges of the elites to have this effect, and thereby to deflect criticism from Stalin and the system itself. Stalin certainly appears to have believed that the terror had grassroots support. At the TsK plenum in October 1937, Novosibirsk party secretary, Eikhe, announced that the mood in the factories and countryside in Siberia was much more positive than it had been in a long time. At this point, Stalin interjected: 'There's a lot of bread' (the harvest had indeed been unusually good), to which Eikhe replied that in some regions there had been good harvests in previous years. Then Stalin suggested, 'They're ridding themselves of wreckers, they're happy.'[28] This diagnosis of the popular mood was probably quite accurate. The terror against the elites was clearly popular. However, in some cases, it seems to have stimulated hostility towards all those in power, including Stalin himself.[29]

Popular thirst for violent retribution against the *verkhi* emerged in the numerous complaints that Kamenev and Zinoviev had been treated too leniently in 1934–5. It was felt that workers in such a situation would have been treated far worse, that Zinoviev and Kamenev had been spared only because they were famous leaders.[30] One soldier described the situation in a letter to his parents in February 1935:

the old counter-revolutionaries – Zinoviev, Kamenev, and Evdokimov – have been sentenced as follows: Zinoviev ten years, Evdokimov eight years, Kamenev five years, and the rest they don't describe who where and how long, previously they wrote – shooting for this one and that one, and there is no sense in it at all, and a simple worker gets ten years for nothing.[31]

After the trial, a worker asked a question that would, as the terror developed, become ever more common: 'Why is it only the educated [*uchenye*] who are involved in all these affairs, and not workers?' The fall of Enukidze in mid-1935 was followed by demands that all the *verkhi* be checked, including the TsK, since the real root of the country's problems lay with them and not with the *nizy*.[32] These sentiments grew more pronounced as the regime itself encouraged vigilance towards those in positions of power. At the TsK plenum in June 1935, Stalin had said: 'We must especially bear in mind when so-called "little people", i.e. rank-and-file party members and non-party people, signal that things are going badly, so that "activists" pay attention to this. They, the "little" people, see more.'[33]

During the August 1936 trial of Zinoviev and Kamenev, fears were expressed that once again they would be let off: 'If a worker does something, then he is sent to court for trifles, but if the *verkha* does something, he is treated less strictly.'[34] There were doubts that the 'terrorists' would be shot:

More likely they'll shoot us fools. Nikolaev killed Kirov, and do you think he was shot, no, they sentenced him but only on paper. They have covered the eyes of us dark [backward, uncultured] people. If they are shot, the communists will get it from the capitalists.[35]

So the news of their death sentence was greeted with some jubilation, regarded as yet another blow against authority. One peasant commented: 'All the leaders in power and Stalin should be shot', while a worker said, in a similar vein, 'Let them sentence the Zinovievites to shooting, and anyway the *vozhdi* will be stifled one by one, especially Stalin and Ordzhonikidze.'[36] Throughout the show trials of 1936–8, people highlighted the presence of Jews, 'big people', party members, and *sluzhashchie*, as in the comment: 'Look at the people sitting there. They are *sluzhashchie* and *sluzhashchie* create these things. Now if they sent old workers from Karl Marx factory and a couple of young ones to tell Stalin to rebuild and change things.'[37] Following the Bukharin–Rykov trial, workers observed that those involved in the trial were only communists, and one even asked if all members of the party had been accused.[38] Evidently the terror was perceived as being targeted against these groups in particular; 'He's not a party member and he's not a Jew, so why has he been arrested?' was a common reaction to the arrest of those not belonging to these categories.[39]

By the time of elections in 1937–8, the cumulative effect of the official and unofficial attacks on authority was popular distrust of anyone in a position of power. The fall from grace even of the 'hero' Tukhachevskii caused particular shock. Everywhere people asked 'Whom do we trust now?', for the old regime and its servants were discredited in the eyes of many at the grassroots. Stalin, Molotov, any member of the TsK might turn out to be a 'Trotskyist' or a 'wrecker'. As one person put it 'Now being in power means to wreck.'[40] It was felt that those in power had been corrupted 'because amongst the *verkhi* there is not one worker'.[41] The we/you feelings were thus exacerbated, and there was a tendency to blame the authorities for every misfortune. A *kolkhoznik* explained: 'that's why life is bad in the *kolkhoz*, wreckers destroy and we have to try to pay for it. We achieve nothing, they wreck and we restore with our backs.'[42]

The popular representation of society as split between the people on one side and the 'powers' on the other legitimised the terror against the *verkhi* for at least some people, who were already predisposed against the powerholders. To a certain extent the popular hostility towards 'them', and the regime's image of the 'enemy' coincided. However, it is clear that this popular hostility was directed not simply towards officially sanctioned enemies, but sometimes also towards Stalin, his colleagues, and the whole party leadership. Likewise some of those denounced as enemies, such as *kolkhozniki* and workers, evidently did not fall within the category of powerholders despised by the ordinary people. Nevertheless, the construction of the image of the enemy was not simply a one-way process.

THE MORAL DICHOTOMY

In their characterisation of the social divide, people often had recourse to moral metaphors. The importance of the moral and religious dimension as a source of legitimacy in popular struggles against authority has been widely noted.[43] Mark Steinberg has shown how pre-revolutionary workers in the Russian printing industry rarely used Marxist language, preferring to define their opponent using ethical criteria:

Although workers often accepted the notion of irreconcilable conflict between labor and capital, they viewed it less as a structural conflict of interest between classes than as a moral battle between, to use their own vocabulary, good and evil, light and darkness, honour and insult.[44]

This practice continued after 1917, as Steinberg shows in a study of religious imagery in the writings of Russian workers. Ideas of suffering, redemption, and salvation enabled workers to make sense of their own experience in a more comprehensible way than the unfamiliar language of Marxism – capital, accumulation, labour value – would allow.[45]

Moral vocabulary had always been a part of the idealist populist language. This, and the influence of the church, left an impact on the language of ordinary workers and peasants in the 1930s. It appealed both to the more literate and also to those who only had elementary ideas about good and evil. It emerged in the practice of attributing positive moral characteristics to the 'people', and negative ones to their oppressors. The people were represented as naturally honest, defenceless, childlike, and innocent. Those in power were by contrast dishonest, sinful, drinkers of blood (*krovopiitsy*), hangmen, and murderers. They were unequivocally guilty. Their relationship with the people was based on deception and mockery or insult (*izdevatel'stvo*). An important distinction between the two groups was that the people worked, whilst 'they' lived off them in a morally reprehensible way. Work itself was thus regarded as a moral good. Work created suffering, and suffering was implicitly noble.

The honesty of the toiler was contrasted with the immorality of those who had made it into the ruling elite using dishonest means, or who had become corrupted as a result of being in power. In its most idealist form, this notion emerged in the populist belief that truth resides only in the people. This is illustrated in an anonymous letter sent to the head of the Leningrad NKVD after the death of Kirov, which criticised the government for being unaware of the people's real feelings behind the facade of peace:

It does not see that every destroyed church resounds with the most terrible echo throughout the whole country. It does not hear the curses of millions of people every day. It does not hear what the tortured people say in the queues created by Soviet power. It does not hear that *people's truth* ... Soviet power is *blat* [influence or pull] plus bureaucratism, boorishness, and vandalism. No Soviet 'truths' can wipe out this genuine *people's truth* ... Soviet power is racing towards its destruction. The more and the quicker it does so, the faster does the cup of the people's patience fill up [emphasis added].[46]

Because of this stereotype of the innate honesty of the people, and the corresponding dishonesty of those in power, ordinary people were receptive to the official discourse on wreckers and sabotage within the leadership. The words of a worker, Kuznetsov, seem to be representative:

I do not trust your VKP(b) – they are all wreckers. I believe only in the worker, who works in production. None of the communists are honest. You get together on your own at your meetings, and what you are sorting out is a mystery. You don't tell the workers about it.[47]

Those in power were constantly represented as deceiving the people, as breaking their promises, pulling the wool over people's eyes, saying one thing and doing another. This feeling was particularly profound in a period when the media was saturated with stories of happiness and prosperity which contradicted sharply with the reality of everyday life. An 'honest worker' from the Samoilov factory expressed this feeling:

What is there to say about the successes of Soviet power. It's lies. The newspapers cover up the real state of things. I am a worker, wear torn clothes, my four children go to school half-starving, in rags. I, an honest worker, am a visible example of what Soviet power has given the workers in the last twenty years.[48]

'Deception' and 'betrayal' were some of the most commonly employed words in this period. The Constitution was a deception, the elections were a deception, the government's economic policies were a deception. The people's enemies had deceived them, and betrayed their trust. In 1935, workers from the Kirov plant wrote a lengthy letter to Zhdanov, full of strong words of complaint against the regime and the 'soap-bubble comedy' it was enacting: 'The time of respect for the Bolsheviks has passed, for they are traitors and oppressors of everyone except their *oprichniki* [a reference to Ivan the Terrible's gendarmes].' The end of rations was 'Molotov's vile deception', especially as the leadership was well aware of the conditions in which the worker lived, particularly those with a family: 'Oh, how criminal, how base to deceive the toiler [*truzhenik*], especially his family. And the children, about whom you shout a lot in the press, constant deceivers and scoundrels.' With reference to the party's attention to youth in mid-1935, they wrote:

And you Bolsheviks – fighters for the people [*narodnoe delo*], for liberty, equality, and fraternity, you still shout at the present time, speak about the education of contemporary youth, and in the spirit of communism as well. Are you not embarrassed to deceive the young so shamefully, surely you Bolsheviks can see, and how can [youth] be educated and be a genuine reserve and helper of your treacherous party.[49]

The feeling that 'you are deceiving us' recurs time and time again.[50] The deception of the people was represented as a constant attribute of power: 'the tsarist government deceived the people and Soviet power deceives them'. The people were easy to deceive because of their naive and trusting nature: 'We have been deceived for nineteen years, and, fools, we understand nothing, like sheep'; 'We are deceived like fools.'[51]

The moral distinction between the honest people and the dishonest rulers was often based on the perception that the people, unlike their rulers, actually worked. The assumption behind this was that toil in itself is redemptive, and suffering is good and that since those in power did not actually work, they became corrupt and dishonest. The characteristics applied by the people to their rulers suggest moral degeneration – they were lazy, fat, drinkers of blood, cowardly, thieving. Sloth was seen as a sin, and those in power did no real work, just sat in offices and issued decrees. It was observed that 'party members lead and non-party members work'.[52] Sometimes this representation was given a nationalist colouring. Georgians and Jews were portrayed as loafers (*lodyri*) living at the expense of the Russians.[53]

The much-vaunted moral precept in the new Constitution, 'he who does not work shall not eat', was treated with irony by many ordinary people, who argued that on the contrary 'he who works does not eat, and he who does no work [i.e. those in power] eats'.[54] The greed of those in power was constantly emphasised: 'Look at the military, responsible workers, the secret police, they live well, just get fatter', and, on Kirov's corpse, 'Kirov is so fat lying there. No doubt he didn't get the pay a worker does.'[55] The attribution of the sin of greed to 'them' was one way of coping with the fact that they themselves were hungry, for hunger was associated with moral virtue. This sense of moral righteousness can also be discerned in a letter from a group of domestic workers to the Leningrad Soviet in 1936. Among their demands was one that cafes selling vodka should be reduced by 80 per cent, and serve tea and coffee instead, for 'we see how responsible workers with briefcases wait at eight o'clock for the opening of the cafe with vodka and beer; having drunk a couple of pints of beer, the *sluzhashchii* goes to work. Is that normal?'[56]

Since those in power did no work themselves, they lived off the labour of others. This idea of exploitation was often expressed through the use of the concept of theft. Rather than working, 'they' simply robbed the workers with loans and other means. It was felt especially that peasants were being robbed of what was theirs by right, the fruits of their labour: 'Soviet power robs the peasants, takes everything, while people are left to go hungry. You won't build socialism that way.' Other nationalities were innately predisposed to theft: 'There is not one sensible person in power, they are all Yids, Armenians, and other *zhuliki* [thieves, swindlers].'[57]

In contrast to those in power, the labouring people were by definition good and free from sin. The idea of redemptive suffering was an essential aspect of the moral superiority of the worker. He suffered because his work was so hard and life so difficult. In contrast to the official doctrine of work in the USSR as creative, joyful, and liberating, many people continued to see labour as a curse to be endured rather than enjoyed. The writer of a letter to Zhdanov in 1935 signed as 'Stradalist pravdist' (roughly, 'sufferer for truth'), and described his life as a poor worker in Leningrad, his miserable, exhausting day at the factory with little to eat but bread and water:

That, dear comrade Zhdanov, is how we Leningrad workers work and suffer and torture ourselves in our lives. Our life is very tortured and suffering, what else can one say, when living people begin to envy the dead, that they sleep without any torture, while we live and suffer terribly.[58]

The idea of suffering was often expressed in terms of torture and blood – those in power 'drink the blood' of the worker. The letter from the workers at the Kirov plant cited above stated that 'you have become carried away with exaggerated successes at the expense of the blood and sweat of the Russian people'. There was a pronounced tendency to equate this suffering and patience with Russianness.[59]

The final aspect of the moral dichotomy which should be considered is that of the authorities' insulting attitude to the people. As Steinberg points out, some workers firmly believed in the dignity and equality of all men.[60] This belief provided a vocabulary with which to protest against the behaviour of the *verkhi*. The millions of petitions sent to the highest party leaders were full of complaints about the rude, boorish, and insulting behaviour of individual bureaucrats. The comments and letters also indicate that *izdevatel'stvo* (mockery, insult) was considered morally unacceptable. One letter to the Leningrad *ispolkom*, sent shortly after the end of bread rations, reiterated this idea several times:

better first to bury all our rulers of Soviet power, so that they do not insult the working class ... That's enough watching the mockery of the working class. So here's a task for you, the bosses, if prices on food are not lowered and on bread by 40 per cent, it will be bad for you ... No, that's enough slavery and mockery of the working class.[61]

Another anonymous letter to Zhdanov from the end of 1935 echoed this theme: 'that's enough laughing at the workers, enough starving, enough teasing them like dogs, who suffers like the poor worker, our enemies are our aristocrats who harm the working people'.[62] This objection to the people being treated like dogs also emerges in a comment in 1940 that, under Catherine II, landowners exchanged their peasants for dogs, while Soviet directors sold workers to each other over drinks in restaurants.[63]

Underlying many of these representations of a moral dichotomy were often questions of political and economic difference. Nevertheless, the moral dimension should not be underestimated. The moral difference between 'us' and 'them', between good and evil, was for many ordinary people as valid as the more obvious political and material inequality. Official representations of the 'enemies of the people' in 1937 consequently played up the moral degeneracy of those concerned and portrayed them as the embodiment of evil. Rittersporn, echoing Moshe Lewin, argues that the 'conspiracies' of the 1930s relied on the 'allegorisation of an ineffable evil that came to possess the life-world of every social category, the projection of the regime's elusively hostile universe in identifiable deeds and agents' and that this corresponded with traditional popular beliefs.[64] In the official discourse, moral turpitude was criticised, not only that of Trotsky (the 'Judas'), but also that of ordinary communists. Thus, in September 1937, *Pravda* in its leader 'The Moral Aspect of a Bolshevik' attacked the 'bourgeois' morality of some communists and Komsomols and their excessive drinking.[65] Once again, official and popular languages echoed each other.

THE ECONOMIC DICHOTOMY

While inequalities of power were frequently articulated using political and moral language, the reality of economic difference was the most immediately perceptible and intelligible facet of everyday life. As one peasant put it, succinctly, 'They say that everyone is equal, but in fact not everyone is equal – some are well dressed, and others badly.'[66] That one family had 150 r. a month, while another had 3,000 r., that the state bought grain from peasants for one price and sold it for twenty times more, that leaders were chauffeured around in cars while the workers struggled to get to the factory by woefully inadequate public transport, risking imprisonment if they were late – all these basic inequalities were the most visible sign of the existence of two groups in society, the rich and the poor. Popular interpretations of economic difference were not usually related to questions concerning the relationship to the means of production, although Marxist concepts such as exploitation and capitalism were sometimes used. More often, though, they focused on inequality in income and life-style, and in particular, access to privileges. The main observation was that those in power seemed to get a lot more money or privileges than ordinary people. From this it followed that workers and peasants were being exploited in order to maintain those in power.

This theme can be found replayed hundreds of times. A sophisticated version emerges in the words of a worker at the Lenin works in the middle of 1934:

How can we liquidate classes, if new classes have developed here, with the only difference being that they are not called classes. Now there are the same parasites who live at the expense of others. The worker produces and at the same time works for many people who live off him. From the example of our factory it is clear that there is a huge apparat of factory administrators, where idlers sit. There are many administrative workers who travel about in cars and get three to four times more than the worker. These people live in the best conditions and live at the expense of the labour of the working class.[67]

This refrain was powerful in the period 1934–41, which witnessed the turn towards the market and greater income differentials. At the Seventeenth Party Congress, Stalin had attacked egalitarianism; however, demands for levelling persisted. Referring to the congress, a cleaner stated:

the speeches are good, but there's no bread, at the factory [people have] three [types of] bones: pure white – they have a canteen of a closed type; white bone – they have their own one; and black (workers) – they have a general one where there is nothing. We are all workers and we should be fed equally.[68]

Likewise, a request to the Leningrad Soviet in 1934 highlighted the need to improve children's food 'and not open various better canteens for ITR. They should have achieved equality of food for all.'[69] The end of rations seemed to signal the end of the preferential treatment of workers and it provoked many comments that prices would be only accessible to craftsmen and businessmen (kustari i chastnikov), sluzhashchie, 'White guards', 'Stalin's shockworkers and Red Partisans', 'scientists', 'kulaks and bourgeoisie', 'alien elements'.[70] There were fears amongst women that the more highly paid and the ITR would buy up everything and leave nothing for the rest. It is interesting that the end of rations was viewed in a similar light by certain academics, including the orientalist, Krachkovskii, who interpreted the decree abolishing rations on meat, fish, and other food as a regression to a new class system:

This decree, like all recent measures, is aimed mainly at high-paid groups. For those who get 1,000–1,500 r. a month the reduction is very important. For the average Soviet citizen, in particular for a young academic, the decree is useless. It does not even provide a hungry minimum, that ration which used to be given. In a word, however much we shout about socialism, in fact we're moving to new classes.[71]

A common perception existed that the elite made policies which promoted their own economic interests rather than those of the workers and peasants. The end of rations was interpreted in this light by many workers: 'Power sees that the people have begun to live only on rations, and no one buys bread at the expensive price, and it gets little profit, so they have to sell unrationed bread, as it will be more profitable. Power only worries about its own profit, and does not want to bother about the people.' A similar reaction greeted all price rises during this period – it must be good for the 'new capitalists', responsible workers, communists, and so on. Even price reductions were thought by one worker to be 'a fiction carried out for the benefit of the higher class'. Likewise labour policies, such as the Stakhanovite movement and the labour decrees of 1938–40 were regarded as a way of extracting more profit from the worker in order to benefit the elite. Typical comments included 'the Stakhanovite movement has been thought up by our rulers in order to squeeze the last juice from the toilers'.[72]

The Stakhanovite movement was accompanied by the public promotion of consumer values and something of a status revolution.[73] This made the growing economic inequality glaringly obvious to the *nizy*. The economic disparity between elite and people was summed up in a question addressed to propagandists in a region of western Siberia in 1936: 'Isn't what is prevailing in practice in the USSR the principle of socialism for the masses and the principle of communism for the *vozhdi*?'[74] The privileged life-style of the elite was one of the most visible signs of social injustice, of a two-tier system. Symbols of this life-style were holidays, cars, servants, special closed shops, flats, clothes. Amongst the ordinary people there was a tendency to associate all this visible wealth with enemies, that is, those in power. At a meeting at Krasnyi Putilovets, a worker complained that 'trips to resorts and rest homes are given to alien [*chuzhdye*] people; lawyers, *sluzhashchie* travel with their wives; and there is no room for the worker'. At another meeting at the Munzenberg factory, the complaint was similar: 'Our children never get to go to rest homes, it costs 112 r., a female worker cannot afford it, and only the children of responsible workers go.'[75]

In *The Revolution Betrayed*, Trotsky argued that the use of cars by a minority perpetuated 'class' divisions:

In barbarian society the rider and the pedestrian constituted two classes. The motor car differentiates society no less than the saddle horse. So long as even a modest 'Ford' remains the privilege of a minority, there survive all the relations and customs proper to a bourgeois society.[76]

As Fitzpatrick points out, the car was the ultimate Soviet status symbol in this period.[77] Not surprisingly, then, numerous complaints were directed at those with access to cars. Once again, the insinuation was often that those with cars were enemies. Remarking on the fall of Enukidze, a chauffeur said 'how many are there of his kind in Leningrad. They go out to the dacha at the weekend in cars, bought with the people's money, wasting petrol, which we lack.' Some people interpreted the new phenomenon as symptomatic of the development of middle-class values: 'A new bourgeoisie has appeared in our country, they travel around in cars, go around the sections, grow paunches'; 'Soviet power is bad because it has created many Soviet bourgeois, for example ... the secretary of the RK VKP(b) Osip. He travels round in cars, while the *kolkhoznik* doesn't have that chance.'[78]

The Torgsin shops, which from 1930–6 sold goods for gold and hard currency, were particularly reviled. In fact, as Osokina shows, the luxurious, opulent Torgsin portrayed so memorably by Bulgakov in *The Master and Margarita* was something of a myth.[79] In many cases, the quality and quantity of its products were inadequate and its service indifferent, although it is also likely that Leningrad would have had more showcase Torgsiny than most places. However, the real significance of the Torgsin lay in its symbolic value, its epitomisation of an inequitable system. In jokes and leaflets, which relied on transmitting ideas in a symbolic and concentrated way, the symbol of the Torgsin frequently appeared. One leaflet of 1934 read 'Comrades! Unite. Russia is perishing. Stalin is wearing the people out. Torgsin caters for Russia gentlemen, who served the emperor Nicholas.'[80] A joke was made by deciphering Torgsin as 'Tovarishchi opomnites', Rossiia gibnet, Stalin istrebliaet narod' ('Comrades

remember, Russia is perishing, Stalin is exterminating the people').[81]
At the time of the end of rations, another joke ran 'there are four
categories (1) *Torgsiane* (2) *Krasnozvezdiane* (3) *Zaerkane* (4) *Koe-kane*
[approximately, the Torgsiners, the Red Stars, The Closed Workers'
Cooperative people, the Somehow-or-others]'.[82] There was some
popular pressure for the shops to be closed. In 1935, Zhdanov
received a letter demanding this. It was sent anonymously by a group
of workers from the Kirov works, and it clearly reveals how workers
tended to associate class with privilege:

Comrade Zhdanov. At all the meetings they speak of a classless society, but
in fact it turns out not like that; we have a handful of people who live and
forget about communism. It's time to stop the fattening up of responsible
workers. It is time to close the Soviet Torgsiny ... for it's a disgrace, the
worker must buy expensive products with his pennies, while the responsible
worker, who receives 600–750 r. a month, gets butter in this shop for 7 r.
per kg, and they give him 4 kilos a month, while the worker for his pennies
gets butter for 27 r.; in general it's a disgrace to have such shops now, it's
simply squandering the people's resources, if they get everything there
virtually *gratis*. It's clear that responsible workers cost the state a lot, they
get dachas, even those without children, they go to resorts, and get benefits;
take our factory director, he doesn't come to our shop, why should he, it's
expensive there. No, we've still got a long way to go before a classless
society if this carries on.[83]

There are numerous examples of such attitudes berating those in
power for their economic privileges, but one which stands out is the
letter already mentioned, written by a group of lowly paid domestics.
This type of worker was most exposed to the glaring differences in
life-style between rich and poor in this period. In the letter they
described how they earned about 125 r. a month for a fourteen-hour
day for employers who were receiving anything from four to twenty
times as much. Their bosses (doctors, engineers, directors) also had
access to free cars, holidays, and luxury flats. They stated directly
that they felt themselves to be the *nizy*, and complained that the press
ignored them, that, according to 'responsible' workers, there were no
longer any *nizy*, only 'low-paid groups'.[84]

Although the writers of this letter were more unusually exposed to
the privileged life-style of the new elite, many others shared their
views and were keen to accord enemy status to those enjoying a life
so conspicuous in its opulence. The terror was regarded by some as
an attack on those with economic privileges. The expulsions of
'former people' and other undesirables from Leningrad in 1935

triggered the following reaction: 'Finally all the parasites will be expelled from Leningrad and the working class will have at least a little improvement in housing at their expense.'[85] It is revealing to compare the type of criticism made by workers in 1937 with official accusations against 'enemies', since both highlighted the material excesses of the elite. Popular complaints tended to be more vehement and to articulate more general grievances about, for example, the low standard of living and the state loans. Workers said to agitators: 'What are you saying that life has become better; in our hostel the stoves have not been lit for three days, there's no food and linen. In the administration of the *artel'* they say there's no money, while 15,000–20,000 r. is being spent on the chairman's office alone.' Likewise old cadre workers and communists at the Kirov works complained during the loan campaign that too much had been spent on officials' flats. One remarked that 'the people who demand loans are those who decorate their flat for 20,000 r., like the head of the factory committee Podrezov'.[86] Fitzpatrick cites some of the official accusations levelled against the accused, such as the director of Molodaia Gvardiia, who 'ripped off the state shamelessly. In the rest houses that the publishing firm is building, a luxurious apartment has been equipped for Leshchintser. Furniture of Karelian birch has been bought for that apartment. He is a bourgeois degenerate.'[87] The words echo those of the ordinary people, with the only difference that the latter tended to blame the whole regime as well as concrete individuals. As one party worker explained in a letter to Stalin of 1937:

The logic of the peasantry is very simple. For him, all leaders are plenipotentiaries of the regime, and correspondingly, he considers that the regime is responsible for all his woes ... And the situation of the kolkhozniki is such that mentally they have sent us all to the devil.[88]

Despite the official representation of a socialist society without antagonistic classes, ordinary people continued to view their world as polarised between those with power, and those without. For these people, the dream of socialism seemed far away. As one person wrote in a note to a speaker at a pre-election meeting at the end of 1934, 'Comrades, how can you say this, we are enserfed, hungry, and cold. This is called a classless socialist society. It's all lies.'[89] Likewise, Arzhilovskii wrote in his diary: 'I'm becoming more and more convinced that there's no such thing as Socialism;

there are aristocrats, bureaucrats, and then there are people like me
to do the dirty work.'[90] Communism was dismissed as an utopian
ideal by a metal worker:

you should not think that you will live to communism. And even if someone
does, he won't see much happiness, because the difference between people
of different positions will never be liquidated. An engineer will never agree
to wear the same suit as a worker. No, we won't live to communism. More
likely we'll get to state capitalism.[91]

People felt divided from the elite on political, economic, and
moral grounds. The way these divisions found expression owed as
much to traditional conceptions of social justice as it did to the ideas
of Marx and Lenin. The terror of 1937 enabled people to satiate their
appetite for revenge against at least some of those in power. For a
while, the regime's image of the enemy and that constructed by the
people partially coincided. However, by early 1938, the 'quasi-popu-
list' aspect of the terror was already receding, with the stress now on
stability of cadres.[92] A new policy of appeasing and extolling the
intelligentsia began in 1938. One symbol of this was the award of
Stalin prizes worth thousands of rubles. Those disbursed in March
1941 for science, technology, art, and literature provoked the
comment from workers that 'We agree that they should get prizes,
but why do they need such big sums when they are well off? We
ourselves are creating capitalists living off interest, and then those
millions will be squeezed out of us workers as loans.'[93] Such feting of
the intelligentsia in the difficult period of 1938–41, when harsh laws
were being applied to workers and peasants, probably ensured that
their sense of social polarisation did not diminish. Possibly only the
appearance in 1941 of a real external enemy in the form of fascist
Germany provided the necessary stimulus for some of the disaffected
nizy to feel part of a 'united people'.

III

The leader cult

CHAPTER 9

The leader cult in official discourse

The adulation accorded to Stalin, many of his colleagues, and indeed outstanding individuals at all levels of Soviet society was one of the most striking aspects of Stalinist propaganda. This 'cult of the *individual*' emerged powerfully in the period 1933–4, contrasting dramatically with an earlier emphasis on the anonymous masses, classes, and party. At the apex of all these cults was that of Stalin. This chapter will provide an overview of the evolution of the leader cult in the propaganda of this period and explore the chief characteristics of the cult as 'official culture'. It will concentrate on the cult of Stalin, since those of other leaders developed according to a pattern which was similar, but less intense.[1]

THE EVOLUTION OF THE CULT

The propaganda of the Stalin cult was never static. It developed from modest beginnings in 1929 to its gigantic proportions at the end of the 1940s. However, it was in the period 1934–41 when many of the fundamental characteristics of the cult were established. During this period, the intensity and emphasis of the cult changed quite markedly in accordance with the needs of the regime.

Although the genesis of the public cult of Stalin is generally dated to the occasion of his fiftieth birthday in December 1929, when effusive praise was heaped upon the leader by his colleagues, this was an exception to the rule. In this period, the emphasis was usually upon anonymous collective leadership. Few pictures of the leaders appeared in the press. As Heizer points out, in 1929 Stalin was portrayed as 'iron-willed, cold, distant, and ruthless'.[2] His personality was secondary to his function. Kol'tsov's article 'The Enigma – Stalin', expresses this clearly: 'Stalin cannot be understood without his milieu, without the class and the party who promoted him, without the combination of tasks and goals for which they struggled together.'[3] From about 1930, adulation of the leader did increase noticeably; however, it was still modest in comparison with later developments. Posters of this period tended not to accord much prominence to the *vozhdi*, but when they did feature, it was usually as a Politburo group. Until 1933, Stalin was always referred to as the unambiguous leader of the party, but without any special appellations. He was merely *primus inter pares*, as in the designation 'under the leadership of the Bolshevik Party headed by its *vozhd'* comrade Stalin'.[4] Nevertheless, the groundwork had been laid in 1929–33 for the further extension of the cult.[5]

The full-blown cult began to emerge in the middle of 1933, by which time Stalin was occasionally referred to as the 'beloved [*liubimyi*] Stalin'. Gerasimov's famous portrait of Stalin at the Sixteenth Party Congress was executed in this year. Thereafter an entire industry was devoted to producing portraits of Stalin and the other *vozhdi*. The Seventeenth Party Congress in January 1934 saw the real explosion of the cult. At the beginning of 1934, just before the congress, a sense of Stalin's historic role and mission started to emerge amongst party members. Radek's eulogistic article 'The Architect of Socialist Society' played a seminal role. At the Moscow party conference, Kaganovich stated that the 'the role of comrade Stalin still awaits a broad and profound evaluation. We not only know this role of comrade Stalin, but we feel it, it is in our heart and our soul.' Likewise in Georgia, Beria told the local party that a Stalin Institute would be set up to give a 'true picture of Comrade Stalin's gigantic role in our revolutionary movement'. The actual congress, which was marked by sycophantic speeches even by his opponents, marked a turning point in attitudes to Stalin. The emigre newspaper *Sotsialisticheskii vestnik* noted in February that 'lately there has undoubtedly been a breakthrough [*perelom*] in attitudes to Stalin'.[6]

After the congress, the chief characteristics of the cult began to emerge clearly. Gill categorises these as, firstly, his link with Lenin; secondly, his role in the achievement of success; thirdly, his writings; and, fourthly, his relationship with the people.[7] Citations from Stalin began to flood the newspapers. Previously a reclusive figure, Stalin now appeared more frequently in public. For example, huge publicity was given to his meeting with the team from the icebreaker *Cheliuskin* and the pilots who had dramatically rescued them when the *Cheliuskin* sank in the spring of 1934. The popularisation of

Stalin's image was accompanied by the publication of often falsified biographical/hagiographical material, designed to illustrate his rise to greatness from a humble background.[8] However, in 1934, his image was still usually that of leader of the party and proletariat.

Kirov's death marked another turning point in the treatment of Stalin's image. This involved both a prohibition of negative portrayals of the *vozhd'* and a greater popularisation of his image and that of his colleagues as *vozhdi naroda* (leaders of the people). An example of the former practice was the expulsion from the party of a regional party committee member on 5 February 1935 after he had given a speech in which he recalled the negative characterisation of Stalin in Lenin's 'testament'. As one other member of the committee said, 'Why did he have to speak about Lenin's testament at a Komsomol meeting? ... It is clear to us all that Stalin is the brilliant pupil of Lenin, and because of his work deserves the immeasurable love of the proletariat and toilers of all the world.'[9] From 1935 onwards, it became mandatory to speak of Stalin only in the most glowing terms. The young writer, A. Avdeenko, has described this deliberate policy. He came into contact with Mekhlis, one of the chief architects of Stalin's cult, shortly after making a speech to the intelligentsia in Sverdlovsk. Avdeenko had ended his speech, 'I thank you, Soviet power.' Mekhlis praised the speech, but suggested that it would have been better if he had not divorced Soviet power from Stalin, explaining that 'Soviet power is, above all, Stalin. We should thank him in particular for everything good that has been and is being achieved in the country.'[10]

The media set the tone for the veneration, with a new stress on the genius of Stalin, his wisdom, and prophetic powers. However, this type of image always carried with it the danger of alienating the people. Likewise in Germany, the manufacturers of the Hitler cult recognised that the 'emphasis on Hitler's many-sided "genius" ... had the danger of playing down the "human qualities" of the "People's Chancellor"'. So Goebbels simultaneously tried to promote the image of a simple leader in touch with his people.[11] Similarly, in the Soviet Union, a more popular image of Stalin was deliberately cultivated. The image extended not only to Stalin, but to all the *vozhdi*, who were now to be represented as close to the people. The change in tone is evident from the remarks of Ugarov (the second secretary of the Leningrad *obkom*) in connection with the preparation for the Day of the Constitution on 6 July 1935:

This affair has to be organised in an essentially different way from in previous years. The political explanation should be organised so that people feel that *Soviet leaders are coming to them* [emphasis added] and telling them about the achievements of Soviet democracy.[12]

This approach found ample expression in the media. A new genre emerged in the form of Stalin's Kremlin meetings with 'the people' to celebrate various occasions. Stakhanovites, delegations from the non-Russian republics, and wives of Red Army commanders came from all over the USSR to participate in these rituals. They were theatrical events, at which Stalin's appearance and words were greeted by an outpouring of emotion and endless applause. The meetings were widely reported in the press, often from the vantage point of a participant, who was required to relay his or her own feelings of awe and wonder at being in the presence of the *vozhdi*.

The year 1935 also inaugurated the practice of displaying visual images of Stalin physically close to the people. The most famous photographs of this period are those in which he hugs a twelve-year-old Tadzhik girl and talks to Stakhanovite Maria Demchenko.[13] These were part of the strategy of representing the *vozhdi* as defenders of the weak (it is probably not coincidental that both these pictures portrayed women). The paternalist, caring imagery of the cult reflected the fact that Stalin's overtures towards the 'small people' had begun this year, with his speech on 4 May, demanding that cadres be protected, and that leaders pay attention to all workers, both big and small.[14] This theme would become increasingly important in the following years, although the 'family' imagery, with its essentially human scale, would also have to compete with 'superhuman', charismatic traits.

In 1936–7, the cult reached its apogee. A local party report from August 1936 on the propaganda of the cult conveys very vividly the new extremism:

During agitation and propaganda in the press there must be more popularisation of the *vozhdi*, and love for them must be fostered and inculcated in the masses, and unlimited loyalty, especially by cultivating the utmost love for comrade Stalin and the other leaders amongst children and young people, inculcating Soviet patriotism, *bringing them to fanaticism in love and defence of comrade Stalin and our socialist motherland* [emphasis added].[15]

In order to inculcate this 'fanaticism', the media was saturated with Stalin, who was habitually referred to as 'the great leader', 'father of the people', 'the wise helmsman', 'the genius of our epoch', 'the titan of the world revolution', and so on. The symbolic and mythic character of the cult became ever more apparent. Poems and folklore in the national languages of the USSR exalted him at any opportunity, while historical paintings were used to manufacture a heroic and largely mythical past for the great leader.

Stalin's role as *creator* was stressed: he was 'creator of the Constitution', and 'creator of our happiness'. As Clark points out, his image had much in common with that of the 'artist-seer'.[16] It is interesting that Pasternak also made this connection, for his most famous cult poem, written for the 1 January 1936 edition of *Izvestiia*, was called 'The Artist', and it drew parallels between the role of the poet and that of Stalin. Stalin was also frequently represented as a source of inspiration for others: 'the care of the *vozhd'* for every person, and love for all people – that is what lifts people and gives them wings'.[17]

A different image of Stalin as hero emerged in the form of idealised accounts of his past, where he was shown fighting for the revolution and surmounting enormous difficulties with unstinting courage. The syncretism of the cult is very evident in the attempts to incorporate into it traditional folk motifs. Stalin was endowed with the qualities of the mythical Russian hero, the *bogatyr'*, sometimes in conjunction with his colleagues:

Stalin, Molotov, Kaganovich, Voroshilov, Ordzhonikidze, Kalinin, and others – friends, comrades-in-arms, pupils of the great Lenin, a powerful *druzhina* [army] of *bogatyry* of communism – they constantly stand at the commanding bridge of the great Soviet ship, travelling on a precise course.[18]

Although the propaganda never explicitly referred to Stalin as a god, certain god-like qualities were nevertheless attributed to him. In particular, he was often called 'Sun', especially in the cult folklore.[19] His role as 'creator' also had connotations of the divine. It was common practice to give thanks to Stalin for life, as to a god: 'You built our life – / We live happily / … Oh, thank you, Stalin / For such a life!'[20] At other times, he was attributed an almost Christ-like character, as in the words of his biographer Barbusse, reprinted in *Pravda* as part of the election campaign in 1937: 'You do not know him, but he knows you. He has thought about you. Whoever you are, you need this friend.'[21] The omniscient, all-seeing, and paternalist nature of Stalin is captured in a poem by Lebedev-Kumach also from this period:

And so – everywhere. In the workshops, in the mines
In the Red Army, the kindergarten
He is watching . . .
You look at his portrait and it's as if he knows
Your work – and weighs it
You've worked badly – his brows lower
But when you've worked well, he smiles in his moustache.[22]

The sense of a divine, superhuman being was accentuated by the portrayal of Stalin in visual forms of propaganda, where he appeared gigantic, looming over the mass of small people gazing up at him.

In 1937, Stalin's links with Lenin acquired a new prominence in connection with the twentieth anniversary of the revolution, in which Stalin and Lenin were shown to have played major and equal roles. In Molotov's speech to celebrate the twentieth anniversary of the revolution, the main emphasis was upon Stalin as the incarnation of the 'moral-political unity of the people'. He was thus transformed into a symbol of the nation.[23] The association of Stalin with patriotic sentiment became an increasingly important feature of the cult in the immediate pre-war years.

During 1938, the rewriting of history was concluded with the publication and propaganda of the *Short Course*, the canonical party history edited by Stalin which laid down the orthodoxy on his past. However, despite a huge tribute on Stalin's sixtieth birthday in 1939, the momentum of the cult seemed to peter out somewhat in 1939–41. Stalin took a back stage, with Molotov assuming relatively greater prominence.[24] The latter was described on the occasion of his birthday in 1940 as a 'great figure [*krupneishii deiatel'*]' of the party.[25]

THE CULT AS 'OFFICIAL CULTURE'

The whole cult phenomenon exhibits many characteristics typical of the hegemonic culture in an authoritarian society as described by Bakhtin: seriousness, asceticism, hierarchy, a sense of its own permanence.[26] Particularly striking is the gravity of the cult, its sanctity. According to Bakhtin, 'seriousness in a class culture is official, authoritarian, associated with violence, prohibitions, limitations. Such seriousness always contains an element of fear and deterrence.'[27] The sacred must not be ridiculed, and to laugh at a *vozhd'* was considered counter-revolutionary. According to one party report: 'Anecdotes about the *vozhdi* may gradually blunt revolutionary vigilance, if they are treated in a conciliatory manner. Behind an anecdote there may lurk a Menshevik, Trotskyist, class enemy.'[28]

The official satirical journal, *Krokodil*, never made fun of the *vozhdi*. On the rare occasions when they did appear in its pages, it was often to laugh at someone else. For example, in December 1934, a laughing Kaganovich was shown with a semi-humorous caption 'the most active foreman of Moscow's construction ... Has glanced into the pages of *Krokodil* to ridicule those who don't believe in the transformation of Moscow into an exemplary socialist capital.'[29] Satire of the leaders was prohibited, and when it emerged that P. Kornilov had used caricatures of Lenin from 1917 as illustrative material for a lecture at the Academy of Arts in January 1935, the matter was given the highest priority by the NKVD and *obkom*.[30] Problems were also caused by ambiguous and potentially comic newspaper headings, such as 'They managed without comrade Stalin.' It was perceived as particularly damaging when a *vozhd'* had a fairly common name which gave rise to headings including 'Trotskyite Khrushchev excluded from the party'; 'Bring Voroshilov to order and teach him to work.'[31]

An important aspect of the cult was its deliberate neglect of the leaders' private lives, what Bakhtin calls the 'material-bodily root of life [*material'no-telesnoe nachalo*]'.[32] For the charismatic magic to work, the *vozhdi* had to be portrayed as extraordinary and above the everyday world of eating, drinking, and family life. Devoted to the party and the Soviet state, their private 'human' dimension was relegated to a minimum. Occasional pictures of Stalin on holiday with his daughter Svetlana were published, but these were immediately conspicuous by their rarity.[33] By contrast, the public 'human' dimension was played up, with Stalin constantly represented as the 'father' of his people.[34]

The cult was based on a sense of an immutable spatial-temporal order. Strict hierarchical principles prevailed. Stalin stood at the apex of the feudal-like pyramid. But the period 1934–41 witnessed a cult not only of his personality, but of individuals at all levels of society – from Stakhanovites to writers and aviators. Stalin's cult was merely one aspect of this more general focus on exceptionality and the heroic.[35] Below his cult were the mini-cults of other party leaders, only some of which were officially sponsored. Stalin's colleagues, particularly Voroshilov, appeared regularly in the media, and also received poetic tributes and cultic appellations. Cities, mountains, boats, indeed anything that could be named, bore the names of members of the Politburo. Particular regions tended to highlight their own boss: Kirov or Zhdanov in Leningrad, Kaganovich in Moscow.[36] The language of these lesser cults followed the pattern of that of Stalin; so, Kirov began to be called 'beloved' in 1933, at the same time as Stalin.

This order was portrayed as eternal, static, permanent. It was retrospective, conservative, oriented towards its own history and tradition. It was the antithesis of revolution.[37] Unexpected death was a severe interruption to this order, for death is an equaliser, a leveller, and an indication of change. The only way death could be overcome was by its rapid ritualisation, and the elevation of the leader to the concomitant hierarchical pantheon of god-like former leaders. So, Kirov, who had been a competent but not outstanding leader, was given heroic status as martyr. On the first anniversary of his death, Stalin sent telegrams to the local party organisations on the need 'to show comrade Kirov as one of the greatest leaders of our party, the tribune of the party, beloved by all the toilers in the USSR'.[38] Every year after this, the 'Kirov anniversary' became part of the ritual of the official culture. Thus his death paradoxically served to reinforce the spatial-temporal order of the official culture.

To what extent did these official images accord with popular representations of the leader(s)? The next two chapters focus on the reception of this propaganda. Chapter 10 examines representations in which the leader was portrayed in a positive light, while chapter 11 considers representations which were more negative (from the regime's point of view). The official cult discourse was employed in a far from passive way. People selected certain elements of it, and rejected or ignored others; they appropriated those aspects of it which served their own purposes; they familiarised it so that it harmonised with their own preconceptions; they distorted its messages, criticised it directly, and subverted it in a more indirect manner.

CHAPTER 10

Affirmative representations of the leader and leader cult

The official cult discourse fluctuated and transmitted heterogeneous messages. Not surprisingly, then, when the people themselves used this discourse, they chose to emphasise different facets in accordance with their own situation, needs, and ideas about leadership. The following analysis is based predominantly on positive representations of the leader in letters. The latter are used because they are usually more individual and less imitative of the propaganda than the comments reproduced in opinion reports and newspapers. Three different types of discourse can be identified: firstly, the leader as benefactor; secondly, the leader as 'traditional' defender of the people; and, finally, the charismatic leader. In many cases these different discourses overlapped, but they will be examined here separately.

THE LEADER AS BENEFACTOR

This type of representation was rarely employed by the social groups with whom this study is mainly concerned. It was mainly used by those who improved themselves in this period, and identified with the regime and its policies. These beneficiaries included many Stakhanovites, some soldiers, the new young intelligentsia, and the *vydvizhentsy* (upwardly mobile), who moved into responsible positions in the hierarchy.[1] Often from humble origins, they had acquired power and status, and were eager to express gratitude to Stalin, and endorsed the progress the USSR had made under his leadership. They were also well versed in the official language. Soldiers in particular had a good command of the phraseology, thanks to intensive indoctrination in the Red Army. Soldiers' letters intercepted by the censor contain expressions of gratitude and loyalty to the *vozhdi*. These letters were written by the soldiers to their families, and it seems unlikely that the propaganda was intoned with the censor in mind. If this had been so, then presumably all of the soldiers would have reproduced the obligatory phrases, which was not the case.

One soldier wrote to his brother, a fellow soldier, enjoining him to study and work hard: 'study the rules consciously and be able to apply the rules precisely in everyday life, be impeccably disciplined, be a hero. Fight for the great work of Lenin–Stalin.'[2] Another letter expressed wonder at the changes that had happened in the last few years, remarking that:

Even from the depths of our village how many people have gone up the hill, not counting myself, and with every new step, you begin to comprehend the essence of Soviet power, the profundity of the complex mechanics of the leadership of the party of Lenin and the *vozhd'* comrade Stalin, without whom we might today have been bowing down in an alien land, while now we must be proud of our position.[3]

This letter also demonstrates the use of an image of society as a 'hill' to be climbed, a consensual, hierarchical image (unlike those discussed in chapter 8) which was probably typical of the representations of this mobile group. For many of these, the progress that had been achieved in a very short time under Stalin was astounding. Industrialisation and collectivisation had produced tangible results, which were easy to admire. As one soldier wrote, 'I was recently in our *kolkhoz* and saw how things are moving forward, in both economic and political life. I say from the heart that we must keep to this, use all our strength to fulfil with honour that created by Vladimir Il'ich and his follower I. V. Stalin.'[4]

Not only those who had actually moved up the hierarchy, such as soldiers, were grateful to Stalin; their relatives, who benefited indirectly, also were. As has already been mentioned, education was highly valued by ordinary people,[5] and in 1939 a 65-year-old illiterate woman wrote to Kalinin (through her son), expressing her gratitude for the fact that all her sons had been educated and had embarked upon careers:

I want to share my feelings: I live very well and think that I will live even better. Why? Because I live in the Stalin epoch. May Stalin live longer than me! ... All my children had and are having education thanks to the state and, I would say, thanks to the party, and especially comrade Stalin, for he, along with Lenin, opened the way for us simple people ... I myself, an old woman, am ready to die for Stalin and the Bolshevik cause.[6]

While this study is concerned primarily with the attitudes of ordinary workers and peasants, it is worth noting that large numbers of the intelligentsia, including the creative intelligentsia, admired Stalin.[7] Especially after 1934, he was regarded as a conciliatory figure. Many benefited directly from his policies. Writers and artists were lauded, awarded Stalin prizes, and provided with dachas and other material rewards. Others regarded the industrial progress initiated by Stalin as necessary and beneficial for the USSR or supported the USSR's anti-fascist stance (until 1939). Konstantin Simonov was one of these. His memories of Stalin from the 1930s are entirely positive. He asks:

What good things were associated in those years with the name of Stalin for us, and for me in particular? Very much, practically everything, if only because at that time in our imagination almost everything came from him and was shrouded in his name. The general line of the industrialisation of the country which he carried out explained everything that was happening in that sphere. And of course, many wonderful things happened. The country changed before my eyes ... Sweeping everything from the path to industrialisation, Stalin carried it out with an iron hand. He spoke little, did a lot, met people on business a lot, rarely gave interviews, rarely made speeches, and managed to get his every word considered and valued not only here, but in the whole world.[8]

M. Gor'kii, I. Erenburg, A. Tvardovskii, A. Avdeenko, I. Babel', L. Seifullina, and a host of other writers all professed their support for Stalin.[9] Even Pasternak, Bulgakov, and Mandel'shtam seem to have had an admiration for some aspects of Stalin's leadership.[10]

THE TRADITIONAL DEFENDER OF THE PEOPLE

Unlike the latter relatively privileged groups, many ordinary workers and peasants emphasised other aspects of the official cult discourse, and in particular, its traditional paternalist features. The representation of the leader as father had long been a part of popular political discourse in Russia. The tsar was *batiushka* ('little father'), and peasants were accustomed to petitioning him for help.[11] This tendency continued in the Soviet period, when ordinary people turned to Lenin, Stalin, Kalinin, and other leaders for defence using paternalist language.[12]

The evidence suggests that they adopted this vocabulary spontaneously. Even before the 'father of the people' imagery had begun to be exploited in the official cult discourse, people referred to Kirov as a father. For example, some workers described feeling as though they had been 'orphaned' by his death. Others recalled Kirov's care for them. In one case, workers had been settled in new homes without light or water. They wrote to him, and in two days he came in person, went round all the families 'like a father', and expressed interest in their life, and within three days all was put right.[13] Once this language had become an integral part of the propaganda in the mid-1930s, some spontaneity seems to have continued. People referred to Stalin and other leaders as *diadia* ('uncle') or *batiushka*, terms which were never used officially. Thus, when a church was being closed in 1940, a group of women assembled and cried out: 'Let them shoot us, or hang us, but we have always prayed and will pray. We will go to *batiushka* Stalin, who allows us to keep our church, while all this is being done by local soviet power [*mestnaia sovetskaia vlast'*].'[14]

This example reveals how ordinary people justified their appeals to the highest authority not only in terms of the father–child relationship, but also with reference to the incompetences and abuses of local power. Both these formulae emerge clearly in letters and petitions, which played such an important role in Russian and Soviet culture. As Freeze points out in relation to the tsarist period: 'supplication and petition was an endemic feature of Russian political culture, providing a partial substitute for popular representation and a vital bond between tsar and people from medieval times'.[15] In the Soviet period, too, petitioning was one of the few means by which ordinary people were able to communicate directly with the *vozhdi*, and their petitions therefore provide plentiful insights into popular representations of the leaders.

The *vozhdi* received millions of petitions and dealing with them was considered a crucial part of their work. The quantity of letters Zhdanov received seems to have progressively risen. While in 1935 he received an average of over 1,000 every month, by 1938–40, the average had risen to from 5,000 to 7,000. Some months he received over 10,000 (e.g. December 1937, March 1938).[16] The letters were classified into about fifty categories, such as 'on restoration to the VKP(b)', 'on providing housing', 'on material help'. The secretariat forwarded them to the relevant bodies concerned, who were supposed to examine the complaint or request in the letter and report back to the *obkom*. Intercession by the *vozhd'*, or his secretariat at least, was thus supposed to galvanise other recalcitrant branches of the bureaucracy into action.

It is worthwhile comparing the representations of authority in Soviet petitions with their tsarist equivalents. The latter tended to follow a common pattern, since the form of a petition to the tsar followed strict rules laid down by government decree.[17] Volkov's study of the lexicon of seventeenth-century *chelobitnye* (petitions) highlights the formulaic aspects of the petition. In particular, he analyses what he calls the 'emotional-expressive' parts of the *chelobitnye*. These included an address setting out the dependent (vassal) nature of the relationship between supplicant and tsar, in which the tsar was attributed flattering and sympathetic characteristics such as 'noble' and 'merciful', and the supplicant was described as 'poor, impoverished', 'orphaned', and his situation as 'helpless', 'without refuge'. The actual request was often accompanied by a narrative of the dire consequences which would ensue if the request was left unheeded; for example, the possibility of death was sometimes mentioned.[18] Later petitions do not appear to have departed markedly from this model. Nineteenth-century petitions also flattered the tsar, stressed the petitioners' dependence on him, their suffering, and the tsar's unique capacity for positive intervention. The following are just two representative examples of language dating from 1859–60:

we, in our general lack of fortune, experience so much grief that it is impossible to bear, and it forces us peasants ... personally to submit a request to the most august monarch, on whom our fate depends.

Velikii gosudar' [Your great majesty], our sufferings and complaints arouse grief in no one, as they do in you ... everything which is written [in the petition] we can tell no one: neither the local leadership, nor the church.[19]

It is significant that supplicants always directed their criticisms at local administrators, while showering extravagant praise upon the monarch, thereby perpetuating the good tsar/wicked ministers notion.[20]

The language of Soviet letters and petitions is reminiscent of that of its pre-revolutionary equivalent, although there are also clear differences between them. While tsarist petitions were very formulaic, appeals to the *vozhdi* were not required to conform to a set pattern. As a result, the latter were far less standardised and mechanical. Nevertheless, certain formulae did recur in many Soviet letters and petitions, and these often echoed their tsarist predecessors, while incorporating simultaneously the new 'Soviet' language.

The form of address to the leader was usually the first stereotypical element of the letter. It defined the relationship between supplicant and addressee. Although some letters simply began 'Dear comrade Zhdanov/Stalin', or even 'comrade Zhdanov!', many others used the address as a way of emphasising the exalted and powerful position of the recipient. Sometimes petitioners recalled the recipient's status in straightforward language 'I am turning to you as my own *vozhd'*',[21] while on other occasions, particularly with the increasing extravagance of the propaganda, they employed the more effusive official cult epithets 'Greetings, dear comrade Stalin! Our beloved *vozhd'*, teacher, and friend of the whole happy Soviet country'; 'Dear, glorious and good Mikhail Ivanovich [Kalinin]!'; 'Our highly respected *zemliach* [fellow countryman] and ruler of all the USSR, comrade M. I. Kalinin'; 'Greetings friend and best leader of our country, M. I. Kalinin!'; 'dear world leader' (to Stalin); 'our great *vozhd'* and teacher and my own dear father I. V. Stalin'.[22] These addresses, and especially the latter appeal to the leader as 'father',[23] not only highlighted the powerful position of the addressee, and his concomitant responsibility for the welfare of his 'children', but were also designed to elicit a strong emotional response.

This quite calculated playing on the emotions of the recipient was one of the most striking features of the petitions. It can be discerned in attempts to flatter the *vozhd'*, not only through the use of the elaborate addresses mentioned above, but also by underlining the special abilities and authority of the leader: 'You are the cleverest leaders of our government and the policies of Soviet power'; 'You are a highly cultured person'; 'I turn to you as leader of the political life of our Union and as a person whose authority may be able to help clear up my case.'[24] Likewise the moral qualities of the leader were frequently played up in the initial address, particularly his humanity, sensitivity, and concern for the welfare of his people.[25]

The address was often accompanied by some sort of apology or justification for the letter. This tended to be couched in terms of the *vozhd'* being the only person capable of dealing with the supplicant's appeal: 'I am turning to you about matters of principle, as leader of the Leningrad party organisation, and about personal matters, as the only person who can help'; 'only you alone, dear and respected comrade Zhdanov, can help me in this matter'; 'Only you, and no

one else in Leningrad can help me find the truth.'[26] The writer
would often emphasise that she or he had explored other avenues
first before turning to the leader: 'We are obliged to turn to you for
help, because nowhere do we find any support for our struggle';
'Only after trying all ways and means that exist did I decide to
bother you with my request';[27] and that she or he was aware of the
fact that the *vozhd'* was very busy: 'I know that you have a huge
workload, but . . . '; 'I understand that you have a terrible lot of work
and that you cannot be generous with your attention to individuals,
but . . . '.[28]

Having established why it was incumbent upon the *vozhd'* to take
heed of the appeal by referring to his own unique, powerful position,
the writer would frequently give this greater impact by revealing his
or her own relative impotence and helplessness. Often the language
bordered on the hysterical, with intimations of death and sickness:
'You are being addressed by a completely persecuted person, who
stands on the edge of the total catastrophe of his life'; 'I beg you
please as the most sensitive comrade to help me in hopeless situation,
which makes me think about death';

I never thought that I would bother you with personal questions, but it's
turned out that as I'm at a dead-end as they say, I've decided to turn to you
for help all the more because at the moment I don't have any support
anywhere and find myself in a difficult state both morally, and also
physically unwell.[29]

It may indeed have been the case that petitioners were close to
sickness and death, but it is also possible that this type of language
was a discursive convention used deliberately in order to elicit the
recipient's sympathy.

The similarities between these elements of Soviet letters and
petitions and their pre-revolutionary antecedents are obvious.
However, a discourse is not automatically passed down from generation to generation. It tends only to be perpetuated if it is still relevant to
a new situation. Why did this type of discourse continue in the Soviet
period? Evidently, certain structural features of the tsarist political
system continued and were even exacerbated in the Soviet period –
notably a centre–periphery divide, a lack of effective representative
institutions, and a new and even more inflated and beleaguered
bureaucratic ruling stratum. An appeal to the *vozhd'* was often the only
way of cutting through the red tape, and it made sense to adopt the

tactics likely to elicit a sympathetic response: employing the cult language, flattering the leader, and stressing the helplessness of the 'little people'. This, after all, was the message put out by Stalin himself from about 1935 – that officialdom was riddled with corruption and abuse, and that the great father Stalin was on the people's side.

Numerous petitioners therefore explicitly affirmed their loyalty to the *vozhdi*, while criticising individual bureaucrats and local distortions, as had been the practice under the tsar. The following examples all refer to the situation in the *kolkhozy*; however, similar comments were made about all aspects of Soviet life:

Dear *vozhdi*, you see very blindly, you only hear at various congresses and meetings a number of completely satisfied delegates, and also all our press pulls the wool over your eyes about what's going on in the countryside.

We think that you and com. Stalin don't know that the *kolkhozniki* live so badly. We think that our village communists are deceiving you, perhaps they write to you that the *kolkhozy* are doing very well, there are still many communists who ... have a card, but in fact are wrecking.

The *kolkhoz* leadership is such that we cannot be wealthy. Our administration often does not do what is written to us by dear com. Stalin, who really cares about us, thank you.[30]

What does the use of this language reveal about the reception of the leader cult? It indicates that the populist, paternalist aspects of the cult resonated with ideas at the grassroots, and that the 'traditional' conceptions inherent in the cult were readily accepted and employed. However, this type of language does not in itself illuminate the extent to which Soviet citizens venerated Stalin and his colleagues, just as petitions from the tsarist period cannot explain whether the Russian peasant was a monarchist or not, as Field has convincingly argued.[31] The rather formulaic nature of the language suggests that some people may have regarded it above all as a device necessary for attaining certain rational goals without appearing to threaten the status quo.[32]

Likewise, people may have considered the citation of the leaders' own words a way of furthering their own aims in their battles with local power. This reappropriation of the official discourse did not necessarily imply a 'cultic' attitude, a sense of reverence for the words of the *vozhd'*. Rather it was a reasoned and effective means of protest, often just what was required to galvanise the officials in question. Thus, shortly after Stalin's 'Cadres' speech in May 1935, policemen complained to Zhdanov that they were having to work sixteen to eighteen hours a day with no time off, and little pay. They ended the letter with the hope that 'after comrade Stalin's brilliant speech on cadres, you will take measures to help us'. As a result of the letter, Zhdanov initiated an investigation.[33] Similarly, there was a case of the pay of ITR being held up at the Krasnogvardeets factory, during which one worker announced that 'Comrade Stalin speaks of the need to protect cadres, but our pay is being held up every month.' The protest was effective, for in this instance Zhdanov, the 'benevolent father', stepped in and those responsible for the abuses were called to account.[34]

THE CHARISMATIC LEADER

Unlike the 'traditional' image of the leader, the charismatic facets of the leader cultivated in the propaganda seem to have had less of a resonance amongst the broad mass of the population, in this period at least. Gordon and Klopov assert that Stalin was perceived as a 'charismatic *vozhd'*, a demi-god, possessing superhuman abilities and superhuman wisdom. For tens of millions of people ... he was the symbol of the motherland, Soviet power, socialism.'[35] In fact, this notion of Stalin as a demi-god is comparatively rare in letters: there are few fanatical outpourings of love for him and other leaders.[36] However, the need to create icons or symbols out of the *vozhdi*, which Gordon and Klopov mention, appears to have been shared rather more widely.

This grassroots input into the iconisation of the leader can be discerned in the popular treatment of pictures of the *vozhdi*. Although the regime itself encouraged the practice of carrying icon-like pictures of leaders during demonstrations and displaying them in prominent places, the way people treated this practice reveals a process of negotiation between official and popular values. Some people hung pictures of the *vozhdi* in icon frames, placed these next to icons of saints, and even prayed and crossed themselves in front of the them.[37] This treatment of the picture of a *vozhd'* as a saint in the Christian tradition, as in itself the embodiment of spiritual power, was clearly a spontaneous movement from below, rather than a policy promoted from above. The reports of party agitators tended to represent such popular practices in a negative light, implying that they were perceived as an undesirable distortion of the official message. There was one incident in particular when a *bezbozhnik* visited a *kolkhoznik* fisher, and was shown the barn where he kept his fishing equipment, and where a portrait of Gamarnik also hung. The *bezbozhnik* asked why the portrait was hanging there, to which he replied 'You see, before St Nicholas hung there, he really helped, and now that portrait has been hanging there, it's been difficult catching fish.'[38] It is possible that the fisher regarded the portrait as the potential locus of supernatural powers. Its actual failure to help may thus have diminished the authority of the *vozhd'* in the eyes of the fisher.

The iconisation of the leaders was actively promoted by the regime, but does not seem to have been considered unnatural by at least some of the people, who volunteered their own suggestions about how to exalt the *vozhdi*. Many ideas about popularising the *vozhdi*, putting up statues to them, renaming places after them, or awarding them honours emanated from the people themselves. After Kirov's death, there were apparently spontaneous proposals that places, children, and so on be named after Kirov, and statues erected to him. It was claimed that Kirov was Lenin's equal, and many questioned, 'Why are they taking our dear Kirov to Moscow?', asking that he should be buried instead in a mausoleum in Leningrad.[39] There was a wide-
·ad desire to see his body lying in state, even amongst 'backward'
:ers and intellectuals, who had never previously appeared at
᠃onstrations and meetings. Even the Hermitage – a nest of reactionaries and 'former people' – found 270 people keen to bid farewell to the body, more than twice as many as had ever attended political events previously.[40] According to a confidential report prepared for the chief of the Leningrad militia, one and a half million people (more than half the population of Leningrad) passed through the Uritskii Palace, where the body lay in state, on 2–3 December, and many others who wanted to participate were refused permission to join the columns because of overcrowding. Those who did get the chance to take part often had to wait for four to five hours on the same spot in temperatures of $-4\,°C$, but this did not deter them.[41] Like the reaction to the deaths of Lenin and Stalin, but on a smaller scale, this interest in Kirov's dead body suggests a mystical, religious attitude to authority. It is significant that only in the 1960s were secular funerals introduced for ordinary Soviet citizens.[42] In this period their limitation to the *vozhdi* must have reinforced the impression of the latter's elevation high above normal mortals.

In August 1935, Zhdanov received a letter complaining about the fact that in Leningrad there were streets named after the populist terrorists Zheliabov and Perovskaia, but none named after revolutionaries, and no 'Lenin Street'. The letter also complained that the statue of Lenin outside the Finland station did not compare favourably with those of Peter I and Catherine II. Clearly Zhdanov sympathised with this view, for at the bottom of the letter was his resolution 'For the agenda of the buro'.[43] Kalinin received a letter in 1936 proposing the creation of museums of Stalin and Voroshilov and a Lenin house in Red Square.[44] One man who knew Zhdanov as a child wrote to him in 1935 to inform him that he had commenced a 'tale for children, the hero of which will be little Andrei, and the theme: his adventures'.[45]

In 1939, the Eighteenth Party Congress received a letter arguing that the party should adopt the names of Lenin and Stalin and become 'The Lenin–Stalin All-Union Communist Party'.[46] At the time of the discussion of the new Constitution, there were suggestions that the Soviet flag should be decorated with pictures of (a) Marx, Engels, Lenin, and Stalin, (b) Lenin, Stalin, Kalinin, and Voroshilov, or (c) Lenin and Stalin, and that Moscow should be renamed in honour of Stalin.[47] A few letters at the end of 1937 and the beginning of 1938 also requested that Moscow be renamed Stalinodar or Stalingrad.[48] One was from a pensioner, E. M. Chulkova, who confessed that her dream was 'to live in Stalinodar'. She reported that: 'As for myself, I have been living there for ages, and would probably have carried on living there quietly', but she had been inspired by Stalin's speech of 11 December 1937, and the triumphal cries of the voters, to imagine how popular a decision to rename Moscow would be. She explained that Leningrad was associated with the heroic past, but that the epoch of victorious socialism was the Stalinist epoch:

In the beautiful capital are concentrated the flowering of scientific thought, the flowering of art, of world achievements, the powerful sweep of the plan for its reconstruction, its metro, the Volga–Moscow canal, the grandiose construction of the Palace of Soviets – all this and much more besides is the gift [*dar*] of the great genius Stalin – Stalinodar.

The letter ended with a poem expressing these thoughts in an even more florid manner. Another letter in the same file also proposed that Moscow should become 'Stalindar':

The genius of Stalin is a historic gift to mankind, its guiding star on the paths of development and ascent to the highest level. Therefore I am deeply convinced that all the workers of mankind on earth of our epoch and all mankind of many ages in the future will welcome the renaming of Moscow to Stalindar with joy and satisfaction.[49]

As well as this desire to employ the icons of the *vozhdi* more widely, there was also pressure to honour the chief symbol, Stalin himself. This was expressed in a letter of 1935 to Kalinin which questioned why Ordzhonikidze, Voroshilov, and Kalinin had received the Order of Lenin, while Stalin had not. Since Stalin, 'The Great Genius, Mind and Heart', was responsible for most of the country's good fortune, it was appropriate that he should be similarly honoured.[50] By 1939, the cult had reached such proportions that the issue was no longer the Order of Lenin, but the establishment of a special Order of Lenin–Stalin, reflecting one writer's gratitude to Stalin.[51] Another called for Stalin's sixtieth birthday in December 1939 to be celebrated as a national holiday, remarking that Stalin would probably refuse from modesty, but that the party and state should insist, since it was the wish of all the people.[52] Also in connection with this event, Kalinin received a request to call an extraordinary session of the Supreme Soviet in order that this institution might confer upon Stalin the title 'the Great'.[53]

Most of these suggestions were left unfulfilled, considered too extravagant even for the extremes of the cult. For example, Zhdanov insisted that the story about his childhood should not be written, saying 'that theme is not at all topical',[54] while Stalin was apparently opposed to the renaming of Moscow.[55]

In ordinary letters, the idea of the leader embodying special spiritual and emotional power was far less common than the representation of the leader as a father-like defender of the people. Nevertheless, there were a few overtly charismatic representations, including those contained in the letters on renaming Moscow. There was also one particular case of a correspondent of Kalinin, who had allegedly been writing to him for ten years, describing these letters as his 'only joy'. He called Stalin 'Sunshine-Happiness', and told Kalinin that 'you are for me like a man-god, and I. V. Stalin is god'. He declared that his one desire was to touch Kalinin. He clearly spent ages poring over the pictures of the *vozhdi* in the newspapers, evaluating them in adoring terms:

And take the last issue of *Pravda* from 28 February, the photo where the border troops are given awards. What an unforgettable face you have on that photo, it's impossible to forget and stands before my eyes all the time, with what pure love our Sunshine-Happiness looks at you here and what an inspired face of the Greatest Genius he has here, and for his smile, for just one smile, a thousand lives could be given up.

And in *Pravda* of 1 March. Your face is only shown in profile, but in it there is so much good, warm, and attractive, which is the very essence of you Dear Mikhail Ivanovich, that it is difficult to convey in words. And the face of our Sunshine-Happiness, on the same photo has a totally special, just marvellous expression. In particular the eyes, the eyes of the Greatest Genius, the Greatest sage and thinker, which seem to see and decide the fates of whole worlds, and before which there are no secrets. How much power, how much greatness, how much sunshine, and how much supernatural reason there is in those dear and beloved eyes.[56]

The cult phenomenon is frequently represented as a mass hypnosis, as something completely irrational, as part of the general 'psychosis' of this period.[57] Evidently, as the last letter in particular illustrates, it did have irrational aspects. Yet some of these more 'charismatic' representations, like those of the traditional leader, may have been employed for quite rational goals. Obviously it is difficult to uncover the complex motivation behind any individual pronouncement. However, by making an apparently innocent and unself-interested suggestion about honouring a *vozhd'*, or by writing 'fan letters', an individual may have hoped to store up a capital of good will to be exploited in the future.

The idea of 'mass hypnosis' is an over-simplification which does no justice to the variety of messages within the official cult discourse itself, and within popular representations of the phenomenon. By disentangling the latter, it is clear that reception of the myth(s) of the leader cult was far from uniform. Ordinary people selected those aspects of the official cult language which conformed with their own ideas about leadership and modified or rejected others. They also reappropriated the official language for their own quite rational ends. Although the charismatic, god-like image of the leader had adherents, it was not the only nor even the main image favoured by ordinary people, in this period at least. In the post-war period, the experience of war, the elevation of the 'Generalissimus', and generational change may all have combined to alter perceptions, to instil the charismatic image more firmly.

CHAPTER II

Negative representations of the leader and leader cult

Although the official cult discourse was employed on certain occasions, it was also ignored, misinterpreted, rejected, criticised, and subverted in various ways. Its messages did not always get through, or did so in a distorted form, either because of the inefficacy of the agitprop, or because people deliberately chose to ignore or misinterpret it. However, there were individuals who were only too well aware of the cult's omnipresence, and criticised it directly, or attacked it in other ways, which included subverting its gravity and sense of hierarchy and permanence. Some people also proposed alternative leaders, although it is significant that the language in which these proposals were couched was very reminiscent of that of the official cult, which suggests that the propaganda of the cult itself probably conformed with popular ideas about the nature of leadership; as in the cases cited elsewhere in this study, it was often simply the failure of the reality to live up to the claims of the propaganda which generated hostility.

INDIFFERENCE TO AND MISUNDERSTANDING OF THE CULT

Until the mid-1930s, a number of people were still unaware of the existence or roles of the *vozhdi*. In 1933, even party members were expelled from the party for ignorance about the biographies of the leaders. For example, during a purge at the Leningrad Historical-Linguistic Institute, one party member described Stalin as 'President of the STO [Sovet truda i oborony – Council of Labour and Defence]', and was unable to answer the question 'Who is Kirov?' Another member thought that Molotov 'leads agriculture'.[1] The ignorance even among party members concerning the identity of their leaders was regarded as a failing in propaganda work, and it was partly to rectify this that the party undertook such a concerted campaign to popularise the *vozhdi* during the next few years. This campaign was not immediately successful. At the time of Kirov's death, it transpired that many peasants and school-children had not even heard of him. In 1935, even party members remained in the dark about their leaders. Some Komsomol members were unable to answer questions such as 'Who is Stalin?', while in the communist university a student described Kalinin as 'the leader of all the *kolkhozy*'. Even some teachers were unaware of what Kalinin and Molotov did at the end of 1936. As late as 1937, a few *kolkhozniki* did not know who Stalin was. When one particular *kolkhoznik* was asked in 1937 'Who is the boss now in Russia?', he replied 'They say its Il'in.' Il'in was in fact the chairman of the village soviet.[2]

This last remark illustrates another aspect of the problem, namely the way in which the propaganda messages were often transmitted in a distorted form. The idea of the cult of the *vozhd'* was frequently misinterpreted as a cult of authority in any form. Such a practice was quite contrary to the official discourse which carefully regulated the entitlement to cult status. While Kirov, Ezhov, Ordzhonikidze, and others close to Stalin were accorded this right at various times, it was inadmissible for regional party leaders to imitate the practices of the centre. Mini-cults emerged publicly in mid-1933, at the same time as the cult of Stalin. For example, in June 1933 the newspaper of Babaevskii district, *Novyi put'*, published a greeting to the secretary of its regional party committee: 'Long live the *raikom* of the VKP(b) and the dear [*blizkii*] *kolkhoznik*, untiring organiser of the struggle for the strengthening of the *kolkhozy*, comrade Vorontsov.'[3] In 1937, it was revealed that the party secretary of Murmansk was being greeted with cries of 'Long live Abramov, the *vozhd'* of the Murmansk Bolsheviks' and 'Long live the steel Abramov', and that during the local May Day demonstration in Poddorsk slogans were heard such as 'Hurrah! To the leader of the Poddorsk Bolsheviks, Sergei Petrovich Krylov'. In some areas party meetings emulated Kremlin receptions, with *paradnost'* (ostentation), *torzhestvennost'* (solemnity), and long applause for the party secretary. Local leaders would lay claim to all successes in their region, much as Stalin was made responsible for the achievements of the Soviet Union, and *podkhalimstvo* (toadying) flourished.[4]

The February–March plenum in 1937 drew attention to these abuses, and exhorted party officials to emulate the 'modesty' of Stalin.[5] Nevertheless, the practice was difficult to eradicate. In

November 1939 excessive praise of candidates was noted in connection with the local soviet elections in Leningrad. One candidate was described as a '*vozhd'* whom the masses will follow as he leads them to communism'. Another election meeting ended with the words 'Long live the VKP(b) and *vozhd'* comrade Stalin, who has raised such a worthy person as comrade Levchenko [the candidate].'[6] These practices undermined the cult of Stalin (and his *soratniki*), for they relativised it in the eyes of ordinary people. His cult may have been perceived as just one of many manifestations of self-aggrandisement, no better or worse than the local cults, and his authority as a variation on all types of authority, rather than something unique and special. Therefore, as Fitzpatrick suggests, when the attacks on the local bosses began in 1937, some ordinary people probably did not distinguish between the different types of authority, and regarded Stalin and his colleagues just as guilty as the local chiefs.[7]

It is worth noting that the distortion of official cult language extended not only to Soviet political figures. For example, schoolchildren sometimes wrongly applied epithets normally reserved for Stalin and his colleagues to capitalist leaders. Tests conducted by the Commissariat of Enlightenment in 1936 on pupils in Moscow *oblast'* revealed that some children had a quite erroneous understanding of Gladstone's significance. He was described as '*vozhd'* of the working class – a liberal'; 'on the one hand, a liberal, and, on the other, a *vozhd'* of the workers'; '*vozhd' naroda* [leader of the people]'.[8] Thus Stalin and Gladstone were placed in one category – an intriguing example of the 'janus-like' quality of signs.

CRITICISM OF THE CULT

While the wider population only began to criticise the cult directly, to treat it with irony, from about 1937, some of the more informed sections of the population, including intellectuals, experienced workers, and party and Komsomol members, were sensitive to the radical changes in the propaganda in this period, and aware of the absurdities of the cult from its outset. Marx's condemnation of the 'cult of personality', and the Bolsheviks' theoretical rejection of *vozhdizm* were presumably known to some people.[9] As early as 1934, a worker attending a meeting devoted to Stalin's Seventeenth Party Congress speech openly protested about the fact that 'everyone is praising Stalin, they consider him a god, and no one makes any criticisms'. It was already obvious that the treatment of Stalin had religious overtones. Likewise, the posthumous deification of Kirov encountered opposition and ridicule. Someone referred ironically to the funeral of Kirov as the funeral of 'the second god' and others compared the portraits of Kirov to icons. A group of students even organised a mock requiem in front of Kirov's picture, accompanied by the performance of anti-religious *chastushki* and the lighting of candles. The widespread desire to honour Kirov was not universal. Some thought that he was being given excessive public acclaim. Others resented the money being spent on the memorialisation.[10]

Initially, a few of the more literate workers were suspicious of the amount of attention accorded to Stalin in the media in 1934–5, since previously his public profile had been comparatively low – he had not played a particularly visible role in the revolution or its aftermath compared with luminaries such as Trotsky, Zinoviev, or Kamenev.[11] His sudden conspicuousness, the rewriting of history, caused them to complain that the achievements of Trotsky were being ascribed to him. Stalin was a *vyskachka* (an upstart). Protest became more vociferous at the end of 1935 and the beginning of 1936, when the cult reached new proportions. A worker from the Baltiiskii plant (with a twenty-year work record), after complaining about Stakhanovism, remarked ironically 'Life has become good, life has become merry. For whom? Is Stalin happy because there are many fools and they write "the great Stalin" during his lifetime?' Workers objected to the incessant declarations of love for Stalin, the use of the epithets *rodnoi* (dear), 'beloved', 'father', and so on, the transformation of Stalin into what one Komsomol member, employing Marxist terminology, called a 'fetish'. It was felt that Lenin would never have allowed himself to be treated in this way.[12]

In 1936, people also began to draw comparisons between the worship of Hitler and Stalin: both had concentrated enormous power in their hands, both were loved by their people.[13] An NKVD agent with the code name 'Volgin', working in the Academy of Sciences, reported a revealing conversation on this theme which took place on 1 September 1936. Although academics are not the focus of this study, their elaborate analysis of the Stalin cult deserves a mention. The conversation, between Krachkovskii, Kazakevich, Shcherbatskii, and Struve, centred on the future role of the party. Rumours had been circulating that the party was to be abolished, or to be allowed to die away naturally, that Stalin could no longer trust

it. The dictatorship of the party was to be replaced by presidential
rule. Struve attributed these rumours to the 'right Academicians',
and to circles around Deborin and Bukharin. That day, however, a
new recruitment into the party had been announced which Shcherbatskii interpreted in the following way: 'They've driven out the old
party members, now they'll choose new ones, who'll do anything to
grovel to Stalin. These ones will only last a year or two, then they'll
get bored.' Krachkovskii warned that now it was necessary to be very
careful about expressing one's views:

We are living during the final flare-up of terror. This time it's broken out
against that section of party members who could prevent Stalin and his
assistants from hanging on to power after the introduction of the new
Constitution. It is clear that in communist circles there is now a struggle
going on for the president's seat. I am almost sure that the president will be
Stalin, who will that way be transformed into Joseph the First, the new all-
Russian emperor. It's not a question of intentions, but of the general course
of history. Communism is becoming the national religion of Russia, just as
fascism is becoming the national religion of Germany and Italy, and
Kemalism the national religion of Turkey. With all these movements what
is characteristic on the one hand is hatred for the pre-existing religions –
Orthodoxy, Catholicism, Lutheranism, Islam – and on the other – a cult of
the *vozhd'*. For when Stalin is publicly called the father and *vozhd'* of the
peoples, then the last line between him and the Führer Hitler is eliminated.

The agent had a similar discussion with another academic,
Makarova, who also considered that the new Constitution signalled
the 'end of revolution and the transition from the masses to the
individual [*perekhod ot mass k lichnosti*]', and that it was likely that
Stalin would be made president and 'official dictator'. Professor
Zarubin, although confessing not to have thought about these
matters for many years, had also heard many opinions recently
comparing Russia and Germany, and stating that Stalin was merely
copying the behaviour of Hitler.[14]

These analyses by the academic old guard are interesting because
the cult is considered as part of long-term, broader historical process.
Krachkovskii (an orientalist) explained the phenomenon of the Stalin
cult as a continuation of the Russian imperial tradition. However, he
was also aware of the parallels with the cults in Germany, Italy, and
Turkey. Why the perpetuation of a Russian tradition should take the
form of a more universal quasi-religious leader cult was not made
clear. However, Zarubin suggested that Stalin was consciously
emulating Hitler. In general, those comparing the Hitler and Stalin

cults tended to be the more informed. For example, an anonymous writer to Zhdanov had read Feuchtwanger's description of the fascist system which terrorised people into shouting 'Heil Hitler'. He immediately noted the similarities between this and what was happening in the Soviet Union, where ordinary people joined in the chorus of praise, while really thinking 'May they go to the devil, they do not make our lives any better.'[15]

By 1936, official demonstrations had turned into occasions for glorifying the leaders. More and more portraits of the *vozhdi* were displayed and carried. In his diary entry following the November 1936 demonstration, Arzhilovskii explicitly made the connection between the carrying of these portraits and the bearing of icons in religious processions:

By the way, the portraits of party leaders are now displayed the same way icons used to be: a round portrait framed and attached to a pole. Very convenient, hoist it onto your shoulder and you're on your way. And all these preparations are just like what people used to do before church holidays ... They had their own activists then, we have ours now. Different paths, the same old folderol.[16]

The portraits were rather heavy, and the NKVD reported that during the May Day demonstrations in 1936 and 1937, several people refused to carry them, or deliberately dropped them. A few objected specifically to the fact that they were supposed to bear them aloft 'like icons'. By 1937, some people, especially party members, were tired of the cult, which had assumed alarming proportions. Towards the end of the year, the terror and the leader cults were both reaching their apogee. The electoral campaign was a huge publicity stunt for the *vozhdi*, who became candidates in several regions simultaneously, to the chagrin of some voters, who thought this farcical. The propaganda alienated some, including a *sluzhashchii* from Borovicheskii district, who had had enough of the elections: 'The radio only reports eulogistic speeches about the rulers, and the rulers themselves eulogise. I'm sick of it. Even illiterates are taught to read using phrases like "dear comrade Stalin".' A Leningrad worker also complained that 'All the party and government leaders are idealised' and objected to the excessive praise of candidates, such as Tevosian, who, it was claimed at one meeting, had been a leader of the liberation of Georgia at the age of fifteen. An engineer from Elektrosila protested against the flattering speeches and the professions of love and loyalty to Stalin, reminiscent of the exaltation of the *batiushka-tsar'*. Stalin's role was being exaggerated at the expense of that of Lenin, his authority was being created since 'the uncultured masses cannot live without authorities'.[17]

Criticism of the cult continued in 1938, especially around the time of the elections to the RSFSR Supreme Soviet. A leaflet ridiculed the impotence of the Supreme Soviet of the USSR where, 'the "people's elect" were allowed to shout out "Hurray" a thousand times in honour of the *"vozhd'"* and his stooges'. After the elections, a celebratory demonstration was held, which caused one worker to comment, 'Now the time has come when *vozhdi* have become gods and are carried like icons.' Ironic remarks were heard – at one school, when pupils asked their teacher for books, she would tell them to ask Stalin for them, or say 'Stalin has taught you everything, but not how to clean the blackboard.' At another school, a pupil drew a picture of Stalin in epaulettes and spread a song in which Stalin was called the 'General of our unhappy life'.[18] The counter-productive effect of the excessive propaganda was pointed out in an anonymous letter from July 1938, which is worth quoting in full. It was written by a communist supporter of the regime:

Dear comrade Zhdanov!
Do you not think that comrade Stalin's name has begun to be very much abused? For example:

> Stalin's people's commissar
> Stalin's falcon
> Stalin's pupil
> Stalin's canal
> Stalin's route
> Stalin's pole
> Stalin's harvest
> Stalin's stint
> Stalin's five-year plan
> Stalin's constitution
> Stalin's block of communists and non-party members
> Stalin's Komsomol (it's already being called this)

I could give a hundred other examples, even of little meaning. Everything is Stalin, Stalin, Stalin.
You only have to listen to a radio programme about our achievements, and every fifth or tenth word will be the name of comrade Stalin.
In the end this sacred and beloved name – Stalin – may make so much noise in people's heads that it is very possible that it will have the opposite effect.

It would be interesting to know how Stalin himself reacts to this?

With communist greetings: V. K. 1/VII-38 Leningrad.[19]

It may have been evident to the leadership that the cult was becoming counterproductive. Certainly, from 1939, there was a marked decline in its prominence (apart from the massive sixtieth birthday celebrations at the end of the year). Stalin seemed to be trying to disassociate himself from the unpopular policies of the period. Nevertheless, people still continued to hold him responsible, and after the 1940 labour decrees, the cultic refrain 'Thank you, comrade Stalin, for X' was constantly parodied.[20]

SUBVERSIVE DISCOURSE

While the majority did not criticise the 'cult of personality' as such, they nevertheless found other indirect ways of subverting the official image of leadership. All the characteristics of the cult were over-turned. Where the official cult was serious, the unofficial images were comic; where the official cult denied the existence of a private life to the leaders, the unofficial images concentrated on their personal, human details; where the official cult portrayed the cult as perma-nent, the unofficial images stressed the transitory nature of the leadership, the imminent deaths of the *vozhdi*. This process of subversion or 'carnivalisation' is particularly evident in the oral popular culture of the period, including jokes, songs, and *chastushki*. When popular culture touched on political questions, it usually featured top party leaders, such as Stalin, Kirov, or Lenin. This was partly because of the prominence accorded to these leaders in the official discourse. However, this is also a typical feature of oral cultures, according to Ong. What he calls 'heavy characters' are crucial to the oral transmission of popular culture, since colourless individuals are simply not memorable.[21]

The gravity of the cult was undermined by practices such as the naming of horses after the *vozhdi* or hanging of their pictures in the toilet. Leaders were portrayed in a comic light, as in the *chastushka*, 'Ekhal Lenin na barane / U barana odin rog / Kuda edesh' ty pleshivyi / Zagoniat' nas vsekh v kolkhoz' ('Lenin was riding on a ram / The ram had one horn / Where are you going, baldy, / Driving us all into the *kolkhoz*'). This focus on the body (Lenin's baldness, his ungraceful pose) contrasted markedly with the deliberate avoidance of any mention of the physicality of the leader in the official cult, as did the emphasis on the leaders' drinking in *chastushki* and rumours. According to one rumour, 'Kirov was killed by a drunken gang. All the *vozhdi* are always getting drunk', while a *chastushka* made a similar allegation: 'Kogda Kirova ubili, / Stalin vyshel na kryltso, / My s tov. Kirovym / liubili pit' vintso' ('When Kirov was killed, / Stalin came onto the porch, / Comrade Kirov and I / Used to like drinking vodka').[22]

Likewise, the official neglect of the leaders' private lives was overturned by ordinary people, who gossiped and joked about the wives and families of their leaders. After Kirov's murder, workers were curious for information about his family, whether he was married even, or if he had any children.[23] A joke was made about the wives of Lenin and Stalin, who were both called Nadezhda (Hope): 'Lenin had a hope – and it remains, but Stalin has no hope. Lenin had the hope of building socialism, but Stalin does not have that hope' (this was a reference to the fact that Lenin's wife was still alive, while Stalin's had killed herself in 1932). Rumours also spread widely about the sex lives of the leaders, exploding the official taboo on this subject. Kirov's murder and Allilueva's suicide were attributed to sex scandals. Stalin's name was linked with a variety of women, and Lenin was purported to have died of syphilis.[24]

Maureen Perrie has shown how Russian folkloric tales often consisted of two main protagonists: one drawn from the elite, and the other from the *narod*. The cunning peasant getting his own back against a cruel master was often a feature of these tales. Likewise, official hierarchies implicit within the Stalin cult were also reversed. Thus in one joke a peasant went up to Stalin and asked him when socialism would be built. Stalin replied that it would be soon, in two years' time. And the peasant asked, 'So then there will be no GPU or other guard?' Stalin said that there would not be. Then the peasant said 'Then we will shoot you all.'[25]

The permanence of the cult, its sense of immobility, was countered by much conversation about the actual and potential deaths of leaders, especially that of Stalin. For ordinary people, the death of a leader was the most usual way of imagining the overturning of the status quo. In 1934, amongst young people it was popular to decipher SSSR as 'Smert' Stalina spaset Rossiiu' (Stalin's death will save Russia). To some people, the actual death of a leader, Kirov, must have seemed like the fulfilment of all their wishes. It evoked a whole range of *chastushki*, many of which linked his death with the impending death of other leaders, especially Stalin: 'Kirova ubili / Stalina ub'iut / Vse krest'iane rady budut / Kommunisty zarevut' ('Kirov's been killed / Stalin will be killed / All the peasants will rejoice / And the communists will cry'). His death was also related to other events, such as the sinking of the *Cheliuskin* in 1934. Both were regarded as presaging the overthrow of Stalin: 'Nemnogo vremeni proshlo, kak Cheliuskin potopili ... Segodnia Kirova ubili, zavtra Stalina ub'iut' ('It's not long, since the *Cheliuskin* was sunk ... Today Kirov was killed, tomorrow Stalin will be killed'). The deaths of Stalin and Kirov were represented as merely the beginning of more sweeping changes, including the end of the *kolkhoz* system: 'Kirova ubili / Skoro Stalina ub'iut / Vse kolkhozy razbegutsia / Nam svobodnei budet zhit'' ('Kirov's been killed / Soon Stalin will be killed / All the *kolkhozy* will collapse / We will live more freely'),[26] and better food: 'Kirova ubili / po kotletke podarili / Stalina ub'iut / po kuritse dadut' ('Kirov died / We had cutlets / Stalin'll die / We'll have chicken').[27] In general, the deaths of leaders represented the realisation of the carnival idea of holiday and rest from the drudgery of work: 'Lenin died – there was a holiday; Kirov died, there was also a holiday; and if they get all the leaders there'll be an eternal holiday'; 'Lenin died and we had a rest; if another good chap dies, we'd rest even more.'[28]

How should this 'subversion' be interpreted? Was it indicative of hostility towards the leaders, or was it simply a way of letting off steam, a safety-valve? This is obviously impossible to tell without more contextual information. The regime tended to view all such expressions as politically subversive. Their interpretations cannot be taken too seriously but nor should they be rejected entirely. Evidently there were many cases when jokes and *chastushki* in particular circulated purely for the purposes of entertainment. However, the dangers of relating them in this period were so great that for some people they may have assumed greater political significance.

ALTERNATIVE MODELS OF LEADERSHIP

In contrast to these essentially negative and destructive attitudes towards leaders, there were also suggestions of alternative leadership models, based on a range of symbolic figures, including Lenin, the tsar, Trotsky, Kirov, Bukharin, and other 'enemies', even Hitler.

People exalted these figures partly because their leadership style was deemed more attractive. The official 'cult' language was often employed in relation to them – they were ascribed characteristics usually attributed to Stalin in the official discourse. These leaders also seemed to represent policies which ensured a better standard of living, although the policies for which they actually stood tended to be distorted; for example, the 'enemies of the people' were sometimes perceived as being non-communist, while Trotsky was thought to hold 'rightist' views. This was partly because of genuine ignorance about the real nature of their policies, but also because as symbols, people may have projected on to them whatever they understood to be a better alternative to Stalin.

The posthumous cult of Kirov, although officially sanctioned, could acquire subversive overtones, particularly when Kirov was juxtaposed with Stalin and other leaders. Whether or not it is true that Kirov was favoured by the TsK as an alternative to Stalin as general secretary in 1934, it is clear that amongst some Leningraders he was rated more highly. He was represented as a conciliatory leader, able to get on with the intelligentsia and the people alike. His populist style won the favour of workers, who noted that he was democratic and travelled by tram and that he 'was brave, he went everywhere alone, did not hide himself behind thick walls, we have seen other *vozhdi* little, except at congresses'. Zhdanov, by contrast, was regarded as too distant, as was shown in chapter 8. Kirov was perceived as being more humane than Stalin: 'much more soft-hearted than Stalin'; caring for the poor and the workers: 'Voroshilov stood for the Red Army, Stalin for construction, and Kirov for the people – that they should live better.'[29] It is significant that one of the most popular poems during the siege of Leningrad was Tikhonov's 'Kirov Is with Us.' Published at the end of 1942, it was written in cultic language, and included a refrain evoking the populist image of Kirov: 'Po gorodu Kirov idet' ('Kirov is walking round the city'). It also contained the couplet ' "Za rodinu" – nadpis' na bashne, / I "Kirov" – na bashne drugoi' (' "For the Motherland" – the inscription on one tower, / And "Kirov" – on the other tower'). This close parallel between Kirov and the motherland contrasted markedly with the usual identification, 'For the Motherland, for Stalin', and reinforces the idea that some Leningraders felt greater allegiance to Kirov than to Stalin.

The Lenin cult was assimilated to the cult of Stalin in the

propaganda, but it could also be used to undermine the Stalin cult, as *Sotsialisticheskii vestnik* recognised in 1934: 'the romantic cult of Lenin is becoming dangerous for the sober reality of the Stalinist regime'.[30] While party members had traditionally used the ideas of Lenin to oppose the regime (notably Riutin, with his 'Union of Marxist-Leninists'),[31] some ordinary people, especially workers, also recalled Lenin in a positive way. An inscription on the wall of a lavatory in one factory in 1934 read 'Lenin is dead but his spirit lives on.' In theory, there was nothing particularly subversive about such a statement, which was an official slogan, but it may have contained an implicit critique of the current regime, and the party's Information Department certainly interpreted it in this light.[32] Sometimes, the subversion was more overt, as in a letter to Zhdanov of 1937 from the 'TsK' of the 'Legion of Revolutionary Democracy', which praised Lenin and called for the capital to be moved to Leningrad where Lenin, 'the leader of revolutionary democracy, had established the first people's power and introduced democratic freedoms'.[33]

The refrain 'If Lenin had been alive ... ' was common in this period. It was suggested that if Lenin were still in power, there would be freedom of speech, no party struggles, no collectivisation, no price rises, and especially no harsh labour laws like those of 1940.[34] Lenin represented a more peaceful, moderate path to socialism, which Stalin had deviated from: 'Stalin must be removed, he has left Lenin's path, our country is regressing.' One worker encapsulated the difference thus: 'Lenin led the country upwards, but today's *vozhdi* are leading it down.'[35] NEP was also perceived as a relatively golden age when:

there was everything, and now there is no food, and when Lenin was alive – everything was peaceful and good, everyone lived in a friendly collective, but when Lenin died, then the squabbles and splits started and the party became impure – there are many cheats and enemies of the people.[36]

This remark betrays a tendency to idealise Lenin, to portray him as a hero and Stalin as the villain responsible for all the country's woes. This black-and-white picture was particularly evident in jokes. One joke ran, 'Why did Lenin wear over-shoes [*botinki*] and Stalin boots [*sapogi*]? Because under Lenin it was possible to wear over-shoes (it was dry, clean, and nice), but now that Stalin's at the top, there is such a marsh that wherever you go, you get stuck. That's why he wears boots.'[37]

The Lenin–Stalin linkage in the official cult may have to some extent inhibited a subversive discourse based on the cult of Lenin. Trotsky, by contrast, was regarded as unequivocally opposed to Stalin. Like Lenin, he had also enjoyed a cult, and the same type of language was applied to his leadership.[38] His military prowess, oratorical ability, flamboyant style, and intelligence were emphasised by dissenting workers. He was habitually referred to as a genius, and it was asserted that victory in the civil war was due entirely to him.[39] Despite the attempt to rewrite history, people continued to trust their own memories. One impassioned supporter of Trotsky was adamant:

The newspapers lie, the accused are not guilty, they did not make any assassination attempts. Trotsky was a good man, a great military leader, leader of the Red Army, defender of the motherland, dedicated to the revolution with all his heart. The army loved him. Were it not for Trotsky, Kazan would not have been taken in 1918 by the Red Army, Moscow would have been left without bread and the Revolution would have perished. Trotsky used to put himself under fire. Were it not for Trotsky, we would not have seen Kronstadt. The fight is going on from soft chairs, they did not want to give in to Trotsky, they blackened him and expelled him.[40]

Trotsky's role in the civil war was contrasted with that of Stalin: 'Thanks to him and only to him was victory over our enemies achieved, for Stalin at that time was at a resort stuffing himself with apples.'[41] His capacity to lead the 'masses' was often remarked upon 'all the masses are behind Trotsky'; 'It's good that Trotsky is alive, he can still organise the masses'; 'Trotsky enjoyed the masses' great love. He was a very strong personality. When the masses listen to him ... everyone is rooted to the spot.' One worker recalled Trotsky's ability to galvanise soldiers into action: 'there were units which did not want to go into battle, and Trotsky came along and everyone rushed into fight'.[42]

Although this charismatic, cultic language was a feature of the discourse on Trotsky in particular, other leaders were also occasionally its recipients. Zinoviev, Kamenev, Bukharin, Tukhachevskii, and Rykov were all praised for their revolutionary services, described as 'historical figures' and idealists.[43] In Leningrad, Zinoviev still enjoyed some support. A leaflet appeared which read 'Long live the tribune of the revolution Zinoviev!'[44] Peasants regarded Bukharin and Rykov as having the peasant interest at heart, and there appears to have been some support for them during the 1937 elections.[45]

The cult language was also applied to the tsar, with the conventional symbols being replaced by those of the *ancien régime*, as in leaflets 'Down with Stalin. Long live Tsar Nicholas II', and 'Down with Soviet power. We need landowners and capitalists. Before it was better. Down with Lenin, down with Stalin! Long live the old days under the Tsar! Comrades! Pay attention to this piece of paper.'[46] Paradoxically, the use of slogans and words such as 'comrades' endowed the symbol of the tsar with revolutionary potential. This most conservative of institutions was thus represented as a means of mobilising the people to overthrow the regime. The tsar was sometimes associated with a better standard of living, and portrayed as a defender of the people's interests. Peasants in particular praised the tsar, for 'Land was given to the peasants not by Soviet power but by the Tsar ... When we prayed to God we lived better.'[47] Workers also contrasted their standard of living unfavourably with that before the revolution, and some remembered how strikes were allowed under the tsar, how then 'the workers were the bosses'.[48]

Popular understanding of the policies espoused by these leaders was not always very clear. Hitler's leadership and policies also came to symbolise an alternative to that of Stalin, and similar cult language was used in relation to him, as chapter 6 illustrated. However, some people placed Hitler and the 'enemies of the people' in one camp and identified their policies. In the words of a priest, 'The fascists will win under Hitler's leadership, because he is for the people. Trotsky and Zinoviev also had the right policy. They are for the people and against *kolkhozy*, and for that they were shot.' One worker said 'I am for Hitler and Trotsky', evidently not knowing what either of them represented but simply regarding both as strong leaders and as symbols of opposition to Stalin.[49] The confusion over leaders' policies was especially evident in the case of Trotsky, who was identified with both a 'leftist' and a 'rightist' stance. Thus he was sometimes represented as having been on the side of Stalin against Lenin. He was also perceived as standing for an anti-*kolkhoz*, pro-private property line, and for being a Bukharinist. Some thought that Trotsky, Bukharin, and Zinoviev were all in favour of the peasantry. Similarly, Zinoviev and the tsar were linked as symbols of better policies, as in the words of a *kolkhoznik*: 'We lived better under the tsar than now, when Zinoviev was in charge, we cut the hay and divided it equally, some for the kolkhoz, some for personal use.'[50] Probably this confusion was partly due to the peasants associating these figures with periods when they were better off, such as NEP. This was the conclusion of one anonymous writer to Zhdanov, who suggested in 1935 that the majority of peasants were on the side of Trotsky, since 'under Trotsky from 1919 to 1930', they had had their own property, free trade, and cheaper prices.[51] Clearly this conclusion was somewhat exaggerated, in order to frighten Zhdanov with the spectre of 'Trotskyism', and it seems unlikely that the 'majority' of peasants shared such a view of Trotsky.

As well as confusion over policies, there was also a tendency to distinguish incorrectly between the favoured leaders and the communists. This reflected ideas which dated back to the civil war period, when people had expressed support for the 'Bolsheviks' against the 'communists', or for 'Soviet power' but against the 'communists'.[52] As was shown in chapter 8, the word 'communist' had acquired negative overtones. So one carpenter contrasted Trotsky with the communists, portraying him as a pro-worker force. Speaking openly at an election meeting in 1937 he declared 'You communists are the rotten intelligentsia: I want to vote for Trotsky.' Bukharin, Rykov, and Zinoviev were also regarded as being enemies of the communists, and therefore worthy of support.[53]

Although a few criticised the whole idea of the 'cult of personality', the majority of ordinary people do not seem to have had a clear vision of an alternative type of leadership. The most common line of attack on the cult was a simple reversal of its attributes. In many ways this type of inversion merely bolstered the status quo, because it implied a recognition that there was a fundamental order to be reversed. Even those people who were capable of imagining different models of leadership often simply chose those which were essentially authoritarian and which they represented in the language of the cult itself. The idea of collective leadership was singularly absent. After the death of Kirov, one suggestion was made that he be replaced by a collective, as Lenin had been, but this proposal was conspicuous by its rarity.[54] The power of the hegemonic discourse to constrain opinion was therefore considerable. However, this discourse was not solely a product of the ruling elite. As the previous chapter illustrated, the traffic of ideas was not only unidirectional – propaganda was also shaped by popular opinion.

Conclusion

Conclusions imply finality, but this one can only be provisional, summarising as it does the results of a preliminary investigation, which has perhaps raised more questions than it has been able to answer. Until now, it has been impossible to address the issue of popular opinion in Stalin's Russia in a systematic way. Now, for the first time, we have access to voices from the past. Often these voices come to us through the mediation of secret police and party officials. Despite the obvious problems with these sources, they do appear to correspond with a genuine *vox populi*, and, in the absence of any superior evidence on the popular mood, historians should use them, albeit with caution and in conjunction with other types of sources.

The new sources indicate that the Stalinist propaganda machine failed to extinguish an autonomous current of popular opinion. The machine itself was far from omnipotent, lacking sufficient resources and personnel to make it fully effective. Whole regions and social groups remained excluded from its influence at various times, and the propaganda that it did manage to transmit was sometimes communicated in a distorted form. The propaganda had to compete with a remarkably efficient unofficial parallel network of information and ideas. The importance of rumour, anecdotes, anonymous letters, and other aesopian strategies in Soviet society has perhaps not been fully appreciated. Likewise, the tenacity of alternative discourses has been underestimated. Religious and nationalist discourse continued to be employed, and gender stereotypes persisted. Alternative political ideas, including those associated with the populists, Lenin, the Workers' Opposition, fascism, and tsarism also remained in circulation.

Yet it is also true that many people were receptive to some or all of the official propaganda messages. Even so, the cultural hegemony of the regime was far from all-embracing. The communication of propaganda (or any 'dominant ideology') is a two-way process, and an understanding of the functioning of propaganda is incomplete without a consideration of its consumption. Soviet propaganda was multivalent, and ordinary citizens invested it with meanings quite foreign to those intended by the regime. They reappropriated it, made it work for their own purposes, selected those aspects of it which corresponded with their own beliefs, and rejected others.

The very pervasiveness and extravagance of the propaganda left it vulnerable to criticism and provided a language of protest. As Scott points out:

> For most purposes ... it is not at all necessary for subordinate groups to set foot outside the confines of ruling ideals in order to formulate a critique of power. The most common form of class struggle arises from the failure of the dominant ideology to live up to the implicit promises it necessarily makes. The dominant ideology can be turned against its privileged beneficiaries not only because subordinate groups develop their own interpretations, understandings, and readings of its ambiguous terms, but also because of the promises that the dominant classes must make to propagate it in the first place.[1]

Observers have long wondered how pronounced in the Soviet Union was this practice of invoking the dominant ideology for the purpose of criticism, particularly as official Soviet ideology was one which did seem to offer the chance of a better life for ordinary people. A non-Sovietologist, E. P. Thompson, in a general discussion of the way in which the official rhetoric of a society 'so much at odds with reality that it is mere inert myth, mere hypocrisy', suddenly becomes activated, questioned whether the hollowness of the official Soviet rhetoric had succeeded in merely generating cynicism and opportunism, or whether 'millions of Soviet citizens still think of their land and factories as *ours* rather than .*theirs*; still hold a pride in the intentions of the October revolution; are socialised in some socialist values; find something more than myth in Marxist texts; and hence already do and increasingly will criticise the practices of their own society in terms of its own rhetoric'.[2] We can only speculate about the situation in the early 1970s when Thompson posed this question, but in the 1930s ordinary citizens certainly availed themselves of the official rhetoric in order to criticise the status quo.

It is difficult to generalise about the content of popular opinion in this period, since one of its features was its heterogeneity, which contrasts so strikingly with the dull uniformity of the 'public opinion' reported in the official media. However, there do appear to have been certain common currents. In particular, some workers seem to have regarded this period as one of 'retreat' from the ideals of socialism and communism. 'Everything is going backwards' was a frequent complaint. This sense of retreat was accompanied by a feeling of polarisation between 'us' (the people) and 'them' (the new elite), which doubtless helped to fuel the momentum of the terror.

Although some were galvanised into thinking seriously about 'democracy' by the Constitution and election campaigns, others evidently expressed little or no interest in politics or public life. However, one question which preoccupied almost all citizens was that of food (especially bread) and, to a somewhat lesser extent, consumer goods – how much they cost and how to acquire them. Despite some relative improvements in living standards during the second five-year plan, life for most ordinary people revolved around the struggle for basic existence. Scarcity encouraged egalitarian feelings.

Attitudes towards the state were contradictory. On the one hand, people seemed to expect to receive state benefits, free education, medicine, and so on. On the other, objections were voiced to paying taxes and to compulsory state loans. Peasants hated the state's interference in agriculture, and animosity towards the *kolkhoz* continued to run high. Attitudes to Stalin and other *vozhdi* were also ambivalent: for some they were father-defenders; for others, objects of abuse because they failed to carry out their paternal role.

Some of these conclusions echo those of the Harvard Interview Project conducted after the Second World War amongst Soviet refugees. This found considerable support amongst the refugees for officially vaunted Soviet values such as state control of heavy industry, the welfare state, and a strong, paternalist leader. The preferred type of economic organisation seems to have been a mixed system on the model of NEP. In *The Soviet Citizen*, Inkeles and Bauer point out that 'popular values do not clash with most of the values *implied* in the Soviet system itself. On the contrary, there is a general marked congruence between popular values and the goals the system purports to pursue.' As I have already observed, the conflicts emerge only when the regime fails to implement these values.[3]

The dissonant views expressed in the 1930s cannot simply be equated with or regarded as a symptom of unequivocal opposition or non-conformity. This would be to repeat the errors of the regime itself which classified the most trivial criticism as an anti-Soviet subversive act. By relating an anti-Stalin joke or *chastushka*, criticising price rises, or demanding *glasnost'*, an individual was not necessarily rejecting the Soviet system or socialism or Stalin. Simply, different discourses were articulated on different occasions. A critic of one policy could also be an enthusiast of another. Elements of consent and dissent, conformity and resistance, could coexist within the same individual.[4] People moved freely between the two worlds of official culture and what Rigby terms the 'shadow culture'.[5]

This shadow culture evidently flourished in the USSR even during the worst moments of Stalinist authoritarianism (and not just since the 1950s, as Rigby argues). Its existence contributed towards the frailty of the Soviet system, and must have played some role in the emergence of the Khrushchev and Gorbachev reform movements and the eventual demise of the USSR. However, to investigate this question more fully, it will be necessary to take a longer perspective than has been feasible in this study, in order to analyse the nature of popular opinion in earlier and later periods, and to trace continuities and discontinuities. More regionally based studies are also needed if we are to establish to what extent Leningrad was exceptional, and to try to assess the variation in opinion across Russia and/or the USSR.

Another question which deserves more attention is the impact of popular opinion upon propaganda and policy. How far did the regime take account of and respond to popular opinion? It does seem that a conscious effort was made to adjust propaganda in the light of feedback from the grassroots through measures such as the adoption of a more populist tone from about 1934–5. However, without access to high-level documents, it is more difficult to trace the relationship between popular opinion and policy. The regime was clearly prepared to modify some of its policies in a minor way, by granting concessions to peasants and believers, for example. Yet it seems unlikely that the leadership was swayed by the grassroots when it came to major policy issues, for there was no discernible reaction to, for example, the widespread hostility towards the *kolkhozy*. However, on a slightly different point, was the terror itself not, at least in part, the desperate response of a leadership aware of grassroots discontent? These are all important questions which require more research.

The aim of this work has been more modest: to provide a preliminary 'map' of the enormous and mostly uncharted terrain of popular opinion in Russia and the USSR. All the topics touched on here deserve more analysis, and enrichment with new sources. The Soviet Union may be dead, but the discourses of the Soviet period are not merely a question of Russia's past, but a key to understanding its present and future.

Notes

INTRODUCTION

1 N. Timasheff, *The Great Retreat. The Growth and Decline of Communism in Russia*, New York, 1946; Robert Conquest, *The Great Terror*, London, 1968.

2 L. Trotsky, *The Revolution Betrayed*, London, 1937.

3 This is discussed in Conquest, *Great Terror*; *ST*; R. Medvedev, *Let History Judge. The Origins and Consequences of Stalinism*, London, 1972; A. Solzhenitsyn, *The Gulag Archipelago*, 3 vols., New York, 1973. The actual numbers of victims are still a matter of long-running dispute. For some recent discussions, see the contributions to *ST* by A. Nove and S. Wheatcroft; J. A. Getty, G. Rittersporn, and V. Zemskov, 'Victims of the Soviet Penal System in the Pre-War Years. A First Approach on the Basis of Archival Evidence', *American Historical Review*, 98/4, 1993, 1017–49; and Edwin Bacon, *The Gulag at War*, London, 1995, 6–41.

4 A. Blium, *Za kulisami 'Ministerstva Pravdy'*, St Petersburg, 1994, 125–6.

5 This was the definition laid down in article 58.10 of the 1927 criminal code: *Ugolovnyi kodeks RSFSR*, Moscow, 1935, 21.

6 See table 1 (p. 16) for some figures on anti-Soviet agitation cases.

7 GARF 8131/27/71/130–2; TsGAIPD SPb 24/2b/553/6–7.

8 GARF 8131/28/22/20.

9 Until now, these were restricted to memoirs (usually written by intellectuals and members of the elite), accounts in the emigre Menshevik journal *Sotsialisticheskii vestnik*, the Smolensk archive, and interviews with Soviet emigres.

10 For an overview of the debates, see *RR*, 45/4, 1986.

11 A notable exception is M. Fainsod's *Smolensk Under Soviet Rule*, London, 1958.

12 E.g. Sheila Fitzpatrick, *Education and Social Mobility in the Soviet Union 1921–1934*, Cambridge, 1979, and 'Stalin and the Making of a New Elite 1928–1939', *SR*, 38/3, 1979, 377–402; Lewis Siegelbaum, *Stakhanovism and the Politics of Productivity in the USSR 1935–1941*, Cambridge, 1988.

13 Robert Thurston, 'Fear and Belief in the USSR's "Great Terror".

Response to Arrest 1935–1939', *SR*, 45/2, 1986, 213–34, and 'Vezhlivost' i vlast' na sovetskikh fabrikakh i zavodakh. Dostoinstvo rabochikh 1935–1941 gg.', in *Rossiiskaia povsednevnost' 1921–1941 gg. Novye podkhody*, St Petersburg, 1995, 59–67.

14 E.g. Donald Filtzer, *Soviet Workers and Stalinist Industrialisation. The Formation of Modern Soviet Production Relations 1928–1941*, London, 1986; *SP*.

15 Detlev Peukert, *Inside Nazi Germany. Conformity, Opposition, and Racism in Everyday Life*, London, 1989, 65; Luisa Passerini, 'Oral Memory of Fascism', in D. Forgacs (ed.), *Rethinking Italian Fascism*, London, 1986, 185–96, and *Fascism in Popular Memory. The Cultural Experience of the Turin Working Class*, Cambridge, 1987.

16 Stephen Kotkin, *Magnetic Mountain. Stalinism as a Civilisation*, London, 1995. This is partly because of the sources he used. He relied heavily on the official newspaper *Magnitogorskii rabochii*, and did not have access to secret police reports.

17 *Ibid.*, 6.

18 *Ibid.*, 358.

19 P. Kenez, *The Birth of the Propaganda State. Soviet Methods of Mass Mobilisation 1917–1929*, Cambridge, 1985, 353.

20 On rumours, see R. Bauer and D. Gleicher, 'Word-of-Mouth Communication in the Soviet Union', *Public Opinion Quarterly*, 17/3, 1953, 297–310.

21 V. Voloshinov (often attributed to M. Bakhtin), *Marksizm i filosofiia iazyka*, Leningrad, 1930, 27.

22 K. Clark and M. Holquist, *Mikhail Bakhtin*, London, 1984, 305.

23 M. Bakhtin, *Tvorchestvo Franzua Rable i narodnaia kul'tura srednevekov'ia i renessansa*, Moscow, 1965, 5–16.

24 T. Rigby, 'Reconceptualising the Soviet System', in S. White, A. Pravda, and Z. Gitelman (eds.), *Developments in Soviet and Post-Soviet Politics*, 2nd edn, London, 1992, 313–14.

25 Soviets and trade unions were also involved in this activity, although apparently much less so in the 1930s than earlier.

26 For more on the history of the party Information Department, see V. Anikeev, 'Partiinaia informatsiia v period podgotovki Oktiabria', *Voprosy istorii KPSS*, 1, 1970, 95–104; A. Chernov, *Partiinaia informatsiia. Voprosy istorii i teorii*, Moscow, 1987. After the revolution various departments within the TsK assumed responsibility for coordinating the exchange of information on all subjects between the centre and periphery. In April 1924, at a time of intra-party conflict following the 'Declaration of the 46', a specific Information Department was created. According to a report to the Thirteenth Party Congress, it had been established because 'at the most critical moments in the life of the party, our central apparatus turned out to be inadequately informed about the mood in the localities': *Trinadtsatyi s"ezd VKP(b). Stenografi-*

cheskii otchet, Moscow, 1924, 134. The department underwent several mutations during the 1920s and 1930s, but its basic functions remained the same: to inform the centre about the party's work in the regions, to communicate the centre's policies to the regions, and to prepare reports on specific economic and political questions, including reports on the mood of the masses.

27 416/1/21/15–16.

28 25/2/31/4, 9–10; 25/2/120/112–16; 24/2v/3721/155–9; 25/2/2225/34– 45.

29 Unfortunately, we have little detail about the NKVD's procedures. In a VChK instruction of 23 February 1922, the Cheka's role in informa- tion-gathering was described in the following way:

> The most important task of state information is the illustration of the feelings of all groups in the population, and of the factors influencing changes in these feelings ... For us it is unusually important to know how these measures [i.e. NEP] are accepted by various groups of the population (workers, peasants, soldiers, petty bourgeoisie, etc.), to what extent these groups understand the sense of what is happening, how it is reflected in their consciousness.
>
> The second task of state information is surveillance of the growth of petty- bourgeois elements, of manifestations of petty-bourgeois feelings amongst the worker, party, union, Red Army masses, of cases of the corrosion of the soviet and party apparatus by petty-bourgeois elements ...
>
> The fourth, purely Chekist task of state information involves informing the centre about manifestations of active and secret counter-revolution.

> Cited in V. S. Izmozik, *Glaza i ushi rezhima. Gosudarstvennyi politicheskii kontrol' za naseleniem sovetskoi Rossii v 1918–1928 godakh*, St Petersburg, 1995, 108.

30 I am grateful to B. Starkov for this reference.

31 Memoirs include Evgeniia Ginsburg, *Into the Whirlwind*, London, 1989; Viktor Kravchenko, *I Chose Freedom. The Personal and Political Life of a Soviet Official*, London, 1949; and Andrew Smith, *I Was a Soviet Worker*, London, 1938. Diaries are only beginning to be published. See V. Garros, N. Korenevskaya, and T. Lahusen (eds.), *Intimacy and Terror. Soviet Diaries of the 1930s*, New York, 1995.

32 E.g. the legal press which reported cases of anti-semitism.

33 416/1/222/40–10b (p/34).

34 TsGAIPD, TsGA SPb (St Petersburg); GANO (Novosibirsk); GARF, RTsKhIDNI, TsKhDMO (Moscow). Richer collections can probably be found in the presently inaccessible Archive of the President of the Russian Federation (APRF). Two NKVD special reports on popular discussion of the draft constitution from this archive were published in *Neizvestnaia Rossiia XX vek*, 3 vols., II, Moscow, 1992, 272–81.

35 See *Neizvestnaia Rossiia XX vek*, II, 200–52, 282–94; III, Moscow, 1993, 324–58; *Dokumenty svidetel'stvuiut. Iz istorii derevni nakanune i v khode kollektivizatsii 1927–1932 gg.*, Moscow, 1989. A recent collection of

reports covering the period 1921–91 is Nicholas Werth and Gael Moullec, *Rapports secrets soviétiques 1921–1991. La Société russe dans les documents confidentials*, Paris, 1994; N. Lebina, 'Problemy sotsializatsii rabochei molodezhi sovetskoi Rossii 20–30-kh gg.', doctoral dissertation, St Petersburg, 1994; S. Iarov, 'Kronshtadtskii miatezh v vospriiatii petrogradskikh rabochikh', in *Zven'ia*, 2 vols., II, Moscow and St Petersburg, 1992.

36 E.g. in 24/2v/4306/130, 144 (n/40).

37 24/5/2696/48 (p/35).

38 24/2g/221/12–13 (l/40).

39 See Getty, Rittersporn, and Zemskov, 'Victims of the Soviet Penal System in the Pre-War Years'.

40 GARF 8131/28/6/4–6.

41 For more on this question, see S. R. Davies, 'Propaganda and Popular Opinion in Soviet Russia 1934–1941', DPhil. dissertation, University of Oxford, 1994, chapter 2.

42 One approach would be to use oral history. However, this would require a separate project in its own right and, in any case, oral history is most interesting for what it reveals about the way people remember. It is unlikely that one could recapture the language of the 1930s from a distance of sixty years.

43 Ian Kershaw, *Popular Opinion and Political Dissent in the Third Reich*, Oxford, 1983, 6. Unger, who attempted to compare the reporting of opinion in Germany and the USSR (using somewhat meagre evidence from the Smolensk archives), argues that the Soviet reports were 'rather more truthful and realistic': A. Unger, *The Totalitarian Party. Party and People in Nazi Germany and Soviet Russia*, Cambridge, 1974, 252.

44 I did not find similar material in such quantities in other archives; however, some of the material I was able to locate in Moscow and Novosibirsk has been included.

45 J. Rossman, 'Worker Resistance Under Stalin. Class and Gender in the Textile Mills of Ivanovo Industrial Region 1926–1941', Ph.D dissertation, University of California at Berkeley, forthcoming; *SP*.

46 In 1935, five of its districts were joined to Kalinin *oblast'* and in 1937 eighteen were joined to Vologda *oblast'*. In 1928, Murmansk *okrug* left the *oblast'*, and in 1940 Karelia joined it.

47 *Leningradskaia oblast'. Istoricheskii ocherk*, Leningrad, 1986; *Ekonomiko-statisticheskii spravochnik Leningradskoi oblasti*, Leningrad, 1932.

48 N. A. Ivinitskii, *Kollektivizatsiia i raskulachivanie (nachalo 30-kh godov)*, Moscow, 1994, 15–17, 80, 93.

49 24/5/2293/1, 10; *Leningradskaia oblast' v tsifrakh*, Leningrad, 1936, 16.

50 *Leningradskaia oblast'. Istoricheskii ocherk*; *Vsesoiuznaia perepis' naseleniia 1939 goda. Osnovnye itogi*, Moscow, 1992; Iu. Poliakov, V. Zhiromskaia, and I. Kiselev, 'Polveka molchania. Vsesoiuznaia perepis' naseleniia 1937 goda', *Sotsiologicheskie issledovaniia*, 6, 1990; *Leningrad v tsifrakh*, Leningrad,

1935, 1936, 1938; *Leningradskaia oblast' v tsifrakh*, Leningrad, 1935, 1936; *Ekonomiko-statisticheskii spravochnik Leningradskoi oblasti.*

1 WORKERS, THE ECONOMY, AND LABOUR POLICY

1 On workers' attitudes before 1934, see H. Kuromiya, *Stalin's Industrial Revolution. Politics and Workers 1928–1932*, Cambridge, 1988; Chris Ward, *Russia's Cotton Workers and the New Economic Policy*, Cambridge, 1990; W. Chase, *Workers, Society, and the Soviet State. Labor and Life in Moscow 1918–1929*, Urbana, Ill., 1987.

2 Emigres interviewed for the Harvard Project also favoured a welfare state and state control of the economy: A. Inkeles and R. Bauer, *The Soviet Citizen. Daily Life in a Totalitarian Society*, Cambridge, Mass., 1961, chapter 10.

3 On the standard of living of workers, see Siegelbaum, *Stakhanovism*, 214–23; V. Andrle, *Workers in Stalin's Russia*, Hemel Hempstead, 1988, 36–51; John Barber, 'The Standard of Living of Soviet Industrial Workers 1928–1940', in C. Bettelheim (ed.), *L'Industrialisation de l'URSS dans les années trente*, Paris, 1982, 109–22; Barber, 'Housing Conditions of Soviet Industrial Workers 1928–1941', paper presented to SIPS seminar, CREES, Birmingham, 1981.

4 Naum Jasny, *The Soviet 1956 Statistical Handbook. A Commentary*, East Lansing, Mich., 1957, 41. See also E. Zaleski, *Stalinist Planning for Economic Growth 1933–1952*, Chapel Hill, 1980, 158, and Janet Chapman, *Real Wages in Soviet Russia Since 1928*, Cambridge, Mass., 1963, 196.

5 Barber, 'The Standard of Living', 117.

6 O. Shkaratan, 'Material'noe blagosostoianie rabochego klassa SSSR v perekhodnyi period ot kapitalizma k sotsializmu', *Istoriia SSSR*, 3, 1964, 39.

7 *Leningrad v tsifrakh*, 1935, 1936.

8 *Leningrad v tsifrakh*, 1936, 81; 24/2v/2423/53. By 1940, the average had risen to 6m^2 in the towns of the *oblast'* and 5.2m^2 in workers' settlements (24/2v/4641/28).

9 *P*, 21 January 1934; *LP*, 17 January 1934.

10 I. V. Stalin, *Sochineniia*, XIII, Moscow, 1951, 340–60.

11 25/5/38/43 (p/34).

12 25/5/38/51 (p/34).

13 25/5/38/41–50 (p/34).

14 GANO 3/2/620/233–4 (l/34).

15 The significance of bread is highlighted by R. E. F. Smith and David Christian, *Bread and Salt. A Social and Economic History of Food and Drink in Russia*, Cambridge, 1984, and William Moskoff, *The Bread of Affliction. The Food Supply in the USSR During World War II*, Cambridge, 1990, 6–7.

16 E. Osokina, *Ierarkhiia potrebleniia. O zhizni liudei v usloviiakh stalinskogo snabzheniia 1928–1935 gg.*, Moscow, 1993.

17 *Trud*, 28 May 1934. The official reason for the price rise was the poor harvest in some regions.

18 25/5/39/12 (p/34); 24/2v/726/2–5 (p/34) on the mood amongst railway workers; *Sputnik agitatora*, August 1934, 2; 24/5/2712/1–4 (p/34).

19 25/5/46/165 (p/34).

20 25/5/45/105 (p/34).

21 GANO 3/9/36/82 (p/34).

22 *LP*, 2 January 1935.

23 However, bread prices in the commercial retail network fell by about a third.

24 Solomon Schwartz, *Labour in the Soviet Union*, London, 1953, 157–8.

25 24/2v/1049/17 (p/35).

26 This proportion was not much lower than that in the aftermath of the civil war – in June 1922, the figure for Leningrad was 62.8 per cent. This fell to 52.6 per cent by the end of the year. In the period 1923 to 1928, the figure ranged from 43 to 48.9 per cent: Shkaratan, 'Material'noe blagosostoianie', 27.

27 *Ibid.*, 40.

28 Osokina, *Ierarkhiia potrebleniia*, 39; Andrle, *Workers*, 36.

29 I. E. Zelenin, 'Byl li "kolkhoznyi neonep"?', *Otechestvennaia istoriia*, 1994/2, 114 (citing RTsKhIDNI 558/1/5324).

30 24/5/2696/93 (p/35).

31 24/2v/1200/66–73 (n/35).

32 N. Jasny, *Soviet Industrialisation 1928–1952*, Chicago, 1961, 170.

33 2/2/552/7 (p/35).

34 TsGA SPb 7384/2/49/262–76 (n/35); TsGAIPD SPb 24/2v/1373/1–5 (p/35).

35 *KPSS v resoliutsiiakh i resheniiakh s"ezdov, konferentsii, i plenumov TsK*, Moscow, 1985, VI, 120.

36 Alec Nove, *An Economic History of the USSR*, Harmondsworth, 1986, 251.

37 24/2v/4036/156–7 (p/40).

38 24/2v/1518/183 (l/35).

39 24/2v/1518/214–15 (l/35).

40 24/2v/1518/9; 11–13 (l/35).

41 *Trud*, 23 April 1935.

42 *Pervoe vsesoiuznoe soveshchanie rabochikh i rabotnits-stakhanovtsev, 14–17 noiabria 1935. Stenograficheskii otchet*, Moscow, 1935, 178.

43 25/10/36/68 (p/36).

44 Siegelbaum, *Stakhanovism*, 172.

45 24/2v/1004/77 (p/35); 563/1/799/2 (p/35).

46 GARF 8131/27/158/35.

47 24/2v/1200/273 (n/35).

48 Siegelbaum, *Stakhanovism*, 196; *Sovetskaia zakonnost'*, 7, 1936, 69.

49 R. Thurston, 'The Stakhanovite Movement. The Background to the Great Terror in the Factories, 1935–1938', in *ST*, 142–60.

50 As Siegelbaum points out, 'an aristocracy [of labour] comprising upward of 25 per cent of all industrial workers is no aristocracy at all': *Stakhanovism*, 168. On changes of status, see *ibid.*, 184.
51 563/1/799/9, 35 (p/35).
52 24/2v/1200/278 (n/35).
53 24/2v/1830/6–7, 104 (n/36).
54 24/2v/1373/104–5 (p/35); 24/2v/1200/272 (n/35); 25/10/10/18 (p/35).
55 F. Benvenuti, 'Stakhanovism and Stalinism 1934–1938', paper presented to SIPS seminar, CREES, Birmingham, 1988, 16; Siegelbaum, *Stakhanovism*, 87–8.
56 TsGA SPb 7384/2/49/426–32 (n/35); TsGAIPD SPb 24/2v/1830/107, 7 (n/36).
57 Filtzer, *Soviet Workers*, 138; 25/10/27/360b (p/36); 24/2v/1837/184–96 (n/36).
58 24/2v/2499/64 (n/37).
59 Roberta Manning, 'The Soviet Economic Crisis of 1936–1940 and the Great Purges', in *ST*, 116–41.
60 24/2v/1837/183–93 (n/36).
61 Nove, *Economic History*, 255.
62 24/2v/2060/24–41 (p/36); 25/5/83/5–12 (p/36).
63 24/2v/1607/81–2 (p/36).
64 24/2v/2060/149 (p/36).
65 24/10/157/111–12 (p/37).
66 Manning, 'The Soviet Economic Crisis', in *ST*.
67 24/2v/2224/9–10 (l/37).
68 24/2v/2664/273–6 (p/37).
69 24/2v/2665/28–9, 35 (p/37).
70 *LP*, 20 July 1937.
71 24/2v/2494/114–24 (n/37). The turnout at the actual demonstration attracted more than a million people, according to the regime's internal reports.
72 1200/3/164/103 (p/37).
73 1200/3/171/89 (p/37).
74 24/2g/149/129–32 (l/38).
75 *Sputnik agitatora*, 18, 1938, 42.
76 25/10/113/30 (p/39).
77 24/2b/432/44–5 (p/38).
78 2/2/618/245–6 (p/38).
79 24/2v/3547/98–107 (n/39).
80 24/2v/3720/352 (p/39).
81 24/2v/3563/30–9; 58–62 (n/39); 24/2v/3721/178–93, 200 (p/39).
82 24/2v/3570/77, 84 (n/39).
83 24/2v/4016/1–2, 70; 116, 149 (p/40); 24/2v/4300/60, 96–9 (n/40); 24/2v/3569/128 (n/39). See also the letters to party leaders in E. A.

Osokina (ed.), 'Krizis snabzheniia 1939–1941 gg. v pis'makh sovetskikh liudei', *Voprosy istorii*, 1, 1996, 3–23.

84 24/2v/4036/73–6 (l/40).
85 24/2v/4300/90 (n/40).
86 24/2v/4300/47, 77–8 (n/40).
87 E. A. Osokina, 'Liudi i vlast' v usloviiakh krizisa snabzheniia 1939–1941 gody', *Otechestvennaia istoriia*, 1995/3, 16–32.
88 24/2v/4020/276–7, 288–90 (p/40); 24/2v/4300/273 (n/40).
89 24/2v/4024/125–6, 224–5 (p/40).
90 *LP*, 5 July 1937.
91 *LP*, 22 September 1937, 11 July 1937.
92 See Siegelbaum, *Stakhanovism*, 261; Filtzer, *Soviet Workers*, 168.
93 24/2v/3547/114–23 (n/39).
94 24/2v/3720/29–35, 121–5 (p/39).
95 24/2v/3721/128–33 (p/39).
96 Timasheff, *The Great Retreat*, 139.
97 24/2v/4313/349 (n/40).
98 24/2v/4828/1–2 (n/41).
99 See also Filtzer, *Soviet Workers*, 233–53.
100 E.g. 24/2v/4029/197, 250, 251 (p/40); 24/2v/4031/50, 97 (p/40); 24/2v/4032/29 (p/40); 24/2v/4035/10 (p/40); 24/2v/4306/42 (n/40); 24/2v/4313/74, 247, 249, 252 (n/40).
101 24/2v/4029/198, 239 (p/40).
102 24/2v/4313/239–40, 280, 275 (n/40).
103 24/2v/4027/107 (p/40); 24/2v/4300/432 (n/40); 24/2v/4306/158 (n/40); 24/2v/4313/472 (n/40).
104 24/2v/4306/127, 142 (n/40).
105 24/2v/4313/239, 270–81 (n/40).
106 24/2v/4306/122–217 (n/40). Sunday was also restored as the day off which compounded the feeling that everything was going backwards: 'Generals and admirals have appeared; they're bringing back the old week, Sunday will be a day off, the only thing is – there aren't enough priests' (*ibid.*).
107 24/2v/4300/427 (n/40); 24/2v/4306/130–1 (n/40).
108 24/2v/4306/125–9, 192–4 (n/40); 24/2v/4029/147 (p/40); 24/2v/4032/149 (n/40); 24/2v/4037/33, 58 (p/40).
109 24/2v/4306/177 (n/40).
110 24/2v/4809/2 (p/41).
111 24/2v/4811/1–3 (p/41).

2 PEASANTS AND THE *KOLKHOZ*

1 *SP*, 26–8.
2 Nove, *Economic History*, 246–7, 259; 24/2v/3538/87–9.
3 24/2v/1846/13 (n/36).

4 The *chastushka* originated in the middle of the nineteenth century, although the term was not coined by Gleb Uspenskii until 1889. It was sung alone or in groups, mainly by young people, either at dances or other festivities, or while walking or working or rocking the baby. One source suggests that they were traditionally composed mainly by women, especially unmarried women. The main themes of *chastushki* were customarily love, satire, and, more rarely, social-political themes – the latter only constituted about 3–5% of all *chastushki* according to one account, even less according to others. Pre-revolutionary workers' versions were apparently more socially aware than those of peasants, and sometimes contained notes of protest. The *chastushka* usually consists of four lines (although two-, six-, eight-, ten-, or twelve-line versions are also possible): A. Bobrov and N. Starshinov (eds.), *Samotsvetnaia chastushka*, Moscow, 1992; E. Eleonskoi (ed.), *Sbornik veliko-russkikh chastushek*, Moscow, 1914; Z. Vlasova and A. Gorelov (eds.), *Chastushka v zapisakh sovetskogo vremeni*, Moscow, 1965; V. Bokov and V. Bakhtin (eds.), *Chastushka*, Moscow, 1966.

5 See *SP*, 270–1, 290–2.
6 к598/1/5407/80–5 (k/35); 24/2v/1190/88 (n/35); к598/1/5407/85 (k/35).
7 24/2v/1595/157 (p/36).
8 See *SP*, introduction, for more on this process.
9 24/5/2291/4 (p/34).
10 24/2v/1187/85–9 (n/35); Antony Netting, 'Images and Ideas in Peasant Art', in Ben Eklof and Stephen Frank (eds.), *The World of the Russian Peasant*, London, 1990; *SP*, 136–9.
11 24/2v/1190/106 (n/35); 24/2v/1855/208, 214 (n/36); 24/2v/1855/214 (n/36).
12 24/10/118/127 (p/35); 24/2v/1829/60–70 (n/36).
13 GANO 47/5/200/41–51, 69 (p/36).
14 Manning, 'The Soviet Economic Crisis', in *ST*, 118–19.
15 24/2v/1841/53 (n/36); 24/2v/1844/27–8 (n/36).
16 24/2v/1859/95–6 (l/36).
17 24/2v/2487/7–80b, 98–9 (n/37); 24/2v/2494/113 (l/37); 24/2v/2491/130ob (n/37).
18 24/2v/1859/95 (n/36); 24/2v/2490/81–3, 113 (n/37); 24/2v/2487/90 (n/37).
19 24/2v/2490/21, 24, 28, 106 (n/37); 24/2v/2486/184 (n/37); 24/2v/2487/68 (n/37); 24/2v/2491/81–2 (n/37).
20 24/2v/3019/43–50 (n/38).
21 24/2v/3549/155 (n/39).
22 24/2v/3025/120 (p/38).
23 24/2v/3539/14.
24 24/2v/3629/83 (p/39); 24/2v/3560/96–7 (n/39).
25 24/5/4177/42, 58–9 (p/39).

26   24/2v/3629/54–7, 109–24, 132–5, 159–62 (p/39); 24/2v/3560/100–2, 135, 150–1, 157 (n/39).

27   24/2v/4301/61–72 (n/40).

28   24/2v/4316/73 (n/40).

29   24/2v/4813/208–9 (p/41).

30   24/5/5435/126–7 (p/41).

31   24/5/5435/73–4 (p/41).

32   24/5/5435/125 (p/41).

33   According to Alexander Dallin, many *kolkhozniki* initially welcomed the German invaders: *German Rule in Russia 1941–1945*, London, 1957, 370–1.

3 WOMEN, FAMILY POLICY, EDUCATION

1   On family policy before 1936, see Rudolf Schlesinger, *The Family in the USSR*, London, 1949, and Wendy Goldman, *Women, State, and Revolution. Soviet Family Policy and Social Life 1917–1936*, Cambridge, 1993.

2   Cf. Steve Smith, 'Class and Gender. Women's Strikes in St Petersburg 1855–1917 and in Shanghai 1895–1927', *Social History*, 19/2, 1994, 141–68. Smith argues that there were no great differences between men's and women's strikes.

3   A good survey of women in the countryside in this period has been provided by Roberta Manning: 'Women in the Soviet Countryside on the Eve of World War II', in B. Farnsworth and L. Viola (eds.), *Russian Peasant Women*, Oxford, 1992, 206–35.

4   24/2v/1366/82–90; *Leningrad v tsifrakh*, 1935, 108.

5   Gail Lapidus, *Women in Soviet Society*, London, 1978, 211.

6   David Hoffmann, *Peasant Metropolis. Social Identities in Moscow 1929–1941*, London, 1994, 119–24.

7   25/5/83/7 (p/36); 24/2v/2286/77 (p/37); 24/2v/2282/66 (p/37); 24/2v/3634/24 (p/39).

8   1200/3/129/98 (p/35).

9   The use of canteens also declined sharply from 1935 (see chapter 1).

10   Hoffmann, *Peasant Metropolis*, 144.

11   Cf. the character of female peasants' resistance before the revolution. See Barbara Alpern Engel, 'Women, Men, and the Languages of Peasant Resistance 1870–1907', in Stephen Frank and Mark Steinberg (eds.), *Cultures in Flux. Lower-Class Values, Practices, and Resistance in Late Imperial Russia*, Princeton, 1994, 34–53. Koenker notes that in the 1920s women were also more likely to speak up at factory meetings about questions of everyday life: Diane Koenker, 'Men Against Women on the Shop Floor in Early Soviet Russia. Gender and Class in the Soviet Workplace', *American Historical Review*, December 1995, 1443.

12   24/5/2286/10 (p/37).

13   25/5/46/62–3 (p/34).

14   24/2v/2064/46 (p/36).

15 к598/1/5407/22 (k/35).
16 Trotsky, *Revolution Betrayed*, 117.
17 24/5/2286/46 (p/34); 25/5/48/52–3 (p/34); 25/5/45/73 (p/34); 24/5/2286/45 (p/34); 24/2v/1373/2 (p/35).
18 24/2v/1366/4, 27–8 (p/35); 25/5/83/5 (p/36).
19 Sheila Fitzpatrick, *The Cultural Front. Power and Culture in Revolutionary Russia*, London, 1992, 231–3.
20 25/10/27/42 (p/36); 25/10/35/49 (p/36); 24/2v/1607/213 (p/36); 24/2v/1748/166–7 (p/36).
21 24/2v/1180/54. A divorce could be obtained simply by completing a form; not even the consent of the spouse was required.
22 See Janet Evans, 'The Communist Party of the Soviet Union and the Women's Question. The Case of the 1936 Decree "In Defence of Mother and Child"', *Journal of Contemporary History*, 16/4, 1981, 757–75.
23 Richard Stites, *The Women's Liberation Movement in Russia. Feminism, Nihilism, and Bolshevism 1860–1930*, Princeton, 1978, 371, 384.
24 24/2v/1598/242–4 (p/36).
25 Interviews with refugees for the Harvard project confirm this. See Robert Thurston, 'The Soviet Family During the Great Terror 1935–1941', *Soviet Studies*, 43/3, 1991, 557; Kent Geiger, *The Family in Soviet Russia*, Cambridge, Mass., 1968, 99.
26 24/2v/2500/94; 24/2v/3540/63.
27 24/2v/1598/237–46 (p/36).
28 24/2v/3721/137 (p/39); 2/2/618/346–7 (p/39); 24/2v/3547/117–18 (n/37).
29 24/2v/3499/113–14 (p/39).
30 24/2v/4313/238–9 (n/40).
31 24/2v/4829/3–5 (this same report recommended producing more condoms to fight abortion; in 1939 10,425 condoms were sold in Leningrad, compared with only 2,591 in 1940); *LP*, 21 July 1940.
32 25/2a/110/3; 24/2v/4285/59; Goldman, *Women*, 293.
33 *SP*, 232.
34 See Elise Kimmerling, 'Civil Rights and Social Policy in Soviet Russia 1918–1936', *RR*, 42/1, 1982, 27.
35 24/2v/1598/1 (p/36); 25/10/10/8–10; 26 (p/35); 24/2v/1829/22–4 (n/36).
36 Fitzpatrick, *Education and Social Mobility*, 235–8.
37 Subsequently, however, girls were also made liable, although they only formed one quarter of the first contingent of 600,000 enrolled in October and November 1940: Mervyn Matthews, 'The "State Labour Reserves". An Episode in Soviet Social History', *Slavonic and East European Review*, 61/2, 1983, 238–41.
38 24/2v/4035/22, 45, 137, 139, 141 (p/40).
39 2/2/637/12, 115 (p/39); 24/2v/4035/44, 136 (p/40).
40 24/2v/4037/1–2 (p/40).

41 Matthews, 'The "State Labour Reserves"', 241–2.
42 24/2v/4316/198–9 (n/40). The reference is presumably to Nicholas II.

4 RELIGION AND THE NATIONALITIES QUESTION

1   Jerry Hough in Sheila Fitzpatrick (ed.), *Cultural Revolution in Russia 1928–1931*, Bloomington, Ind., 1978, 242; Trotsky, *Revolution Betrayed*, 148.
2   N. Timasheff, *Religion in Soviet Russia 1917–1942*, London, 1943, 46.
3   24/2v/1923/79 (p/36); 24/2v/1610/48 (p/36); 24/10/267/170b–18 (p/37); 24/2v/2424/138 (p/37).
4   24/10/267/24 (p/37); 24/2v/2490/61 (n/37).
5   24/10/268/9 (p/37). Primitive forms of religion and superstition were common in the countryside, and peasants would call upon the services of *kolduny* or witches when they or their animals were sick: 24/10/268/4–5 (p/37).
6   Lebina, 'Problemy sotsializatsii', 184; *Sputnik kommunista v derevne*, 4, 1936, 19; Poliakov, *et al.*, 'Polveka molchania', 7, 69. The question itself created such a confusion and anxiety that one should be slightly cautious about the reliability of these figures.
7   TsGA SPb 7384/2/39/39–46; TsGA SPb 7384/2/54/32–6; TsGAIPD SPb 24/2v/2494/117–19.
8   24/2v/1923/79–80 (p/36); к598/1/5407/25–6 (k/35).
9   Dimitry Pospielovsky, *The Russian Orthodox Church Under the Soviet Regime 1917–1982*, 3 vols., New York, 1984, 1, 103; 24/2v/1923/79 (p/36).
10 *SP*, 205.
11 24/2v/1923/79–80 (p/36).
12 TsGA SPb 7384/2/39/39–46.
13 24/2v/2494/117–19 (n/37).
14 24/2v/2494/126–7 (n/37); 24/2v/2272/32–7 (p/37).
15 On the role of church holidays in the 1920s, see Helmut Altricher, 'Insoluble Conflicts. Village Life Between Revolution and Collectivization', in S. Fitzpatrick, A. Rabinowitch, and R. Stites (eds.), *Russia in the Era of NEP. Explorations in Soviet Society and Culture*, Bloomington, Ind., 1991, 195–200.
16 24/8/249/3–4 (p/36); 24/2v/1595/13–15 (p/36); 24/8/250/75 (p/35); 24/10/262/3–5 (p/37)
17 24/8/250/75 (p/35); 24/2v/1610/50 (p/36).
18 24/2v/2494/117 (n/37).
19 TsGA SPb 7384/2/39/40–1.
20 24/2v/1844/181 (n/36); 24/2v/1846/46–7 (n/36); 24/2v/1855/202 (n/36).
21 *Voprosy istorii*, 6, 1993, 8.
22 24/2v/1610/49 (p/36); *Sputnik kommunista v derevne*, 4, 1936, 20; 24/2v/1772/21 (p/36); 24/2v/2286/49 (p/37); 24/2v/2272/33 (p/37).

23 24/2v/1772/21 (p/36).

24 24/2v/2272/35–6 (p/37).

25 On the census, see Catherine Merridale, 'The 1937 Census and the Limits of Stalinist Rule', *Historical Journal*, 39/1, 1996, 225–40.

26 Poliakov, *et al.*, 'Polveka molchania', 6, 7, 12; 24/2v/2486/36–8, 83–4 (n/37); 24/2v/2423/110–13 (p/37).

27 24/2v/2482/74 (p/37); 24/10/263/40 (p/37); 24/2v/2424/137 (p/37); 24/2v/2282/85 (p/37); 24/10/297/4–5 (p/37); 24/10/303/97 (p/37); *SP*, 282–3.

28 24/10/267/43–430b (p/37).

29 E.g. 24/5/3202/92 (p/36); 24/2v/3633/140 (p/39); *SP*, 214. On the history of apocalyptic rumours in Russia, see L. Viola, 'The Peasant Nightmare. Visions of Apocalypse in the Soviet Countryside', *Journal of Modern History*, 62, 1990, 747–70.

30 24/5/3202/92 (p/36); 24/2v/2665/56–7 (p/37).

31 TsGA SPb 7384/33/50/87–8 (l/38).

32 TsGA SPb 7384/33/50/99–990b (l/38).

33 24/2v/3020/111 (n/38); 24/2v/2843/77–9 (p/38).

34 Pospielovsky, *The Russian Orthodox Church*, 66.

35 Stalin, *Sochineniia*, XIII, 361.

36 An alternative explanation is that the reporting of such feelings in the countryside was less efficient, because of the party's weakness in the *oblast'*.

37 The remaining 3.6 per cent consisted of Jews: 0.5 per cent; Veps: 0.5 per cent, Belorussians: 0.4 per cent, Germans: 0.4 per cent; Tatars: 0.4 per cent; Latvians: 0.3 per cent, and others: 1.1 per cent.

38 24/2v/2490/62 (n/37); 24/2a/85/1–10 (p/37).

39 *Leningrad v tsifrakh*, 1935, 9. The figures include only the three main ethnic groups.

40 The remaining 5.0 per cent consisted of Belorussians: 1.0 per cent; Tatars: 1.0 per cent; Poles: 0.6 per cent; Estonians: 0.5 per cent; Germans: 0.3 per cent; Finns: 0.3 per cent, and others: 1.3 per cent.

41 All 1939 statistics are from *Vsesoiuznaia perepis' naseleniia 1939 goda*.

42 See Fainsod, *Smolensk*, 43, 48.

43 See the OGPU reports from 1926 on anti-semitism in *Neizvestnaia Rossiia XX vek*, III, 327–52.

44 Iu. Larin, *Evrei i antisemitizm v SSSR*, Moscow, 1929; L. Liadov, *O vrazhde k evreiam*, Moscow, 1927.

45 *Biulleten' TsKK VKP(b) i NK RKI SSSR i RSFSR*, January 1929, 26; S. Fitzpatrick, *The Russian Revolution*, Oxford, 1982, 132–3.

46 An OGPU report of 1934 listed anti-semitism along with hooliganism, gang violence, criminal behaviour, and sexual promiscuity as examples of anti-social behaviour prevalent amongst young workers, apprentices, and school-children. Between August 1933 and April 1934, 648 Kom-

somol members in Tsentral'nyi district were called to account for anti-semitism: 24/2v/772/2–10 (n/34).

47 See the articles in *Sovetskaia iustitsiia*, and the letters in *LP*, 23 July 1936 and 16 September 1937.

48 Michael Beizer, 'The Jewish Minority in Leningrad 1917–1939', paper presented to BASEES conference, Cambridge, England, March 1995, 8, 10.

49 *Ibid.*, 10.

50 25/5/55/40 (p/34); 24/5/2288/70 (p/34).

51 24/5/2288/3, 44 (p/34); 25/5/51/3 (p/34); к598/1/5343/17 (k/34).

52 24/2v/727/367 (l/35).

53 24/2v/1543/10 (l/35).

54 24/2v/1518/9–10 (l/35).

55 24/2v/1855/203–4 (n/36).

56 24/2v/2499/99, 100 (n/37).

57 24/2v/2665/4 (p/37).

58 24/2v/2061/141 (p/36); 24/2v/2267/14, 250b (p/37); к598/1/5423/11 (k/37).

59 24/2v/2064/46 (p/36); 24/2v/2665/4 (p/37); 25/10/17/80 (p/35); 24/2v/4306/198 (n/40); 24/2v/2499/125 (n/37); 24/2v/3562/324, 343 (n/39).

60 к598/1/5386/171 (k/35).

61 24/2v/2286/72 (p/37); 24/2v/2499/105 (n/37).

62 24/5/2289/131 (p/34); к598/1/5343/17, 19 (k/34).

63 24/5/3202/92 (p/36).

64 M. Cherniavsky, *Tsar and People. Studies in Russian Myths*, London, 1961.

65 Jeffrey Brooks, *When Russia Learned to Read. Literacy and Popular Literature 1861–1917*, Princeton, 1985, 214.

66 Hubertus Jahn, 'For Tsar and Fatherland? Russian Popular Culture and the First World War', in Frank and Steinberg, *Cultures in Flux*, 142–5.

67 24/2v/2286/96 (p/37); 24/2v/3178/23 (p/38); 24/2v/2665/178 (p/37).

68 24/2v/2499/81 (n/37); 24/2v/2286/13 (p/37).

69 It is of course not impossible that these were written by more literate workers or peasants.

70 24/2g/47/197 (l/37); 24/2v/2500/62 (n/37); 24/2b/323/67–9 (n/37); 24/2v/2499/29 (n/37); 24/2v/3569/257–8 (n/39).

5 INTERNATIONAL RELATIONS

1 24/5/2714/30 (p/35); 24/2v/1848/112 (n/36); 24/2v/2490/21–3, 107 (n/37).

2 24/2v/2665/57 (p/37); 24/2v/2490/23 (n/37); *SP*, 293–4.

3 24/5/2291/20 (p/34).

4 24/5/2291/21 (p/34). These are the last few lines of a poem which is
   cited in full in chapter 7, p. 117.

5 Oleg Khlevniuk suggests that Stalin was also well aware of this link in
   'The Objectives of the Great Terror 1937–1938', in J. Cooper, M.
   Perrie, and E. A. Rees (eds.), *Soviet History 1917–1953. Essays in Honour of
   R. W. Davies*, London, 1993, 174.

6 TsGA SPb 7384/2/35/92 (n/34); TsGAIPD SPb 24/2v/3631/168 (p/
   39); 24/5/4897/61 (p/40); 24/2v/3723/12 (p/39).

7 24/2v/3561/210 (n/39).

8 24/2v/1855/208 (n/36); 24/10/157/111–12 (p/36); 24/2v/2064/46–7
   (p/36).

9 24/2v/2487/94 (n/37); 24/2v/2490/22 (n/37); 24/2v/3721/201 (p/39);
   24/2v/3569/128 (n/39).

10 к598/1/5423/266–7 (k/37).

11 24/2v/1190/109–10 (n/35).

12 24/2v/2060/82 (p/36).

13 The 'black raven' is a reference to the vehicles used by the NKVD; 24/
   2v/1833/34 (n/36).

14 24/2v/2487/58 (n/37); 24/2v/2491/44 (n/37).

15 The term *muzhik* (literally, 'peasant') is often applied approvingly to
   'real', i.e. strong, Russian men.

16 24/2v/3721/186 (p/39).

17 It is interesting that a similar phenomenon took place in fascist Italy.
   However, there the subversive symbols were the Red Flag or hammer
   and sickle which were daubed on walls, especially in toilets: Franco
   Andreucci, ' "Subversiveness" and Anti-Fascism in Italy', in Raphael
   Samuel (ed.), *People's History and Socialist Theory*, London, 1981, 199–204.

18 Jane Degras (ed.), *Soviet Documents on Foreign Policy*, III, *1933–1941*,
   Oxford, 1953, 367.

19 24/2v/3721/233–6 (p/39); 24/2v/3631/16–17, 83–6 (p/39).

20 24/2v/3561/202 (n/39); 24/2v/3560/222 (n/39).

21 24/2v/3561/203 (n/39).

22 24/2v/3562/340 (n/39).

23 24/2v/3631/140–3 (p/39); 24/2v/3721/260–2, 271 (p/39).

24 24/2v/3721/278–9; 291–2 (p/39); 24/2v/3562/242–3, 256, 301 (n/39).

25 24/2v/3562/330 (n/39); 24/2v/3721/299–301 (p/39); 24/2v/3631/233
   (p/39); 24/2v/3499/115–16 (p/39).

26 24/2v/3722/177–9, 262–4 (p/39); 24/2v/3723/47–53, 60–2 (p/39).

27 24/2v/3722/177–9, 262–4 (p/39); 24/2v/3633/137–40 (p/39).

28 24/2v/3633/176–7, 184–6, 206–8 (p/39).

29 24/2v/3723/16–18 (p/39); 24/2v/3634/7–9 (p/39).

30 24/2v/3634/42 (p/39).

31 24/2v/3723/62 (p/39).

32 24/2v/3723/50 (p/39).

33 24/2b/278/97–8, 135 (l/39).

34 24/2v/4017/136–9 (p/40); 24/5/4897/59 (p/40).

35 Degras, *Soviet Documents on Foreign Policy*, III, 368. Molotov claimed that 49,000 had been killed and 158,863 wounded, with much heavier losses on the Finnish side. The figures quoted in a 1993 article are 126,875 killed and missing on the Soviet side (cited in *Istoriia otechestva v dokumentakh 1917–1993*, 4 vols., III, Moscow, 1995, 19).

36 24/2v/5135/143–7 (n/41).

6 THE CONSTITUTION AND ELECTIONS

1 G. Hosking, 'The Beginnings of Independent Political Activity', in Hosking, J. Aves, and P. Duncan (eds.), *The Road to Post-Communism. Independent Political Movements in the Soviet Union 1985–1991*, London, 1992, 2.

2 For details on the organisation of the Constitution and elections, see J. A. Getty, 'State and Society Under Stalin. Constitutions and Elections in the 1930s', *SR*, 50/1, 1991, 18–35.

3 Richard Pipes, *The Russian Revolution 1899–1919*, London, 1990, 56; see also 116.

4 Steve Smith, 'Workers and Civil Rights in Tsarist Russia 1899–1917', and Linda Edmondson, 'Was There a Movement for Civil Rights in Russia in 1905?', in O. Crisp and L. Edmondson (eds.), *Civil Rights in Imperial Russia*, Oxford, 1989, 145–69 and 263–85; V. Bonnell, *Roots of Rebellion. Workers' Politics and Organisation in St Petersburg and Moscow 1900–1914*, London, 1983, 168–71.

5 Marc Ferro, *The Russian Revolution of February 1917*, London, 1972, 113–58.

6 Diane Koenker, *Moscow Workers and the 1917 Revolution*, Princeton, 1981, 240–7.

7 Marc Ferro, *October 1917. A Social History of the Russian Revolution*, London, 1980, 225–6.

8 William Rosenberg, 'Russian Labour and Bolshevik Power After October', *SR*, 44/2, 1985, 213–38, and his 'Reply', 251–6. For a contrary view, see Vladimir Brovkin, 'Politics, Not Economics, Was the Key', in the same issue, 244–50.

9 P. Avrich, *Kronstadt 1921*, Princeton, 1970, 36, 42, 73, 162–3. See also the recently published documents on the uprising in *Voprosy istorii*, 4–5, 1994.

10 Iarov, 'Kronshtadtskii miatezh', 543.

11 24/2v/727/121 (p/34).

12 24/5/2696/88 (p/35). See also 24/5/2288/40 (p/34).

13 24/2v/1846/45–6 (n/36); 24/2v/2065/197 (p/36).

14 24/2v/1855/208 (n/36).

15 24/2v/2059/60 (p/36); 25/10/36/30 (p/36); 25/5/83/24 (p/36); 24/2v/1772 (p/36).

16 24/2v/1772/16 (p/36).
17 Getty, 'State and Society', 26–7; *LP*, 2 July 1936; 24/2v/1772/18 (p/36); 24/2v/1860/5 (n/36).
18 24/2v/1855/203–4 (n/36).
19 Getty, 'State and Society', 26.
20 24/2v/1844/182–3 (n/36); 24/2v/1846/40–4, 123 (n/36); 24/2v/1860/5, 8, 19 (n/36); 24/2v/1855/202 (n/36); 24/2v/2065/7, 195 (p/36); 24/5/3732/88 (p/36).
21 24/2g/89/29–40 (l/37).
22 24/2v/2487/60–7 (n/37).
23 24/2v/2059/61, 67 (p/36).
24 24/2g/51/145–8 (l/37).
25 For examples of this, see the relevant sections in chapters 1, 3, and 4.
26 *Voprosy istorii*, 6, 1993, 26, 15.
27 24/2v/2286/49 (p/37).
28 24/2v/2498/150 (n/37).
29 24/2v/2499/48 (n/37).
30 Getty, 'State and Society', 31.
31 24/2v/2278/77 (p/37); 24/2v/2286/51 (p/37).
32 24/10/265/32–3 (p/37).
33 24/2v/2282/101 (p/37).
34 GANO 3/11/695/1310b (p/37).
35 24/10/259/69–70 (p/37).
36 24/2v/2282/19, 67 (p/37); 24/2v/2499/23, 26, 64, 79, 99, 108, 128 (n/37); 24/2v/2286/11, 77 (p/37).
37 24/2v/2499/110 (n/37); 24/2v/2424/72 (p/37).
38 24/2v/2499/26 (n/37).
39 24/2v/2286/4 (p/37).
40 GANO 4/1/74/86–7 (p/37).
41 GANO 4/1/74/282 (p/37).
42 24/10/325/33 (p/37).
43 GANO 4/1/74/253 (p/38). This practice of writing messages on electoral bulletins continued throughout the Soviet period.

7 THE GREAT TERROR

1 See n. 3 in the introduction.
2 See Thurston, 'Fear and Belief', and 'The Stakhanovite Movement', in *ST*, 155–60.
3 *SP*, 203, and Fitzpatrick, 'Workers Against Bosses. The Impact of the Great Purges on Labor–Management Relations', in L. Siegelbaum and R. Suny (eds.), *Making Workers Soviet*, London, 1994, 311.
4 For example, those cited by Thurston in 'Fear and Belief', 224–8.
5 I have included the Kirov murder in the state-sponsored campaign of terror, although dispute continues about who perpetrated the

murder. See J. A. Getty, 'The Politics of Repression Revisited', in *ST*, 40–64.

6 *LP*, 2 December 1934.

7 25/5/52/3, 42, 97 (p/34); 25/5/47/19, 20, 44–5 (p/34); 25/5/55/36 (p/34); 24/5/44/15 (p/34); 25/5/54/35 (p/34); T. Shibutani, *Improvised News. A Sociological Study of Rumour*, Indianapolis, 1966, 1; G. Allport and L. Postman, *The Psychology of Rumour*, New York, 1947, 2.

8 25/5/43/5 (p/34).

9 *LP*, 3 December 1934.

10 24/2v/935/2. The document is dated 3 December, the day that Medved' was sacked.

11 25/5/55/71 (p/34); 25/5/47/56 (p/34).

12 25/5/55/35, 77, 90 (p/34); 25/5/54/99 (p/34); 24/5/2290/22 (p/34); TsKhDMO 1/23/1102/167 (k/35). Zheliabov and Perovskaia were both members of Narodnaia Volia, which assassinated Alexander II.

13 These rumours were very close to those that emerged in the West and subsequently entered the historiography of the Kirov murder.

14 There is an interesting literature on the role of rumour as a form of catharsis for otherwise sublimated anxieties. See Allport and Postman, *Psychology of Rumour*; R. Rosnow and G. Fine, *Rumor and Gossip. The Social Psychology of Hearsay*, New York, 1976; A. Farge and J. Revel, *The Rules of Rebellion. Child Abductions in Paris in 1750*, Cambridge, 1991.

15 24/5/2289/22 (p/34); 25/5/44/12, 23 (p/34); 25/5/45/9 (p/34); 25/5/52/19, 42 (p/34); 25/5/55/30 (p/34); 25/5/47/100 ob, 107, 109, 146 (p/34); 24/5/2290/22 (p/34).

16 24/5/2290/8 (p/34); 25/5/52/119 (p/34); 24/5/2291/4, 24 (p/34).

17 25/5/55/39 (p/34).

18 25/5/55/130 (p/34); 25/5/43/6 (p/34); 25/5/56/1, 6 (p/34).

19 24/5/2291/21 (p/34).

20 25/5/56/7 (p/34); 25/5/47/20, 120 (p/34).

21 25/5/56/11 (p/34); 25/5/47/120 (p/34); 25/5/46/11 (p/34); 25/5/44/17 (p/34).

22 25/5/44/13 (p/34); 25/5/45/84, 104, 113 (p/34); 25/5/47/20 (p/34); 25/5/54/80 (p/34).

23 24/2v/1848/78 (n/36); к598/1/5423/7, 122, 282 (k/37); 24/2v/2659/3 (p/37); 24/2v/3178/28–9 (p/38).

24 24/2v/1848/76 (n/36); 24/2v/2061/4, 184–5 (p/36); к598/1/5423/11 (k/37); 24/2v/2659/1, 3–4 (p/37); 24/2v/2498/3 (n/37); 24/2v/3178/30 (p/38).

25 24/2v/2659/97, 114–15 (p/37); 24/2v/2487/141–7 (n/37); к598/1/5423/13, 32, 34, 54, 57, 75 (k/37); 24/2v/2664/204 (p/37); 24/2v/3178/4–5 (p/38).

26 Kravchenko, *I Chose Freedom*, 126.

27 24/2v/2267/27 (p/37); 24/5/3202/175 (p/36); 24/10/291/44–6 (p/37); 24/2v/2061/143–4 (p/36).

28 Garros, *et al.*, *Intimacy and Terror*, 147–8.
29 25/5/65/57 (p/35); 25/5/66/4 (p/35).
30 24/2v/1851/73 (n/36); 24/2v/2061/97, 125, 127, 137, 138, 140, 143, 199 (p/36); 24/2v/2514/107 (p/37); 24/5/4177/85 (p/38); 24/2v/3178/3, 94 (p/38).
31 24/5/2714/23–6 (p/35).
32 24/5/2714/14 (p/35).
33 24/5/2714/14, 25, 8 (p/35).
34 Less surprisingly, the Orthodox clergy played a significant role in collection of money. One bishop gave each exiled priest 500 r. and a pair of boots, while church leaders arranged send-offs: 24/2v/1190/46–7 (n/35).
35 24/2v/1190/47 (n/35).
36 24/2v/2499/62, 74–6, 78–9 (n/37).
37 Garros, *et al.*, *Intimacy and Terror*, 353; 24/2v/2498/151 (n/37); 24/2v/2499/27, 49–50, 59–60, 65, 75, 78 (n/37).
38 24/2v/2499/68, 75, 128 (n/37).
39 24/2v/2499/80 (n/37).
40 GANO 4/34/31/23 (n/37).
41 24/2v/2498/153 (n/37); 24/2v/2499/29, 55 (n/37); 24/2v/3203/6–7 (n/38).

8 'US' AND 'THEM': SOCIAL IDENTITY AND THE TERROR

1 E.g. Alec Nove, 'Is There a Ruling Class in the USSR?', *Soviet Studies*, 27/4, 1975, 615–38, and 'The Class Nature of the Soviet Union Revisited', *Soviet Studies*, 35/3, 1983, 298–312; David Lane, *Soviet Economy and Society*, Oxford, 1985, 163.
2 On the relationship between language and social identity, see Gareth Stedman-Jones, *Languages of Class*, Cambridge, 1983, 22, 101; Siegelbaum and Suny, *Making Workers Soviet*; Sheila Fitzpatrick, 'Ascribing Class. The Construction of Social Identity in Soviet Russia', *Journal of Modern History*, 65, December 1993, 745–70.
3 On static and conflictual images, see Ralf Dahrendorf, *Class and Class Conflict in Industrial Society*, London, 1959, 283–4.
4 Hoffmann, *Peasant Metropolis*, 107–25.
5 Dahrendorf, *Class*, 285.
6 S. Ossowski, *Class Structure in the Social Consciousness*, London, 1963, 19–37.
7 R. Tucker, *The Soviet Political Mind*, London, 1972, 122.
8 See L. Haimson, 'The Problem of Social Stability in Urban Russia 1905–1917', *SR*, 23/4, 1964, 619–42, and 24/1, 1965, 1–22, and 'The Problem of Social Identities in Early Twentieth-Century Russia', *SR*, 47/1, 1988, 1–20.

9 Cited in T. McDaniel, *Autocracy, Capitalism, and Revolution in Russia*, London, 1988, 389.
10 On representations of enemies in the Soviet period, see Chase, *Workers, Society, and the Soviet State*; Diane Koenker, 'Class and Class Consciousness in a Socialist Society. Workers in the Printing Trades During NEP', in Fitzpatrick, *et al.*, *Russia in the Era of NEP*; Kuromiya, *Stalin's Industrial Revolution*.
11 See Fitzpatrick, 'Workers Against Bosses', in Siegelbaum and Suny, *Making Workers Soviet*, 312.
12 25/5/46/109 (p/34); 24/2v/1914/58 (p/36); 24/2v/2286/12 (p/37); 24/2v/1914/3 (p/36); 24/2v/4306/176 (n/40); 24/2v/3563/32 (n/39); 24/2v/4313/279 (n/40); 24/5/2696/90 (p/35); 24/2v/4306/213 (n/40); 24/2v/4300/275 (n/40).
13 For more on this, see part III.
14 24/5/2288/61, 100 (p/34); 25/5/53/59 (p/34); 24/2v/2286/97, 78 (p/37).
15 25/10/17/80 (p/35).
16 24/2g/149/129 (l/38).
17 25/5/49/117 (p/34).
18 24/5/2286/67, 93 (p/34); 24/2v/4306/128 (n/40).
19 When workers did move up the ladder, there was considerable resentment and sense of betrayal, as in the case of Stakhanovites. For example, one worker asked in 1936, 'Why did Stakhanov develop the Stakhanovite movement, and does not work himself, but is a boss [*nachal'nik*]?': 25/10/36/68 (p/36).
20 24/10/303/162 (p/37); 24/2v/1855/210 (n/36); 24/2v/2499/24, 26 (n/37).
21 24/2v/2499/27 (n/37). See also 24/2v/2499/48, 79, 105 (n/37).
22 24/2v/3179/110–13 (p/38).
23 24/2v/2685/2–3 (p/37).
24 24/2g/47/197 (l/37).
25 24/2v/1914/56 (p/36); 24/2v/1914/58 (p/36); 24/10/163/141 (p/37).
26 E.g. by Rittersporn and Fitzpatrick in much of their work.
27 24/2v/1190/88–91 (n/35); 24/2v/1595/157 (p/36).
28 RTsKhIDNI 17/2/625/40.
29 Fitzpatrick also argues this in *SP*, 312.
30 E.g. 25/5/48/1; 25/5/48/3 (p/34).
31 24/2b/33/43 (n/35).
32 25/5/48/12 (p/34); 24/2v/1367/71–2 (p/35).
33 RTsKhIDNI 17/2/547/61.
34 24/2v/2061/115 (p/36).
35 24/2v/1851/74 (n/36).
36 24/2v/1851/72 (n/36).
37 24/10/291/77 (p/37); к598/1/5423/65 (k/37).
38 24/2v/3178/19, 23, 29 (p/38).

39 Thurston, 'Fear and Belief', 219.
40 24/2v/2664/1–8 (p/34); 24/2v/2498/1–2, 150 (n/37); 24/2v/2514/92–3 (n/37); 24/2v/2286/13 (p/37); 24/2v/2665/2–4 (p/37); 24/2v/3178/23, 28–9 (p/38); 24/10/291/78 (p/37); 24/2v/2664/8 (p/37); 24/2v/2499/ 24 (n/37).
41 24/2v/2499/24 (n/37).
42 24/10/163/68 (p/37).
43 E.g. by N. Cohn in *The Pursuit of the Millennium*, London, 1970.
44 Mark Steinberg, *Moral Communities. The Culture and Class Relations in the Russian Printing Industry 1867–1907*, Berkeley, 1992, 234.
45 Mark Steinberg, 'Workers and the Cross. Religious Imagery in the Writings of Russian Workers 1910–1924', *RR*, 53/2, 1994, 213–39.
46 24/2v/1518/1 (l/37).
47 24/2v/2664/265 (p/37).
48 24/2v/2282/109 (p/37).
49 24/2v/1518/184–8 (l/35).
50 E.g. 24/5/2696/90 (p/35); 24/5/3202/92 (p/36); 24/2v/1833/185 (n/ 36).
51 24/2v/2499/77, 104 (n/37); 24/5/3202/109 (p/36).
52 24/2v/3720/339 (p/39). See also 24/2v/3563/32 (p/39).
53 24/2v/2286/137 (p/37); 25/10/17/80 (p/36).
54 E.g. 'there are many intelligentsia, and they live off us; they say that he who does not work does not eat, but we work and there is nothing to eat': 24/2v/1914/92 (p/36); 24/2v/1846/123 (n/36); 24/5/3732/88 (p/ 36).
55 24/2v/1049/20 (p/35); 24/5/47/31 (p/34).
56 24/2v/1748/171 (l/36).
57 24/2v/3563/61 (n/39); 24/2v/1049/23 (p/35); 24/2v/4306/198 (n/40). See also chapter 4.
58 24/2v/1518/183 (l/35).
59 See chapter 4.
60 Steinberg, *Moral Communities*, 235.
61 24/2v/1518/14 (l/35).
62 TsGA SPb 7384/2/49/432 (n/35).
63 24/2v/4306/213 (n/40).
64 G. Rittersporn, 'The Omnipresent Conspiracy. On Soviet Imagery of Politics and Social Relations in the 1930s', in *ST*, 116.
65 *P*, 20 September 1937.
66 24/2v/1914/92 (p/36).
67 25/5/38/46 (p/34).
68 25/5/38/44 (p/34).
69 24/5/2286/6 (p/34).
70 25/5/48/52 (p/34); 25/5/46/141 (p/34); 25/5/54/27 (p/34); 25/5/49/ 116 (p/34); 24/2v/1200/70 (n/35); 24/5/2286/80 (p/34); 24/5/2691/35 (p/35).

71 24/2v/1200/71 (n/35).
72 24/2v/1049/22 (p/35); 25/10/74/11 (p/37); 24/2v/1829/63 (n/36).
73 See Fitzpatrick, *The Cultural Front*, 216–37.
74 GANO 3/10/926/52 (1936).
75 25/5/46/180 (p/34); 25/5/49/11 (p/34).
76 Trotsky, *Revolution Betrayed*, 61.
77 Fitzpatrick, *The Cultural Front*, 230.
78 24/2v/1367/71 (p/35); 25/5/83/24 (p/36); 24/2v/1851/124 (n/36).
79 E. A. Osokina, 'Za zerkal'noi dver'iu Torgsina', *Otechestvennaia istoriia*, 1995/2, 97–8.
80 24/2v/772/15 (n/34).
81 TsKhDMO 1/23/1128/64 (k/35).
82 25/5/46/73 (p/34).
83 24/2v/1518/32 (l/35).
84 24/2v/1748/166–8 (l/36).
85 24/5/2714/106 (p/35).
86 24/2v/2665/61–2 (p/37).
87 Fitzpatrick, *The Cultural Front*, 230.
88 24/2g/49/114 (l/37).
89 25/5/48/53 (p/34).
90 Garros, *et al.*, *Intimacy and Terror*, 153–4.
91 24/2v/1830/6 (n/36).
92 Fitzpatrick, 'Stalin and the Making of a New Elite', 396.
93 24/2v/4814/116–17 (p/41); 24/2v/5134/30–6 (p/41).

9 THE LEADER CULT IN OFFICIAL DISCOURSE

1 There is a large literature on various aspects of the Stalin cult. See J. Heizer, 'The Cult of Stalin 1929–1939', Ph.D dissertation, University of Kentucky, 1977; B. Kiteme, 'The Cult of Stalin. National Power and the Soviet Party State', Ph.D dissertation, Columbia University, 1989; G. Gill, 'Political Myth and Stalin's Quest for Authority in the Party' in T. Rigby, A. Brown, and P. Reddaway (eds.), *Authority, Power, and Policy in the USSR*, London, 1980, 98–117; Gill, 'The Soviet Leader Cult. Reflections on the Structure of Leadership in the Soviet Union', *British Journal of Political Science*, 10/2, 1980, 167–86; J. Barber, 'The Image of Stalin in Soviet Propaganda and Public Opinion During World War II', paper presented to the IV World Congress for Soviet and East European Studies, Harrogate, England, 1990. The biographies by R. McNeal, *Stalin, Man and Ruler*, London, 1988, and R. Tucker, *Stalin in Power. The Revolution from Above 1928–1941*, London, 1990, also devote attention to this question. Kobo (ed.), *Osmyslit' kul't Stalina*, Moscow, 1989, is the most comprehensive collection of Soviet analyses; J. Barber has addressed the general question of the reception of the cult in 'Working-Class Culture and Political Culture in the 1930s', in H.

Gunther (ed.), *The Culture of the Stalin Period*, London, 1990, 3–14. For Stalin's own input into the cult, see L. Maksimenkov, 'Kul't. Zametki o slovakh-simvolakh v sovetskom politicheskom kul'ture', *Svobodnaia mysl'*, 11, 1993, 26–43. For comparisons between the cults of Mao and Stalin, see G. Gill, 'The Cult of Personality and the Search for Legitimation. The Cases of Mao and Stalin', MA thesis, Monash University, 1973; R. Thompson, 'Reassessing Personality Cults. The Case of Stalin and Mao', *Studies in Comparative Communism*, 21/1, 1988, 99–128.

2 Heizer, 'Cult of Stalin', 55.

3 *P*, 21 December 1929.

4 *Druzhnye rebiata*, 1, 1932, 4.

5 For more on the cult-making of the period 1929–33, including the establishment of Stalinist orthodoxies in history and philosophy, see Tucker, *Stalin in Power*, 146–71.

6 *P*, 1 January 1934; *LP*, 22 January 1934; Tucker, *Stalin in Power*, 333; *Semnadtsatyi s"ezd VKP(b). Stenograficheskii otchet*, Moscow, 1934; *Sotsialis-ticheskii vestnik*, 25 February 1934, 14.

7 Gill, 'The Soviet Leader Cult'.

8 E.g. *Pioner*, 2, 1934, 2–3. Work dealing with the rewriting of history includes: S. Sukharev, 'Istoriko-partiinaia nauka v usloviiakh utverzh-deniia kul't lichnosti I. V. Stalina 1931–1935. Avtoreferat', candidate dissertation, Moscow, 1990. This discusses in particular the significance of Beria's role in the formation of the Stalin cult in history. See also Amy Knight, *Beria. Stalin's First Lieutenant*, Princeton, 1993.

9 GANO 3/9/36/166–9. The TsK was informed about the case. See RTsKhIDNI 17/120/175/44.

10 *Znamia*, 3, 1989, 67. Avdeenko learned quickly. In his speech at the congress of Soviets in 1935, he pronounced the notorious words 'When I have a son, and when he begins to speak, the first word he says will be Stalin': *ibid.*, 50–1.

11 Ian Kershaw, *The Hitler Myth. Image and Reality in the Third Reich*, Oxford, 1989, 59.

12 25/2/119/58.

13 *Krasnaia derevnia*, 35, 1935, 6; *Rabotnitsa i krest'ianka*, 23, 1935, 1.

14 Stalin, *Sochineniia*, XIV, Stanford, 1967, 62.

15 24/5/3207/53.

16 K. Clark, *The Soviet Novel. History as Ritual*, London, 1985, 142.

17 *P*, 25 July 1936.

18 *P*, 1 January 1937.

19 E.g. the poem 'Sun-Man', *Molodoi kolkhoznik*, 6, 1938, 1. On folklore, see F. Miller, *Folklore for Stalin. Russian Folklore and Pseudofolklore of the Stalin Era*, London, 1990.

20 *Molodoi kolkhoznik*, 2, 1937, 2.

21 *P*, 9 December 1937.

22 *P*, 5 December 1937.

23 Kiteme discusses Stalin's role as an integrative symbol for national consolidation in 'The Cult of Stalin'.

24 A similar pattern has also been noted by G. Alekseev, who plotted a graph of the dynamics of the cult on the basis of the quantity of references to Stalin in *Pravda* leaders in any one month: 'Kolichestvennye parametry kul'ta lichnosti', *SSSR v protivorechiiakh*, 6, 1982, 5–11.

25 *Maiak*, 9 March 1940.

26 Bakhtin, *Tvorchestvo*.

27 *Ibid.*, 101.

28 24/5/2678/10.

29 *Krokodil*, 35–6, 1934, 3.

30 24/2v/1829/172–3.

31 24/2v/1017/116–17.

32 Bakhtin, *Tvorchestvo*, 23.

33 E.g. *P*, 3 August 1935. This was notably during a year when family values were being promoted. In October, a conversation with Stalin's mother was also published: *P*, 28 October 1935.

34 Cf. Hitler's lack of family life: 'His celibacy, which Goebbels portrayed as the sacrifice of personal happiness for the welfare of the nation, was also regarded by Hitler as a functional necessity directed against avoiding any loss of popularity among German women, whose support he saw as vital to his electoral success' (Kershaw, *Hitler Myth*, 3).

35 Clark, *Soviet Novel*, 119–29, 136–55.

36 The cult of Kirov reached its apogee at the Leningrad *oblast'* and district party conferences in January 1934, when Kirov's personal qualities were lauded by other party secretaries. See, for example, *Smena*, 10 January 1934. The district and factory press was not always certain how to pitch the tone. One article header referred to him as 'the best Stalinist [*Staliniets*]', while in the article itself he was just 'the best Leninist'. At this time Kirov was also known as 'the best *soratnik* [comrade-in-arms] of our great Stalin' (*Bol'shevichka*, 11 January 1934). Chudov called him 'the closest *soratnik*' (*Krest'ianskaia pravda*, Luga, 22 January 1934), and Komarov referred to 'our brilliant *vozhdi*, comrades Stalin and Kirov' (*Za sotsialisticheskuiu nauku*, 20 January 1934).

37 Cf. Bakhtin, *Tvorchestvo*, 12–13.

38 GANO 3/2/655/49.

10 AFFIRMATIVE REPRESENTATIONS OF THE LEADER AND LEADER CULT

1 See R. Medvedev, *Let History Judge*, 430. *Sotsialisticheskii vestnik* noted that 'a characteristic feature of party and non-party responsible workers – you cannot distinguish them – is the emphasised, obvious adoration [*obozhenie*] of Stalin': 10 February 1936, 15.

2 24/2b/33/430b (n/35).

3 24/2b/33/430b (n/35).

4 24/2b/33/450b (n/35).

5 See chapter 3.

6 GARF 7523/24/121/92 (l/39).

7 On the relationship between Stalin and writers, see A. Kemp-Welch, *Stalin and the Literary Intelligentsia 1928–1939*, London, 1991.

8 K. Simonov, *Glazami cheloveka moego pokoleniia. Razmyshleniia o I. V. Staline*, Moscow, 1988, 74–5.

9 See, for example, Babel's speech at the Congress of Writers in *Pervyi vsesoiuznyi s″ezd sovetskikh pisatelei. Stenograficheskii otchet*, Moscow, 1934, 279.

10 See the personal papers of Bulgakov: J. Curtis (ed.), *Manuscripts Don't Burn. Mikhail Bulgakov: A Life in Letters and Diaries*, London, 1991; and L. Fleishman, *Boris Pasternak. The Poet and His Politics*, London, 1990; G. Freidin, *A Coat of Many Colours. Osip Mandel'shtam and the Mythologies of Self-Presentation*, London, 1987.

11 On the relationship between tsar and people, see Cherniavsky, *Tsar and People*; M. Perrie, *The Image of Ivan the Terrible in Russian Folklore*, Cambridge, 1987; S. White, 'The USSR. Patterns of Autocracy and Industrialism', in A. Brown and J. Gray (eds.), *Political Culture and Political Change in Communist States*, London, 1979, 25–65. On the tsar 'cult', see V. Zhivov and B. Uspenskii, 'Tsar' i Bog. Semioticheskie aspekty sakralizatsii monarkha v Rossii', in B. Uspenskii (ed.), *Iazyki kul'tury i problemy perevodimosti*, Moscow, 1987, 47–153.

12 On popular attitudes to Lenin, see Nina Tumarkin, *Lenin Lives! The Lenin Cult in Soviet Russia*, Cambridge, 1983.

13 24/5/2289/101 (p/34).

14 24/2v/4314/23–5 (n/40).

15 G. Freeze, *From Supplication to Revolution. A Documentary Social History of Imperial Russia*, Oxford, 1988, 5.

16 24/2g/4/3–7; 24/2g/13/9–11; 24/2g/46/1; 24/2g/92; 24/2g/221.

17 V. A. Il'inikh, 'Krest'ianskie chelobitnye XVIII–pervoi poloviny XIX v. Na materialakh Zapadnoi Sibiri', in *Sibirskoe istochnikovedenie i arkheografiia*, Novosibirsk, 1980, 86–7.

18 S. S. Volkov, *Leksika russkikh chelobitnykh XVII veka*, Leningrad, 1974, 24–5, 44, 104–6, 129–32.

19 *Krestianskoe dvizhenie v Rossii 1857–1861. Sbornik dokumentov*, Moscow, 1963, 232–3, 256–9.

20 See Freeze, *From Supplication*, 15.

21 24/2v/1533/4 (l/35).

22 *Kommunist*, 1, 1990, 95; RTsKhIDNI 78/1/591/88 (l/36); 78/1/593/97 (l/37); 78/1/593/155 (l/37); TsGAIPD SPb 24/2v/2225/223 (l/37).

23 See also 24/2v/2229/49 (l/37); 24/2g/51/284 (l/37); 24/2g/121/347 (l/38).

24 RTsKhIDNI 78/1/593/16 (l/37); TsGAIPD SPb 24/2v/2228/89 (l/37); TsGA SPb 960/2/177/118 (l/35).

25 24/2g/51/77 (l/37); 24/2v/1534/72 (l/35); 24/2g/53/135 (l/37); 24/2g/
    47/147, 304 (l/37).
26 24/2v/727/304 (l/34); 24/2v/1520/73 (l/35); 24/2g/52/27 (l/37).
27 24/2g/70/152 (l/37); 24/2g/52/27 (l/37).
28 24/2g/48/302 (l/37); 24/2g/47/147 (l/37).
29 RTsKhIDNI 78/1/596/47 (l/36); TsGAIPD SPb 24/2v/1534/72 (l/35);
    24/2g/52/37 (l/37).
30 RTsKhIDNI 78/1/593/16, 36 (l/37);TsGAIPD SPb 24/2g/1016/137 (l/
    37).
31 Daniel Field, *Rebels in the Name of the Tsar*, Boston, 1976.
32 James C. Scott also makes this point in relation to the act of petitioning:
    'By making appeals that remain within the official discourse of
    deference, the peasantry may somewhat lessen the mortal risks incurred
    by the desperate act of petitioning' (*Domination and the Arts of Resistance*,
    London, 1990, 95).
33 24/2g/5/113–18 (l/35).
34 24/2v/1193/10–11 (n/35).
35 L. Gordon and E. Klopov, *Chto eto bylo?*, Moscow, 1989, 143.
36 Cf. Kotkin, *Magnetic Mountain*, 502–3, n. 108; *SP*, 296.
37 24/8/240/41 (p/35); 24/8/251/1 (p/35).
38 24/10/268/120b (p/37).
39 24/5/2290/55 (p/34); 24/5/2289/7, 28, 32–3 etc. (p/34).
40 24/5/2289/4–5, 37, 39, 41 (p/34); 25/5/53/1 (p/34).
41 TsGA SPb 7384/2/37/437–42 . Those who were not included in the
    organised groups because of insufficient space often tried to make their
    own way in spontaneously. The militia reported that, on 3 December,
    'some of the unorganised population, numbering several thousand,
    joined onto the columns and pushed in and pressed and tried to get
    into the palace as quickly as possible without waiting their turn'.
42 Christel Lane, *The Rites of Rulers. Ritual in Industrial Society: The Soviet
    Case*, Cambridge, 1981, 82.
43 24/2g/5/105–7 (l/35). Shortly afterwards, ulitsa Zheliabova was
    renamed as part of the anti-narodnik campaign.
44 RTsKhIDNI 78/1/613/35–6 (l/36).
45 24/2g/5/96 (l/35).
46 RTsKhIDNI 477/1/44/9 (l/39).
47 24/2v/1772/120, 237, 238 (p/36).
48 GARF 1235/2/2156/3–12 (l/37–8).
49 GARF 1235/2/2156/3–9 (l/37–8). It has been suggested, not implau-
    sibly, that these letters were manufactured as part of a Ezhov-instigated
    campaign for the renaming of Moscow: B. Starkov, 'Kak Moskva chut'
    ne stala Stalinodarom', *Izvestiia KPSS*, 12, 1990, 126–7.
50 RTsKhIDNI 78/1/550/37 (l/35).
51 GARF 7523/24/123/71–2 (l/39).
52 GARF 7523/24/125/126 (l/39).

53 GARF 7523/24/117/111 (l/39).
54 24/2g/5/84 (l/35).
55 Starkov, 'Kak Moskva'.
56 RTsKhIDNI 78/1/591/9–14 (l/36)
57 R. Medvedev, *Let History Judge*, 302–3.

11 NEGATIVE REPRESENTATIONS OF THE LEADER AND LEADER CULT

1 *Za proletars'kie kadry*, 14 October 1933.
2 24/10/118/127 (p/35); 25/5/43/33 (p/34); 24/5/2291/24–5 (p/34); к598/1/5387/97 (k/35); 25/2/24/70; 24/10/262/16 (p/37); 24/10/262/14 (p/37).
3 *Novyi put'*, 28 June 1933.
4 24/5/3212/83–5, 92–3, 120 (p/37).
5 *P*, 9 February 1937, reported how in a region of Checheno-Ingushetiia, *kolkhozy* had been named after the first and second secretaries of the raikom. See also *P*, 28 March 1937.
6 24/2b/548/36–7 (p/39).
7 *SP*, 312.
8 *Bor'ba klassov*, 4, 1936, 106.
9 *Vozhdizm* within the party had always been condemned in principle, if not in practice; for example, Kamenev, an architect of the Lenin cult, who was not averse to the bolstering of his personal authority, said at the Fourteenth Party Congress, 'We are against the creation of a theory of the *"vozhd'"*, we are against making a *"vozhd'"*': *Chetyrnadtsatyi s"ezd VKP(b). Stenograficheskii otchet*, Moscow, 1925, 274.
10 25/5/38/44 (p/34); 24/5/2290/34 (p/34); 24/5/2288/67 (p/34); 25/5/53/53 (p/34); к598/1/5387/138 (k/35); 24/5/2712/52 (p/34); 24/5/2288/45, 67, 114 (p/34); 25/5/47/19 (p/34).
11 In a biography of leaders of the October Revolution, published in 1924, Stalin did not even feature amongst the nine leaders (who were listed as Kamenev, Semashko, Rykov, Trotsky, Krupskaia, Kalinin, the dead Lenin, Rakovskii, Zinoviev): *Vozhdi okt'iabrskoi revoliutsii*, Moscow, 1924.
12 24/5/2285/124 (p/34); 25/5/45/101 (p/34); 24/2v/937/3 (p/34–5); 24/2v/2061/115, 179 (p/36); к598/1/5423/91, 300 (k/37); TsGA SPb 7384/2/49/427 (n/35); TsGAIPD SPb 25/5/45/101 (p/34); 24/2v/937/3 (p/34–5); 24/2v/2061/115, 179 (p/36); 24/2v/2059/218 (p/36); 24/2v/2065/198 (p/36); 24/2v/1846/44 (n/36).
13 24/5/3207/29 (p/36).
14 24/2b/185/50–2 (n/36).
15 24/2g/89/62 (l/37).
16 Garros, *et al.*, *Intimacy and Terror*, 118.
17 24/2v/2494/119–24 (n/37); 24/2v/2499/23, 27, 76, 105, 25 (n/37).
18 24/2v/3023/6 (n/38); 24/2v/3025/2 (n/38); 24/2v/3027/50, 58 (n/38).

19 24/2g/149/66–66ob (l/38).
20 24/2v/4306/193 (n/40); 24/2v/4313/241 (n/40).
21 W. Ong, *Orality and Literacy*, London, 1982, 44–5, 70.
22 24/10/225/9 (p/35); 24/5/2692/13 (p/35); к598/1/5407/85 (k/35); 24/5/2290/22 (p/34); к598/1/5388/188 (k/35).
23 25/5/53/1, 62 (p/34). Kirov's family life remains an enigma to this day. See N. Lebina, 'Mif o mironiche', unpublished ms. Virtually nothing is known about his wife, M. Markus, who died in 1945. Her sister seems to have destroyed all her documents after her death.
24 TsKhDMO 1/23/1102/167 (k/35); 24/5/2289/22 (p/34); 24/5/2288/60 (p/34); 24/5/45/5 (p/34); 24/5/2288/35 (p/34); 25/5/54/78–9 (p/34); к598/1/5423/296 (k/37).
25 Perrie argues that the tales 'involve a utopian element of psychological wish fulfilment for the performer and his audience': 'Folklore as Evidence of Peasant *Mentalité*. Social Attitudes and Values in Russian Popular Culture', *RR*, 48/2, 1989, 126. See also R. Jakobson, 'On Russian Fairy Tales': 'A fairy tale fulfils the role of a social utopia ... It is a dream about the triumph of the wretched, about the metamorphosis of a hind into a tsar' (*Selected Writings*, 8 vols. The Hague, 1966, IV, 82–100); 24/5/2288/130 (p/34).
26 24/2v/772/16 (n/34); к598/1/5388/244 (k/35); 25/5/55/15 (p/34); к598/1/5387/93 (k/35).
27 25/5/47/8 (p/34). Cf. 'Kirov was killed – they abolished ration cards. When Stalin's killed – there'll be no queues': RTsKhIDNI 17/120/175/50 (p/35); and the *chastushka*, 'Kogda Kirova ubili / Khleba vdovol' privalilo / Kogda Stalina ub'iut / Khleb nam na dom prinesut' ('When Kirov was killed / There was extra bread / When Stalin is killed / They'll bring bread to our homes'). But contrast this with the more pessimistic *chastushka*: 'Kogda Kirova ubili / Tri dnia golodem khodili / Kogda Stalina ub'iut / Sovsem khleba ne dadut' ('When Kirov was killed / We went hungry for three days / When Stalin is killed / We'll get no bread at all') к598/1/5407/81, 85 (k/35).
28 25/5/55/92 (p/34); RTsKhIDNI 17/120/175/96 (p/35).
29 24/5/2288/106 (p/34); 25/5/47/20 (p/34); 25/5/46/53 (p/34).
30 *Sotsialisticheskii vestnik*, 25 January 1934, 2.
31 M. Riutin, *Na koleni ne vstanu*, Moscow, 1992.
32 25/5/56/108 (p/34).
33 24/2g/89/28–9, 40 (l/37).
34 24/5/2696/88 (p/35); 34/2v/2659/1 (p/37); 24/2v/3178/28 (p/38); 24/2v/4020/290 (p/40); 24/2v/4027/40, 106 (p/40); 24/2v/4032/149 (p/40); 24/2v/4306/179 (n/40).
35 24/2v/3178/28 (p/38); 24/2v/2061/185 (p/36); 24/2v/2659/1–2 (p/37); 24/2v/2685/2 (p/37); 24/2v/4020/290 (p/40); 24/2v/4027/106 (p/40); 24/2v/4029/29 (p/40); 24/2v/4032/149 (p/40).
36 к598/1/5386/273 (k/35).

37 GANO 22/3/520/8ob (p/35). Another version of this ended: 'Because Lenin avoided the marsh of opposition and Stalin goes barging through it' (RTsKhIDNI 17/120/175/88 (p/35)).

38 On the cult of Trotsky and the origins of *vozhdizm* within the party, see A. Ovsiannikov, 'Istoki vozhdizma. Ideologiia i praktika', in V. Dmitrenko (ed.), *Formirovanie administrativno-komandnoi sistemy 20–30e gody*, Moscow, 1992, 185–203, especially 189, 199. There are many comments praising Trotsky in the opinion reports, and it is possible that some of these were invented during the anti-Trotsky mania of this period, when accusing someone of expressing support for Trotsky was one of the easiest ways of incriminating them.

39 24/10/163/119 (p/37); 24/2v/2065/331 (p/36); 24/5/2288/112 (p/34); 25/5/49/89 (p/34); 24/2v/2061/138, 185 (p/36); 24/2v/2065/9 (p/36); 24/2v/2659/2 (p/37); 24/2v/2286/2 (p/37).

40 24/2v/2659/1 (p/37).

41 25/5/49/89 (p/34).

42 24/5/3202/166–7 (p/36); 24/2v/2061/126 (p/36); 24/2v/2282/109 (p/37).

43 24/10/163/59 (p/37); 24/2v/2061/97, 116, 125–6, 140, 143, 186 (p/36); 24/5/3207/27 (p/36).

44 24/2v/2061/185 (p/36).

45 24/2v/3178/94 (p/38); 24/2v/2499/69 (n/37).

46 24/2v/1190/48 (n/35); 24/2v/772/17 (n/34).

47 24/5/3731/95 (p/37); 24/2v/2286/12–13 (p/37).

48 K598/1/5423/10 (k/37); 24/5/2288/114 (p/34); 24/2v/2065/8–9 (p/36); 24/2v/1914/8 (p/36); 24/5/2696/221 (p/35).

49 24/2v/2491/44 (n/37); 24/5/3202/65 (p/36). See also K598/1/5423/266–7 (k/37).

50 24/5/2288/48 (p/37); 24/2v/1851/72 (n/36); 24/10/291/78 (p/37); 24/2v/2491/44 (n/37); 24/5/3739/10 (p/37); 24/10/118/128 (p/35); 24/2v/2497/7 (n/37); 24/2v/1855/203 (n/36); 24/5/3731/95 (p/37).

51 24/2v/1518/11–13 (l/35).

52 O. Figes, *Peasant Russia, Civil War. The Volga Countryside in Revolution 1917–1921*, Oxford, 1989, 209; *Neizvestnaia Rossiia XX vek*, II, 232.

53 24/10/298/71 (p/37); 24/2v/2499/69 (n/37); 24/2v/2061/177 (p/36).

54 24/5/2289/26 (p/34).

CONCLUSION

1 J. C. Scott, *Weapons of the Weak. Everyday Forms of Peasant Resistance*, London, 1985, 338.

2 E. P. Thompson, *The Poverty of Theory and Other Essays*, London, 1978, 166.

3 Inkeles and Bauer, *The Soviet Citizen*, 291.

4 Cf. Stephen White, *Political Culture and Soviet Politics*, London, 1979, 111.

5 Rigby, 'Reconceptualising the Soviet System', 312.

Bibliography

I ARCHIVAL SOURCES

I TSGAIPD SPB (TSENTRAL'NYI GOSUDARSTVENNYI ARKHIV ISTORIKO-POLITICHESKIKH DOKUMENTOV SANKT PETERBURGA)

fond 24: Leningradskii oblastnoi komitet VKP(b)
fond 25: Leningradskii gorodskoi komitet VKP(b)
fond K598: Leningradskii oblastnoi komitet VLKSM
fond 2: Vyborgskii raionnyi komitet VKP(b)
fond 416: Tsentral'nyi raionnyi komitet VKP(b)
fond 1200: Krasnyi Treugol'nik – komitet VKP(b)
fond 563: Komissiia partiinogo kontrolia TsK VKP(b) – Upolnomochennaia po Leningradskoi oblasti

2 TSGA SPB (TSENTRAL'NYI GOSUDARSTVENNYI ARKHIV V SANKT PETERBURGE)

fond 7384: Leningradskii sovet

3 GANO (GOSUDARSTVENNYI ARKHIV NOVOSIBIRSKOI OBLASTI)

fond 20: Prokuratura zapadno-sibirskogo kraia
fond 47: Zapadno-sibirskii kraevoi ispolnitel'nyi komitet
fond 4: Novosibirskii oblastnoi komitet VKP(b)
fond 22: Novosibirskii gorodskoi komitet VKP(b)
fond 3: Zapadno-sibirskii kraevoi komitet VKP(b)

4 GARF (GOSUDARSTVENNYI ARKHIV ROSSIISKOI FEDERATSII)

fond 374: Tsentral'naia kontrol'naia komissia VKP(b)
fond 3316: Tsentral'nyi ispolnitel'nyi komitet SSSR

fond 1235: Vserossiiskii tsentra'lnyi ispolnitel'nyi komitet
fond 7523: Verkhovnyi sovet SSSR
fond 9401: Narodnyi kommissariat vnutrennikh del SSSR
fond 8131: Prokuratura SSSR
fond 9474: Verkhovnyi sud SSSR

5 RTSKHIDNI (ROSSIISKII TSENTR KHRANENIIA I IZUCHENIIA
DOKUMENTOV NOVEISHEI ISTORII)

fond 17: Tsentral'nyi komitet VKP(b)
fond 78: Kalinin M. I.

6 TSKHDMO (TSENTR KHRANENIIA DOKUMENTOV
MOLODEZHNYKH ORGANIZATSII)

fond 1: Biuro VLKSM

II NEWSPAPERS AND JOURNALS IN RUSSIAN

Biulleten' oppozitsii
Biulleten' TsKK VKP(b) i NK RKI SSSR i RSFSR
Bol'shevichka
Bol'shevik
Bor'ba klassov
Druzhnye rebiata
Istoricheskii arkhiv
Istoricheskii zhurnal
Istoriia SSSR
Iunii proletarii
Izvestiia TsK KPSS
Kommunist
Krasnaia derevnia
Krest'ianskaia pravda
Krokodil
Leningradskaia pravda
Molodoi kolkhoznik
Novyi mir
Novyi put'
Ogonek
Partiinaia ucheba
Pioner
Pod znamenem marksizma
Pravda
Propaganda i agitatsiia
Rabotnitsa i krest'ianka

Rodina
Smena
Sotsialisticheskii vestnik
Sovetskaia iustitsiia
Sovetskaia zakonnost'
Sovetskoe gosudarstvo i pravo
Sputnik agitatora
Sputnik kommunista v derevne
SSSR: Vnutrennye protivorechiia
Svobodnaia mysl'
Trud
Voenno-istoricheskii zhurnal
Voprosy istorii
Voprosy istorii KPSS
Za proletars'kie kadry
Za sotsialisticheskuiu nauku
Znamia

III PUBLISHED PRIMARY SOURCES

Chetyrnadtsatyi s"ezd VKP(b). Stenograficheskii otchet, Moscow, 1925.
Curtis, J. (ed.), *Manuscripts Don't Burn. Mikhail Bulgakov: A Life in Letters and Diaries*, London, 1991.
Degras, J. (ed.), *Soviet Documents on Foreign Policy*, III, *1933–1941*, Oxford, 1953.
Dokumenty svidetel'stvuiut. Iz istorii derevni nakanune i v khode kollektivizatsii 1927–1932 gg., Moscow, 1989.
Ehrenburg, I., *Post-War Years – 1945–1954*, London, 1966.
Ekonomicheskaia zhizn' SSSR, Moscow, 1967.
Ekonomiko-statisticheskii spravochnik Leningradskoi oblasti, Leningrad, 1932.
Entsiklopediia gosudarstva i prava (edited by P. Stuchka), Moscow, 1930.
Evtushenko, E., *A Precocious Autobiography*, London, 1963.
Freeze, G., *From Supplication to Revolution. A Documentary Social History of Imperial Russia*, Oxford, 1988.
Garros, V., Korenevskaya, N., and Lahusen, T. (eds.), *Intimacy and Terror. Soviet Diaries of the 1930s*, New York, 1995.
Ginsburg, E., *Into the Whirlwind*, London, 1989.
Istoriia otechestva v dokumentakh 1917–1993, 4 vols., Moscow, 1995.
KPSS v resoliutsiiakh i resheniiakh s"ezdov, konferentsii, i plenumov TsK, II, Moscow, 1970–2; VI–VII, Moscow, 1985.
Kravchenko, V., *I Chose Freedom. The Personal and Political Life of a Soviet Official*, London, 1949.
Krestianskoe dvizhenie v Rossii 1857–1861. Sbornik dokumentov, Moscow, 1963.
Leningrad v tsifrakh, Leningrad, 1935, 1936, 1938.

Leningradskaia oblast'. Istoricheskii ocherk, Leningrad, 1986.
Leningradskaia oblast' v tsifrakh, Leningrad, 1935, 1936.
Mandel'shtam, N., *Hope Against Hope*, London, 1989.
Neizvestnaia Rossiia XX vek, 3 vols., Moscow, 1992–3.
Pervoe vsesoiuznoe soveshchanie rabochikh i rabotnits-stakhanovtsev, 14–17 noiabria 1935. Stenograficheskii otchet, Moscow, 1935.
Pervyi vsesoiuznyi s"ezd sovetskikh pisatelei. Stenograficheskii otchet, Moscow, 1934.
Scott, J., *Behind the Urals. An American Worker in Russia's City of Steel*, Bloomington, Ind., 1989.
Semnadtsatyi s"ezd VKP(b). Stenograficheskii otchet, Moscow, 1934.
Simonov, K., *Glazami cheloveka moego pokoleniia. Razmyshleniia o I. V. Staline*, Moscow, 1988.
Smith, A., *I Was a Soviet Worker*, London, 1938.
Stalin, I. V., *Sochineniia*, I–XIII, Moscow, 1946–51, and XIV–XVI, Stanford, 1967.
Trinadtsatyi s"ezd VKP(b). Stenograficheskii otchet, Moscow, 1924.
Ugolovnyi kodeks RSFSR, Moscow, 1935.
Ugolovnyi kodeks RSFSR, Moscow, 1968.
Viktorov, B., *Bez grifa 'Sekretno'. Zapiski voennogo prokurora*, Moscow, 1990.
Vozhdi okt'iabrskoi revoliutsii, Moscow, 1924.
Vsesoiuznaia perepis' naseleniia 1937 goda. Kratkie itogi, Moscow, 1991.
Vsesoiuznaia perepis' naseleniia 1939 goda. Osnovnye itogi, Moscow, 1992.
Werth, N., and Moullec, G. (eds.), *Rapports secrets soviétiques 1921–1991. La Société russe dans les documents confidentials*, Paris, 1994.

IV SECONDARY WORKS

Abercrombie, N., Hill, S., and Turner, B., *The Dominant Ideology Thesis*, London, 1980.
Alekseev, G., 'Kolichestvennye parametry kul'ta lichnosti', *SSSR v protivorechiiakh*, 6, 1982, 5–11.
Allport, G., and Postman, L., *The Psychology of Rumour*, New York, 1947.
Andreucci, F., ' "Subversiveness" and Anti-Fascism in Italy', in R. Samuel (ed.), *People's History and Socialist Theory*, London, 1981, 199–204.
Andrle, V., *Workers in Stalin's Russia*, Hemel Hempstead, 1988.
Anikeev, V., 'Partiinaia informatsiia v period podgotovki Oktiabria', *Voprosy istorii KPSS*, 1, 1970, 95–104.
Avrich, P., *Kronstadt 1921*, Princeton, 1970.
Bacon, E., *The Gulag at War*, London, 1995.
Bakhtin, M., *The Dialogic Imagination*, Austin, Tex., 1981.
Tvorchestvo Franzua Rable i narodnaia kul'tura srednevekov'ia i renessansa, Moscow, 1965.
Barber, J., 'The Composition of the Soviet Working Class 1928–1941', paper presented to SIPS seminar, CREES, Birmingham, 1978.

'Housing Conditions of Soviet Industrial Workers 1928–1941', paper presented to SIPS seminar, CREES, Birmingham, 1981.

'The Image of Stalin in Soviet Propaganda and Public Opinion During World War II', paper presented to the IV World Congress for Soviet and East European Studies, Harrogate, England, 1990.

'The Standard of Living of Soviet Industrial Workers 1928–1940', in C. Bettelheim (ed.), *L'Industrialisation de l'URSS dans les années trente*, Paris, 1982, 109–22.

'Working-Class Culture and Political Culture in the 1930s', in H. Gunther (ed.), *The Culture of the Stalin Period*, London, 1990, 3–14.

Bauer, R., 'The Pseudo-Charismatic Leader in Soviet Society', *Problems of Communism*, 3–4, 1953, 11–14.

Bauer, R., and Gleicher, D., 'Word-of-Mouth Communication in the Soviet Union', *Public Opinion Quarterly*, 17/3, 1953, 297–310.

Beizer, M., 'The Jewish Minority in Leningrad 1917–1939', paper presented to BASEES conference, Cambridge, England, March 1995.

Benvenuti, F., 'Stakhanovism and Stalinism 1934–1938', paper presented to SIPS seminar, CREES, Birmingham, 1988.

Blium, A., *Za kulisami 'Ministerstva Pravdy'*, St Petersburg, 1994.

Bloch, M., *Les Rois thaumaturges*, Paris, 1961.

Bobrov, A., and Starshinov, N. (eds.), *Samotsvetnaia chastushka*, Moscow, 1992.

Bokov, V., and Bakhtin, V. (eds.), *Chastushka*, Moscow, 1966.

Bonnell, V., *Roots of Rebellion. Workers' Politics and Organisation in St Petersburg and Moscow 1900–1914*, London, 1983.

Bourdieu, P., *Distinction. A Social Critique of Taste*, London, 1984.

Language and Symbolic Power, Cambridge, 1991.

Brooks, J., *When Russia Learned to Read. Literacy and Popular Literature 1861–1917*, Princeton, 1985.

Brovkin, V., *Behind the Front Lines of the Civil War. Political Parties and Social Movements in Russia 1918–1922*, Princeton, 1994.

'Politics, Not Economics, Was the Key', *SR*, 44/2, 1985, 244–50.

Brown, A., and Gray, J. (eds.), *Political Culture and Political Change in Communist States*, London, 1979.

Burke, P., *Popular Culture in Early Modern Europe*, London, 1978.

de Certeau, M., *The Practice of Everyday Life*, Berkeley, 1984.

Chapman, J., *Real Wages in Soviet Russia Since 1928*, Cambridge, Mass., 1963.

Chase, W., *Workers, Society, and the Soviet State. Labor and Life in Moscow 1918–1929*, Urbana, Ill., 1987.

Cherniavsky, M., *Tsar and People. Studies in Russian Myths*, London, 1961.

Chernov, A., *Partiinaia informatsiia. Voprosy istorii i teorii*, Moscow, 1987.

Clark, K., *The Soviet Novel. History as Ritual*, London, 1985.

Clark, K., and Holquist, M., *Mikhail Bakhtin*, London, 1984.

Cobb, R., *The Police and the People. French Popular Protest 1789–1820*, Oxford, 1970.

Cohen, S., *Rethinking the Soviet Experience*, Oxford, 1985.

'Stalin's Terror as Social History', *RR*, 45/4, 1986, 375–84.

Cohen, S., and Vanden Heuvel, K. (eds.), *Voices of Glasnost'*, New York, 1989.

Cohn, N., *The Pursuit of the Millennium*, London, 1970.

Conquest, R., *The Great Terror*, London, 1968.

'What Is Terror?', *SR*, 45/2, 1986, 235–7.

Crisp, O., and Edmondson, L. (eds.), *Civil Rights in Imperial Russia*, Oxford, 1989.

Dahrendorf, R., *Class and Class Conflict in Industrial Society*, London, 1959.

Danilov, V., and Berelowitch, A., 'Les Documents de la VCK–OGPU–NKVD sur la campagne soviétique 1918–1937', *Cahiers du monde russe*, 35/3, 1994, 633–40.

Dallin, A., *German Rule in Russia 1941–1945*, London, 1957.

Darnton, R., *The Great Cat Massacre and Other Episodes in French Cultural History*, Harmondsworth, 1991.

The Literary Underground of the Old Regime, Cambridge, Mass., 1982.

Davies, R., Harrison, M., and Wheatcroft, S. (eds.), *The Economic Transformation of the Soviet Union 1913–1945*, Cambridge, 1994.

Davies, S. R., 'Propaganda and Popular Opinion in Soviet Russia 1934–1941', DPhil. dissertation, University of Oxford, 1994.

Davis, N. Zemon, *Society and Culture in Early Modern France*, London, 1975.

Djilas, M., *The New Class*, London, 1957.

Dunham, V., *Middle-Class Values in Soviet Fiction*, Cambridge, 1976.

Eklof, B., and Frank, S. (eds.), *The World of the Russian Peasant*, London, 1990.

Eleonskoi, E. (ed.), *Sbornik velikorusskikh chastushek*, Moscow, 1914.

Engel, B., 'Women, Men, and the Languages of Peasant Resistance 1870–1907', in S. Frank and M. Steinberg (eds.), *Cultures in Flux. Lower-Class Values, Practices, and Resistance in Late Imperial Russia*, Princeton, 1994.

Evans, J., 'The Communist Party of the Soviet Union and the Women's Question. The Case of the 1936 Decree "In Defence of Mother and Child"', *Journal of Contemporary History*, 16/4, 1981, 757–75.

Evans, R., *Proletarians and Politics. Socialism, Protest, and the Working Class Before the First World War*, New York, 1990.

Fainsod, M., *Smolensk Under Soviet Rule*, London, 1958.

How Russia Is Ruled, Cambridge, Mass., 1970.

Farge, A., and Revel, J., *The Rules of Rebellion. Child Abductions in Paris in 1750*, Cambridge, 1991.

Farr, R., and Moscovici, S. (eds.), *Social Representations*, Cambridge, 1984.

Ferro, M., *The Russian Revolution of February 1917*, London, 1972.

October 1917. A Social History of the Russian Revolution, London, 1980.

Field, D., *Rebels in the Name of the Tsar*, Boston, 1976.

Figes, O., *Peasant Russia, Civil War. The Volga Countryside in Revolution 1917–1921*, Oxford, 1989.

Filtzer, D., *Soviet Workers and Stalinist Industrialisation. The Formation of Modern Soviet Production Relations 1928–1941*, London, 1986.

Fitzpatrick, S., 'Ascribing Class. The Construction of Social Identity in Soviet Russia', *Journal of Modern History*, 65, December 1993, 745–70.

　The Cultural Front. Power and Culture in Revolutionary Russia, London, 1992.

　Education and Social Mobility in the Soviet Union 1921–1934, Cambridge, 1979.

　'New Perspectives on Stalinism', *RR*, 45/4, 1986, 357–73.

　The Russian Revolution, Oxford, 1982.

　'Stalin and the Making of a New Elite 1928–1939', *SR*, 38/3, 1979, 377–402.

　Stalin's Peasants. Resistance and Survival in the Russian Village After Collectivisation, Oxford, 1994 (referred to as *SP*).

　'Supplicants and Citizens. Public Letter-Writing in Soviet Russia in the 1930s', *SR*, forthcoming.

Fitzpatrick, S. (ed.), *Cultural Revolution in Russia 1928–1931*, Bloomington, Ind., 1978.

Fitzpatrick, S., Rabinowitch, A., and Stites, R. (eds.), *Russia in the Era of NEP. Explorations in Soviet Society and Culture*, Bloomington, Ind., 1991.

Fleishman, L., *Boris Pasternak. The Poet and His Politics*, London, 1990.

Forgas, J., *Perspectives on Everyday Understanding*, London, 1981.

Freidin, G., *A Coat of Many Colours. Osip Mandel'shtam and the Mythologies of Self-Presentation*, London, 1987.

Geiger, K., *The Family in Soviet Russia*, Cambridge, Mass., 1968.

von Geldern, J., *Bolshevik Festivals 1917–1920*, London, 1993.

Getty, J., *Origins of the Great Purges. The Soviet Communist Party Reconsidered 1933–1938*, Cambridge, 1985.

　'State and Society Under Stalin. Constitutions and Elections in the 1930s', *SR*, 50/1, 1991, 18–35.

Getty, J., and Manning, R. (eds.), *Stalinist Terror. New Perspectives*, Cambridge, 1993 (referred to as *ST*).

Getty, J., Rittersporn, G., and Zemskov, V., 'Victims of the Soviet Penal System in the Pre-War Years. A First Approach on the Basis of Archival Evidence', *American Historical Review*, 98/4, 1993, 1017–49.

Gill, G., 'The Cult of Personality and the Search for Legitimation. The Cases of Mao and Stalin', MA thesis, Monash University, 1973.

　'Political Myth and Stalin's Quest for Authority in the Party', in T. Rigby, A. Brown, and P. Reddaway (eds.), *Authority, Power, and Policy in the USSR*, London, 1980, 98–117.

　'The Soviet Leader Cult. Reflections on the Structure of Leadership in the Soviet Union', *British Journal of Political Science*, 10/2, 1980, 167–86.

Ginsburg, C., *The Cheese and the Worms*, London, 1980.

Ginzburg, L., 'Eshche raz o starom i novom', *Tynianovskii sbornik*, 1986, 133–40.

Goldman, W., *Women, State, and Revolution. Soviet Family Policy and Social Life 1917–1936*, Cambridge, 1993.

Gombrich, E., *Art and Illusion*, Oxford, 1989.

Goody, J., *The Domestication of the Savage Mind*, London, 1977.

Gordon, L., and Klopov, E., *Chto eto bylo?*, Moscow, 1989.

Gramsci, A., *Selections from the Prison Notebooks* (edited by Q. Hoare and G. Nowell-Smith), London, 1986.

Guha, R., *Elementary Aspects of Peasant Insurgency in Colonial India*, Delhi, 1983.

Haimson, L., 'The Problem of Social Identities in Early Twentieth-Century Russia', *SR*, 47/1, 1988, 1–20.

'The Problem of Social Stability in Urban Russia 1905–1917', *SR*, 23/4, 1964, 619–42, and 24/1, 1965, 1–22.

Haslam, J., *The Soviet Union and the Struggle for Collective Security 1933–1939*, London, 1984.

Hatch, J., 'The "Lenin Levy" and the Social Origins of Stalinism. Workers and the Communist Party in Moscow 1921–1928', *SR*, 48/4, 1989, 548–58.

Havel, V., *Living in Truth*, London, 1990.

Heizer, J., 'The Cult of Stalin 1929–1939', Ph.D dissertation, University of Kentucky, 1977.

Hoffmann, D., *Peasant Metropolis. Social Identities in Moscow 1929–1941*, London, 1994.

Hosking, G., Aves, J., and Duncan, P. (eds.), *The Road to Post-Communism. Independent Political Movements in the Soviet Union 1985–1991*, London, 1992.

Humphreys, C., ' "Janus-Faced Signs". The Political Language of a Soviet Minority Before Glasnost", in R. Grillo (ed.), *Social Anthropology and the Politics of Language*, London, 1989, 145–75.

Iarov, S., 'Kronshtadtskii miatezh v vospriiatii petrogradskikh rabochikh', in *Zven'ia*, 2 vols., II, Moscow and St Petersburg, 1992.

Il'inikh, V. A., 'Krest'ianskie chelobitnye XVIII–pervoi poloviny XIX v. Na materialakh Zapadnoi Sibiri', in *Sibirskoe istochnikovedenie i arkheografiia*, Novosibirsk, 1980, 86–7.

Inkeles, A., *Public Opinion in Soviet Russia*, Cambridge, Mass., 1958.

Inkeles, A., and Bauer, R., *The Soviet Citizen. Daily Life in a Totalitarian Society*, Cambridge, Mass., 1961.

Ivinitskii, N. A., *Kollektivizatsiia i raskulachivanie (nachalo 30-kh godov)*, Moscow, 1994.

Izmozik, V., *Glaza i ushi rezhima. Gosudarstvennyi politicheskii kontrol' za naseleniem sovetskoi Rossii v 1918–1928 godakh*, St Petersburg, 1995.

Jahn, H., 'For Tsar and Fatherland? Russian Popular Culture and the First World War', in S. Frank and M. Steinberg (eds.), *Cultures in Flux. Lower-Class Values, Practices, and Resistance in Late Imperial Russia*, Princeton, 1994, 131–46.

Jakobson, R., *Selected Writings*, 8 vols., The Hague, 1966.

Jameson, F., *The Political Unconscious*, London, 1981.

Jasny, N., *The Soviet 1956 Statistical Handbook. A Commentary*, East Lansing, Mich., 1957.
Soviet Industrialisation 1928–1952, Chicago, 1961.
Johnson, R., *Peasant and Proletarian. The Working Class of Moscow in the Late Nineteenth Century*, New Brunswick, N. J., 1979.
Joyce, P., *Visions of the People. Industrial England and the Question of Class 1848–1914*, Cambridge, 1991.
Kemp-Welch, A., *Stalin and the Literary Intelligentsia 1928–1939*, London, 1991.
Kenez, P., *The Birth of the Propaganda State. Soviet Methods of Mass Mobilisation 1917–1929*, Cambridge, 1985.
Kershaw, I., *The Hitler Myth. Image and Reality in the Third Reich*, Oxford, 1989.
Popular Opinion and Political Dissent in the Third Reich, Oxford, 1983.
Khlevniuk, O., *1937-i. Stalin, NKVD, i sovetskoe obshchestvo*, Moscow, 1992.
'The Objectives of the Great Terror 1937–1938', in J. Cooper, M. Perrie, and E. A. Rees (eds.), *Soviet History 1917–1953. Essays in Honour of R. W. Davies*, London, 1993, 158–76.
Stalin i Ordzhonikidze. Konflikty v Politbiuro v 30-e gody, Moscow, 1993.
Kimmerling, E., 'Civil Rights and Social Policy in Soviet Russia 1918–1936', *RR*, 42/1, 1982, 24–46.
Kiteme, B., 'The Cult of Stalin. National Power and the Soviet Party State', Ph.D dissertation, Columbia University, 1989.
Knight, A., *Beria. Stalin's First Lieutenant*, Princeton, 1993.
Kobo, Kh. (ed.), *Osmyslit' kul't Stalina*, Moscow, 1989.
Koenker, D., 'Men Against Women on the Shop Floor in Early Soviet Russia. Gender and Class in the Soviet Workplace', *American Historical Review*, December 1995, 1438–64.
Moscow Workers and the 1917 Revolution, Princeton, 1981.
Kolonitskii, B., 'Antibourgeois Propaganda and Anti-"*Burzhui*" Consciousness in 1917', *RR*, 53/2, 1994, 183–96.
Kotkin, S., *Magnetic Mountain. Stalinism as a Civilisation*, London, 1995.
Kozlov, V. A., and Khlevniuk, O. V., *Nachinaetsia s cheloveka*, Moscow, 1988.
Kuromiya, H., *Stalin's Industrial Revolution. Politics and Workers 1928–1932*, Cambridge, 1988.
'Stalinskaia "revoliutsiia sverkhu" i narod', *Svobodnaia mysl'*, 2, 1992, 93–6.
La Capra, D., *Rethinking Intellectual History*, London, 1983.
Lane, C., *The Rites of Rulers. Ritual in Industrial Society: The Soviet Case*, Cambridge, 1981.
Lane, D., *Soviet Economy and Society*, Oxford, 1985.
Lapidus, G., *Women in Soviet Society*, London, 1978.
Larin, Iu., *Evrei i antisemitizm v SSSR*, Moscow, 1929.
Lebina, N., 'Mif o mironiche', unpublished manuscript.
'Problemy sotsializatsii rabochei molodezhi sovetskoi Rossii 20–30-kh gg.', doctoral dissertation, St Petersburg, 1994.

Lefebvre, G., *La Grande Peur de 1789*, Paris, 1932.

Lenin, V. I., *Selected Works*, Moscow, 1971.

Lévi-Strauss, C., *Structural Anthropology*, London, 1968.

Lewin, M., *The Making of the Soviet System*, New York, 1985.

Liadov, L., *O vrazhde k evreiam*, Moscow, 1927.

Lotman, Ju., and Uspenskij, V., *The Semiotics of Russian Culture* (edited by A. Shukman), Ann Arbor, Mich., 1984.

Ludtke, A., *The History of Everyday Life*, Princeton, 1995.

McAuley, M., *Bread and Justice*, Oxford, 1991.

'Political Culture and Communist Politics. One Step Forward and Two Steps Back', in A. Brown (ed.), *Political Culture and Communist States*, London, 1984, 13–39.

McDaniel, T., *Autocracy, Capitalism, and Revolution in Russia*, London, 1988.

McNeal, R., *Stalin, Man and Ruler*, London, 1988.

Maksimenkov, L., 'Kul't. Zametki o slovakh-simvolakh v sovetskom politicheskom kul'ture', *Svobodnaia mysl'*, 11, 1993, 26–43.

Manning, R., 'Women in the Soviet Countryside on the Eve of World War II', in B. Farnsworth and L. Viola (eds.), *Russian Peasant Women*, Oxford, 1992, 206–35.

Marx, K., and Engels, F., *Selected Works*, Moscow, 1962.

Matthews, M., *Privilege in the Soviet Union. A Study of Elite Lifestyles Under Communism*, London, 1978.

'The "State Labour Reserves". An Episode in Soviet Social History', *Slavonic and East European Review*, 61/2, 1983, 238–51.

Medvedev, P., *Formal'nyi metod v literaturovedenii*, Leningrad, 1928.

Medvedev, R., *Let History Judge. The Origins and Consequences of Stalinism*, London, 1972.

Merridale, C., 'The 1937 Census and the Limits of Stalinist Rule', *Historical Journal*, 39/1, 1996, 225–40.

Mertsalov, A. (ed.), *Istoriia i stalinizm*, Moscow, 1991.

Miller, F., *Folklore for Stalin. Russian Folklore and Pseudofolklore of the Stalin Era*, London, 1990.

Moore, B., *Injustice. The Social Bases of Obedience and Revolt*, London, 1978.

Terror and Progress USSR, Cambridge, Mass., 1954.

Moskoff, W., *The Bread of Affliction. The Food Supply in the USSR During World War II*, Cambridge, 1990.

Nakhimovskii, A., and Nakhimovskii, A. (eds.), *The Semiotics of Russian Cultural History*, London, 1985.

Nikolaevsky, B., *Power and the Soviet Elite*, London, 1966.

Nove, A., 'The Class Nature of the Soviet Union Revisited', *Soviet Studies*, 35/3, 1983, 298–312.

An Economic History of the USSR, Harmondsworth, 1986.

'Is There a Ruling Class in the USSR?', *Soviet Studies*, 27/4, 1975, 615–38.

Ong, W., *Orality and Literacy*, London, 1982.

Oni ne molchali, Moscow, 1991.

Osokina, E., *Ierarkhiia potrebleniia. O zhizni liudei v usloviiakh stalinskogo snabzheniia 1928–1935 gg.*, Moscow, 1993.

'Liudi i vlast' v usloviiakh krizisa snabzheniia 1939–1941 gody', *Otechestvennaia istoriia*, 1995/3, 16–32.

'Za zerkal'noi dver'iu Torgsina', *Otechestvennaia istoriia*, 1995/2, 86–104.

Osokina, E. (ed.), 'Krizis snabzheniia 1939–1941 gg. v pis'makh sovetskikh liudei', *Voprosy istorii*, 1, 1996, 3–23.

Ossowski, S., *Class Structure in the Social Consciousness*, London, 1963.

Ovsiannikov, A., 'Istoki vozhdizma. Ideologiia i praktika', in V. Dmitrenko (ed.), *Formirovanie administrativno-komandnoi sistemy 20–30e gody*, Moscow, 1992, 185–203.

Passerini, L., *Fascism in Popular Memory. The Cultural Experience of the Turin Working Class*, Cambridge, 1987.

'Oral Memory of Fascism', in D. Forgacs (ed.), *Rethinking Italian Fascism*, London, 1986, 185–96.

Perrie, M., *The Agrarian Policy of the Russian Social-Revolutionary Party from Its Origins Through the Revolution of 1905–1907*, Cambridge, 1976.

'Folklore as Evidence of Peasant *Mentalité*. Social Attitudes and Values in Russian Popular Culture', *RR*, 48/2, 1989, 119–43.

The Image of Ivan the Terrible in Russian Folklore, Cambridge, 1987.

Pethybridge, R., *The Social Prelude to Stalinism*, London, 1974.

Peukert, D., *Inside Nazi Germany. Conformity, Opposition, and Racism in Everyday Life*, London, 1989.

Pipes, R., *Russia Under the Old Regime*, Harmondsworth, 1987.

The Russian Revolution 1899–1919, London, 1990.

Poliakov, Iu., Zhiromskaia, V., and Kiselev, I., 'Polveka molchania. Vsesoiuznaia perepis' naseleniia 1937 goda', *Sotsiologicheskie issledovaniia*, 6–8, 1990.

Pospielovsky, D., *The Russian Orthodox Church Under the Soviet Regime 1917–1982*, 3 vols., New York, 1984.

Priestland, D., 'Ideological Conflict Within the Bolshevik Party 1917–1939. The Question of "Bureaucracy" and "Democracy"', DPhil. thesis, University of Oxford, 1991.

Propp, V., *Morfologiia skazki*, Moscow, 1969.

Rice, C., *Russian Workers and the Social-Revolutionary Party Through the Revolution of 1905–1907*, London, 1988.

Rigby, T., 'Reconceptualising the Soviet System', in S. White, A. Pravda, and Z. Gitelman (eds.), *Developments in Soviet and Post-Soviet Politics*, 2nd edn, London, 1992, 300–19.

Rigby, T., and Feher, F. (eds.), *Political Legitimation in Communist States*, London, 1982.

Rittersporn, G., 'Politicheskii podtekst povsednevnogo povedeniia', paper presented to the conference 'Rossiiskaia povsednevnost' 1921–1941 gg.', St Petersburg, 1994.

Stalinist Simplifications and Soviet Complications, Chur, 1991.

Riutin, M., *Na koleni ne vstanu*, Moscow, 1992.

Robin, R., *Le Réalisme socialiste. Une Esthétique impossible*, Paris, 1986.

Rosenberg, W., 'Russian Labour and Bolshevik Power After October', *SR*, 44/2, 1985, 213–38, and 'Reply', 251–6.

'Smolensk in the 1920s. Party–Worker Relations and the "Vanguard" Problem', *RR*, 36/2, 1977, 125–50.

'Workers and Workers' Control in the Russian Revolution', *History Workshop Journal*, 5, 1978, 89–97.

Rosenberg, W., and Siegelbaum, L. (eds.), *Social Dimensions of Soviet Industrialisation*, Bloomington, Ind., 1993.

Rosnow, R., 'Psychology of Rumour Reconsidered', *Psychological Bulletin*, 87, 3, 1980, 578–91.

Rosnow, R., and Fine, G., *Rumor and Gossip. The Social Psychology of Hearsay*, New York, 1976.

Rossman, J., 'Worker Resistance Under Stalin. Class and Gender in the Textile Mills of Ivanovo Industrial Region 1926–1941', Ph.D dissertation, University of California at Berkeley, forthcoming.

Rude, G., *The Crowd in the French Revolution*, Oxford, 1967.

Ideology and Popular Protest, London, 1980.

Sartori, R., 'Stalinism and Carnival. Organisation and Aesthetics of Political Holidays', in H. Gunther (ed.), *The Culture of the Stalin Period*, London, 1990, 41–77.

Savinova, E., 'Karnivalizatsiia i tselostnost' kul'tury', in *M. M. Bakhtin i filosofiia kul'tury XX veka. Problemy bakhtinologii*, St Petersburg, 1991, 61–9.

Schlesinger, R., *The Family in the USSR*, London, 1949.

Schwartz, S., *Labour in the Soviet Union*, London, 1953.

Scott, J., *Domination and the Arts of Resistance*, London, 1990.

Weapons of the Weak. Everyday Forms of Peasant Resistance, London, 1985.

Service, R. (ed.), *Society and Politics in the Russian Revolution*, London, 1992.

Shanin, T., *The Awkward Class*, Oxford, 1972.

Shibutani, T., *Improvised News. A Sociological Study of Rumour*, Indianapolis, 1966.

Shils, E., 'Charisma, Order, and Status', *American Sociological Review*, April 1965, 199–213.

Shkaratan, O., 'Material'noe blagosostoianie rabochego klassa SSSR v perekhodnyi period ot kapitalizma k sotsializmu', *Istoriia SSSR*, 3, 1964, 17–44.

Siegelbaum, L., *Stakhanovism and the Politics of Productivity in the USSR 1935–1941*, Cambridge, 1988.

Siegelbaum, L., and Suny, R. (eds.), *Making Workers Soviet*, London, 1994.

Smith, R., and Christian, D., *Bread and Salt. A Social and Economic History of Food and Drink in Russia*, Cambridge, 1984.

Smith, S., 'Class and Gender. Women's Strikes in St Petersburg 1855–1917 and in Shanghai 1895–1927', *Social History*, 19/2, 1994, 141–68.

'Craft Consciousness, Class Consciousness. Petrograd 1917', *History Workshop Journal*, 11, 1981, 33–56.

Red Petrograd. Revolution in the Factories 1917–1918, Cambridge, 1983.

'Writing the History of the Russian Revolution After the Fall of Communism', *Europe–Asia Studies*, 46/4, 1994, 563–78.

Solzhenitsyn, A., *The Gulag Archipelago*, 3 vols., New York, 1974–8.

Starkov, B., 'Kak Moskva chut' ne stala Stalinodarom', *Izvestiia KPSS*, 12, 1990, 126–7.

Stedman-Jones, G., *Languages of Class*, Cambridge, 1983.

Steinberg, M., *Moral Communities. The Culture and Class Relations in the Russian Printing Industry 1867–1907*, Berkeley, 1992.

'Workers and the Cross. Religious Imagery in the Writings of Russian Workers 1910–1924', *RR*, 53/2, 1994, 213–39.

Stites, R., *Revolutionary Dreams. Utopian Visions and Experimental Life in the Revolution*, Oxford, 1989.

Russian Popular Culture. Entertainment and Society Since 1900, Cambridge, 1992.

The Women's Liberation Movement in Russia. Feminism, Nihilism, and Bolshevism 1860–1930, Princeton, 1978.

Sukharev, S., 'Istoriko-partiinaia nauka v usloviiakh utverzhdeniia kul't lichnosti I. V. Stalina 1931–1935. Avtoreferat', candidate dissertation, Moscow, 1990.

Suny, R., 'Nationalism and Class in the Russian Revolution. A Comparative Discussion', in E. Frankel, J. Frankel, and B. Knei-Paz (eds.), *Revolution in Russia. Reassessments of 1917*, Cambridge, 1992.

'Revision and Retreat in the Historiography of 1917. Social History and Its Critics', *RR*, 53/2, 1994, 165–82.

'Toward a Social History of the October Revolution', *American Historical Review*, 88/1, 1983, 31–52.

Surovaia drama naroda. Uchenye i publitsisty o prirode stalinizma, Moscow, 1989.

Thompson, E. P., *The Making of the English Working Class*, London, 1980.

'The Moral Economy of the English Crowd in the Eighteenth Century', *Past and Present*, 50, 1971, 76–131.

The Poverty of Theory and Other Essays, London, 1978.

Thompson, R., 'Reassessing Personality Cults. The Case of Stalin and Mao', *Studies in Comparative Communism*, 21/1, 1988, 99–128.

Thurston, R., 'Fear and Belief in the USSR's "Great Terror". Response to Arrest 1935–1939', *SR*, 45/2, 1986, 213–34.

'Reassessing the History of Soviet Workers. Opportunities to Criticise and Participate in Decision-Making 1935–1941', in S. White (ed.), *New Directions in Soviet History*, Cambridge, 1992, 160–88.

'The Soviet Family During the Great Terror 1935–1941', *Soviet Studies*, 43/3, 1991, 553–74.

'Vezhlivost' i vlast' na sovetskikh fabrikakh i zavodakh. Dostoinstvo rabochikh 1935–1941 gg.', in *Rossiiskaia povsednevnost' 1921–1941 gg. Novye podkhody*, St Petersburg, 1995, 59–67.

Timasheff, N., *The Great Retreat. The Growth and Decline of Communism in Russia*, New York, 1946.

Religion in Soviet Russia 1917–1942, London, 1943.

Tokes, R., *Opposition in East Europe*, London, 1979.

Totalitarizm kak istoricheskii fenomen, Moscow, 1990.

Trotsky, L., *The Revolution Betrayed*, London, 1937.

Tucker, R., *The Soviet Political Mind*, London, 1972.

Stalin in Power. The Revolution from Above 1928–1941, London, 1990.

'The Theory of Charismatic Leadership', *Daedalus*, 97/3, 1968, 731–56.

Tucker, R. (ed.), *Stalinism. Essays in Historical Interpretation*, New York, 1977.

Tumarkin, N., *Lenin Lives! The Lenin Cult in Soviet Russia*, Cambridge, 1983.

Unger, A., *The Totalitarian Party. Party and People in Nazi Germany and Soviet Russia*, Cambridge, 1974.

Veselyi, A. (ed.), *Chastushki kolkhoznykh dereven'*, Moscow, 1936.

Viola, L., '*Bab'i bunty* and Peasant Women's Protest During Collectivisation', *RR*, 45/1, 1986, 23–42.

Best Sons of the Fatherland. Workers in the Vanguard of Industrialisation, Oxford, 1987.

'The Peasant Nightmare. Visions of Apocalypse in the Soviet Countryside', *Journal of Modern History*, 62, 1990, 747–70.

Vlasova, Z., and Gorelov, A. (eds.), *Chastushka v zapisakh sovetskogo vremeni*, Moscow, 1965.

Volkogonov, D., *Triumf i tragediia. I. V. Stalin: Politicheskii portret*, Moscow, 1989.

Volkov, S. S., *Leksika russkikh chelobitnykh XVII veka*, Leningrad, 1974.

Voloshinov, V., *Marksizm i filosofiia iazyka*, Leningrad, 1930.

Vovelle, M., *Ideologies and Mentalities*, Cambridge, 1990.

Vyltsan, M., 'Pobeda kolkhoznogo stroia i meropriatiia partii i gosudarstva po uluchsheniiu zhizni sovetskogo krest'ianstva 1933–1940 gg.', *Voprosy istorii KPSS*, 1968/6.

Ward, C., *Russia's Cotton Workers and the New Economic Policy*, Cambridge, 1990.

Weber, M., *On Charisma and Institution-Building* (edited by S. Eisenstadt), London, 1968.

Welch, D., *The Third Reich. Politics and Propaganda*, London, 1995.

White, S., *Political Culture and Soviet Politics*, London, 1979.

Zaleski, E., *Stalinist Planning for Economic Growth 1933–1952*, Chapel Hill, 1980.

Zelenin, I. 'Byl li "kolkhoznyi neonep"?', *Otechestvennaia istoriia*, 1994/2, 105–21.

Zhivov, V., and Uspenskii, B., 'Tsar' i Bog. Semioticheskie aspekty sakralizatsii monarkha v Rossii', in B. Uspenskii (ed.), *Iazyki kul'tury i problemy perevodimosti*, Moscow, 1987, 47–153.

Index